Changing the Goalpost of New Testament Textual Criticism

Changing the Goalpost of New Testament Textual Criticism

ABIDAN PAUL SHAH

WIPF & STOCK · Eugene, Oregon

CHANGING THE GOALPOST OF NEW TESTAMENT TEXTUAL CRITICISM

Copyright © 2020 Abidan Paul Shah. All rights reserved. Except for brief quotations in critical publications or reviews, no part of this book may be reproduced in any manner without prior written permission from the publisher. Write: Permissions, Wipf and Stock Publishers, 199 W. 8th Ave., Suite 3, Eugene, OR 97401.

This Dissertation was prepared and presented to the Faculty as a part of the requirements for the Doctor of Philosophy Degree at Southeastern Baptist Theological Seminary, Wake Forest, North Carolina. All rights and privileges normally reserved by the author as a copyright holder are waived for the Seminary. The Seminary Library may catalog, display, and use this Dissertation in all normal ways such materials are used, for reference, and for other purposes, including electronic and other means of preservation and circulation, including online access and other means by which library materials are or in the future may be made available to researchers and library users.

Wipf & Stock
An Imprint of Wipf and Stock Publishers
199 W. 8th Ave., Suite 3
Eugene, OR 97401

www.wipfandstock.com

PAPERBACK ISBN: 978-1-7252-7869-1
HARDCOVER ISBN: 978-1-7252-7870-7
EBOOK ISBN: 978-1-7252-7871-4

Manufactured in the U.S.A.   09/18/20

Dedicated to two individuals who inspired me to look at the text:

My father-in-law, Rev. Jerry L. Shedd (1943–1998)
My father, Rev. Paul H. Shah (1937–)

Contents

Abstract		ix
Acknowledgments		xi
1	Introduction	1
2	The Traditional Goals And Methods Of NTTC	9
3	Bart D. Ehrman	28
4	David C. Parker	54
5	Eldon J. Epp	78
6	J. Keith Elliott	103
7	The Coherence-Based Genealogical Method	113
8	Final Analysis and Critique	127
9	Conclusion	169
Bibliography		173

Abstract

Chapter 1 lays out the thesis of the dissertation by giving a brief introduction to each of the subsequent chapters. It is claimed that the primary goal of New Testament Textual Criticism (NTTC) should remain the search for the original text. Failure to do so will undermine biblical authority for faith and practice.

Chapter 2 focuses on the traditional goals and methods of NTTC. Major works of leading text-critics, past and present, are examined with regards to their understanding of the primary goal of the discipline. It is argued that even though text-critics across the spectrum have differed on methodology, most have remained unanimous regarding the importance of seeking the original text of the NT.

Chapter 3 examines the text-critical view of Bart D. Ehrman, the first proponent of the new trend in NTTC. Although Ehrman has written many works geared toward the lay audience, his *Orthodox Corruption of Scripture* is a major scholarly work that has challenged the primary goal of NTTC.

Chapter 4 focuses on the methodology of David C. Parker. His *Living Text of the Gospels* has also undermined the traditional goal of NTTC, albeit from the basis of the Gospels only.

Chapter 5 is a survey of a major proponent and popularizer of the new movement, Eldon J. Epp. Unlike the previous two proponents, Epp's view has to be gleaned from his many articles on the subject.

Chapter 6 examines the change in J. Keith Elliott's position regarding the original text. Compared to the previous three, Elliott's writings are more declaratory than descriptive.

Chapter 7 discusses the Coherence-Based Genealogical Method as the most recent development in the new movement in NTTC. Although it is touted as a great improvement over previous methodologies of establishing the text, its proposal of the "initial text" (*Ausgangstext*) undermines the goal of the original text.

Chapter 8 gives the final analysis and critique of the new movement in NTTC. It evaluates the four major premises that are common among each of the proponents. It also includes a section regarding the relationship of NTTC and inerrancy. Contrary to the proponents' easy dismissal of inerrancy, it is argued the doctrine of inerrancy is rooted in inspiration and not in text-critical conclusions.

Chapter 9 concludes the study with an appeal to retain the primary goal of NTTC of establishing the original text of the NT.

Acknowledgments

It is impossible to list all the individuals who have, in one way or another, impacted the completion of this study. I would like to thank the faculty and staff at Southeastern who have taught me so much through the years. My major professor, Dr. Maurice A. Robinson, has been a true mentor in guiding me throughout this project. I wouldn't have made it without his help. Of course, any mistakes in this study are mine. I am also grateful to Dr. David Alan Black for his friendship over two decades and his encouragement to publish this work.

I especially want to thank my wife, Nicole. Without her love and support I would not have come this far. Also, thank you to my children (Rebecca, Abigail, Nicholas, and Thomas) for being so patient through the years when Dad was busy in his office. I am greatly indebted to the Clearview Church family for their prayers and support, in particular the staff for catching the extra work throughout this process. Special thanks go to Rebecca Shah for proofreading this work, and David Williamson for helping with formatting.

Last, but not least, I thank my Savior Jesus Christ for calling me to his service and giving me a love for the Scriptures.

1

Introduction

Before the 1960s, the goal of New Testament Textual Criticism (NTTC) was singular: to retrieve the "original text" of the New Testament (NT). Since then, the goalpost has incrementally shifted away from the "original text" to retrieving "any text" or "many texts" of the NT. Under this new approach to the text, all variants are considered to be equally valuable, regardless of their external evidence in the history of transmission. Previously, variants were looked upon as a means to recover the original text, but now they are increasingly treated as windows into the various early Christian communities and their struggles with doctrines. Now it is considered far more profitable to gain insight into the various "Christianities"[1] or "trajectories of faith"[2] in the early church than to seek after an elusive and illusive "original text." Some scholars have concluded the original text is hopelessly lost and cannot be retrieved with any confidence or accuracy.[3] Other scholars have gone a step further to claim the idea of an original text itself is a misconception that needs to be abandoned.[4] As a major representative of this movement, Eldon J. Epp contends that instead of a single, authoritative, "original text," there were multiple originals in the beginning, and the

---

1. Bauer, *Rechtgläubigkeit und Ketzerei*. For the English translation, see Bauer, *Orthodoxy and Heresy*.
2. Koester, "ΓΝΩΜΑΙ ΔΙΑΦΟΡΟΙ," 279–318.
3. Ehrman, *Orthodox Corruption of Scripture* (2011), 31.
4. Epp, "Multivalence of the Term 'Original Text,'" 245–81.

concept of an original text is a later development that arose since the coming of the printing press. Some have also proposed creating a text or texts that suit the reader and his or her community.[5] Such an understanding of the history of the NT text has serious implications for the study of the NT and the authority of Scripture. Historic Christianity is a faith that is built upon a first-century text. Without a generally determinable original text, there is no longer an authoritative text, and if there is no authoritative text, then there is no longer any distinct Christian faith and practice.[6] It is imperative this new shift in NTTC be examined, evaluated, and refuted.

This new movement in NTTC has been spearheaded by five proponents and the recent use of a computer program. Leading the charge is Bart D. Ehrman, who popularized his view through his bestseller *Misquoting Jesus: The Story Behind Who Changed the Bible and Why*,[7] but the bulk of his thesis is contained in his scholarly work *The Orthodox Corruption of Scripture*.[8] Ehrman based the latter on Walter Bauer's *Orthodoxy and Heresy in Early Christianity*.[9] Prior to Bauer, the normative understanding of early church history was that orthodoxy came first and heresy followed later, but was rebutted successfully. Bauer challenged this traditional view and proposed heresy was on par with orthodoxy in the early church. In fact, in some regions, heresy was the original orthodoxy, and only after some bitter sociopolitical struggles did the orthodox group rise victorious. Since "winners write the history," the orthodox party passed down a distorted view of the church's origin to prove their precedence over the other parties. Ehrman extends Bauer's thesis to allege the orthodox were not content with just sabotaging sees, bishoprics, and councils to advance their agenda; they even corrupted the NT text in order to prove their superiority and maintain their dominance.[10]

---

5. Parker, "Et Incarnatus Est," 343.

6. Knust, *Unprotected Texts*, 244–49. Knust made several remarks in her work that exemplify the loss of scriptural authority: "Looking to the Bible for straightforward answers about anything . . . can only lead to disappointment"; "It is therefore a mistake to pretend that the Bible can define our ethics for us in any kind of straightforward way: such an interpretative strategy will only lead us astray . . . . Neither the Bible nor a particular interpretation can limit what particular stories and teachings must mean"; [Acknowledgements] "to Bart Ehrman, who assisted me at every turn." Such statements are indicative of the impact of the new trend in NTTC.

7. Ehrman, *Misquoting Jesus*.

8. Ehrman, *Orthodox Corruption of Scripture* (1993), 7–9.

9. Bauer, *Orthodoxy and Heresy*.

10. Ehrman, *Orthodox Corruption of Scripture* (1993), 15.

Unlike Bauer, who had sequestered the NT as being inconsequential due to widespread corruption, Ehrman deems it as Exhibit A for his thesis. He begins his argument with the following declaration:

> Christianity in the second and third centuries was in a remarkable state of flux. To be sure, at no point in its history has the religion constituted a monolith. But the diverse manifestations of its first three hundred years—whether in terms of social structures, religious practices, or ideologies—have never been replicated.[11]

He claims this turbulence in early Christianity can be verified by examining the extant NT manuscripts, wherein many of the variants are simply traces of the orthodox attempt to gain control and root out other equally viable movements. He repeats the commonly accepted observation the orthodox scribes "occasionally altered the words of their sacred texts to make them more patently orthodox and to prevent their misuse by Christians who espoused aberrant views."[12] The previous statement is nothing new and has been repeatedly affirmed in standard text-critical works.[13] The confounding twist is Ehrman extends his list of suspects from the "orthodox scribes" of the third and fourth centuries to the hypothetical "proto-orthodox" scribes of the first couple hundred years of early Christianity. He claims in the early years of "theological instability," the scribes of the "proto-orthodox" party manipulated the text to fit their theological agenda and thus cemented the hold of their successors: the orthodox party. He uses some of the early christological controversies of the third and fourth centuries as a background to identify the motives behind the different variants created by the proto-orthodox scribes. Under his thesis, the text available to us can no longer be claimed as the original text because it has been altered by the orthodox coup in the earliest stages of the Christian movement. Simply stated, "the winners not only write the history, they also reproduce the texts."[14] It is important to note here, even though Bauer's thesis has been repeatedly challenged through the years, Ehrman has continued to use it without any qualifications to promote his own work.[15] So also, those who

---

11. Ehrman, *Orthodox Corruption of Scripture* (1993), 3.

12. Ehrman, *Orthodox Corruption of Scripture* (1993), xi.

13. For example, see Metzger, *Text of the New Testament*, 201–3; Aland and Aland, *Text of the New Testament*, 69–70; Greenlee, *Introduction to New Testament Textual Criticism*, 60–61.

14. Ehrman, *Orthodox Corruption of Scripture* (1993), 27.

15. Among such rebuttals are the following: Turner, *Pattern of Christian Truth*; Robinson, *Bauer Thesis Examined*; Flora, "Critical Analysis of Walter Bauer's Theory," 5276-A.

espouse the latter's view continue to make similar claims without considering the faulty foundation of Bauer's thesis.

The second proponent in the new movement in NTTC is David C. Parker. In *The Living Text of the Gospels*, Parker advocates a "free or living text" approach whereby "there is no authoritative text beyond the manuscripts which we may follow without further thought."[16] Unlike Ehrman's view of early corruption by the proto-orthodox, Parker proposes from the beginning the Gospel texts grew freely and therefore "the material about Jesus was preserved in an interpretive rather than an exact fashion."[17] He examines cases where the final decision was seemingly difficult and concludes the text in this early period of transmission was fluid and the "sayings and stories continued to be developed by copyists and readers."[18] Accordingly, seeming discrepancies in the textual traditions are not to be resolved so much as to be used as a window into the world of the early church and the issues they faced. In his concluding chapter, Parker remarks,

> Rather than looking for right and wrong readings, and with them for right or wrong beliefs and practices, the way is open for the possibility that the church is the community of the Spirit even in its multiplicities of texts, one might say in its corruptions and in its restorations. Indeed, we may suggest that it is not in spite of the variety but because of them that the church is that community.[19]

Parker blames the Reformation along with the printing press as the sources of the misguided concept of authoritative texts. He advocates a "living canon" approach, wherein "the concept of a Gospel that is fixed in shape, authoritative, and final as a piece of literature has to be abandoned."[20] Consequently, according to Parker, NTTC is no longer about an "original text" but many "fluid texts" that developed over time to meet the needs of their individual communities.

The third proponent, Eldon J. Epp, has written much in NTTC, but his contribution to the new movement in the field is not found in one single work. His views have to be gleaned from his numerous text-critical articles through the years, especially in the past two decades. The clearest articulation of his approach came in his seminal article, "The Multivalence of the Term 'Original Text' in New Testament Textual Criticism," wherein he not

---

16. Parker, *Living Text of the Gospels*, 212.
17. Parker, *Living Text of the Gospels*, 200. Also see Parker, "Scripture is Tradition," 15.
18. Parker, "Scripture is Tradition," 45–46.
19. Parker, *Living Text of the Gospels*, 212.
20. Parker, *Living Text of the Gospels*, 93.

only commends Ehrman and Parker for bringing new life in an otherwise "dead field" of NTTC, but he also adds his own flavor to the new approach.[21] He posits many "original texts" at the end of the "lengthy canonization process" and offers four categories that challenged the idea of one single authoritative "original text."[22] First was the "predecessor text-form," which he deems to be the "pre-canonical" text. This text represented the sources available to the author at the time of writing the text. The second was the "autographic" text, which represented the actual text as it was penned by the author or his amanuensis. The third was the "canonical text-form," which represented the "textual form of a book (or a collection of books) at the time it acquired consensual authority or when its canonicity was (perhaps more formally) sought or established." The fourth was the "interpretive text-form," which represented the reformulations of the original text. The article did not provide much by way of supporting evidence but it was very successful in permanently dismantling the traditional concept of a single authoritative "original text." Much of Epp's supporting evidence, which is meager compared to the others, has to be culled from his work on D, and the various articles on the papyri and the state of the text in the second century.

The fourth proponent, J. Keith Elliott, is a latecomer in the new movement in NTTC text, but by no means is he a newcomer to the field of NTTC. Back in 1974, Elliott was quite confident the original text of the NT was retrievable and the primary task of NTTC was to do so.[23] So also, his articles promoting rigorous eclecticism and his numerous book reviews, especially on text-critical works, had always supported the traditional understanding of the original text. However, in recent years, Elliott has gradually shifted in his understanding of the NT text. He has become far more pessimistic regarding the idea of a single authoritative original, which he refers to as a "chimera."[24] Now, he espouses the view of multiple texts of equal value which derive their status of authority from the community that deems them such. He declares in his latest writing, "All manuscripts, however maverick they be branded by modern scholarship, were nonetheless at one time the divine and sacred scriptures of the individuals, churches, and communities that happened to read *and use* each and every copy."[25] Elliott's enlistment within the ranks of

---

21. Epp, "Multivalence of the Term 'Original Text,'" 245–81.
22. Epp, "Multivalence of the Term 'Original Text,'" 263, 276–77.
23. Elliott, "Can We Recover the Original New Testament?," 338.
24. Elliott, "Recent Trends," 127.
25. Elliott, "Majority Text or Not," 81 (emphasis original).

the new movement is symptomatic of the growing trend in NTTC to value *all* texts in lieu of the traditional original text.

The final proponent is the Coherence-Based Genealogical Method (CBGM), a computer-based system of evaluating readings of the NT text. It is the brainchild of Gerd Mink, from the Institut für Neutestamentliche Textforschung (INTF) in Münster, Germany. Since 1982, Mink has attempted to create a genealogical structure of the manuscript tradition for individual variant units which has culminated in his computer program popularly referred to as CBGM. He claims to view all variants as equally important and attempts to place them in their best possible home in the infinite web of textual tradition.[26] The results have already been applied to the Editio Critica Maior (ECM) in Acts and the Catholic Epistles, as well as the latter in the NA[28] and UBS[5] editions, with more to follow in Mark, John and Revelation. While some have referred to it as a "major breakthrough" in NTTC,[27] there is much to be concerned about regarding CBGM's procedures and fundamental assumptions, especially regarding the original text. The idea of a single, authoritative, original text is not necessarily denied but simply set aside for the *Ausgangstext* or the initial text. In fact, the iterative process of CBGM constantly attempts to create a "better" initial text.[28] Such a shifting initial text will never reach a definitive original text. To the contrary, it will become a "retreating mirage."[29]

All of the proponents share certain assumptions that impact how they view the text of the NT—distrust of authority and anything authoritative, the disputable claims of a struggle between political parties in the early church with the dominant group attempting to marginalize and even eradicate the weak, the undue emphasis on individual readers rather than the original writer(s), and the utter hopelessness of ever reaching anything definitive. The pitfalls inherent in these assumptions are that they render the original text nonexistent and leave it at the doorstep of the reader to recreate a text that suits one's preference and need. Such an approach to the NT text is not only bad scholarship, but it also threatens to destroy an authoritative original and thereby any definitive standard for faith and practice.

Of all the proponents listed above, Ehrman has made some of the most baleful statements against the NT text. In his bestseller, *Misquoting Jesus*, he writes,

---

26. For an introduction, see Mink, "Contamination, Coherence, and Coincidence," 141–216.

27. See Wasserman, "Criteria for Evaluating Readings," 595, 605.

28. Wasserman, "Coherence Based Genealogical Method," 208.

29. Clark, "Theological Relevance of Textual Variation," 15.

> The reality is that we don't have the originals—so saying that they were inspired doesn't help me much, unless I can reconstruct the originals. Moreover, the vast majority of Christians for the entire history of the church have not had access to the originals, making their inspiration something of a moot point. Not only we do not have the originals, we don't have the first copies of the originals. We don't even have the copies of the copies of the originals, or copies of the copies of the copies of the originals. What we have are copies made later—much later. In most instances, they are copies made many *centuries* later. And these copies all differ from one another, in many thousands of places . . . these copies differ from one another in so many places that we don't even know how many differences there are.[30]

Based on the above understanding of the textual history, Ehrman goes on to draw the following conclusion regarding the original text of the NT,

> In some places . . . we simply cannot be sure that we have reconstructed the original text accurately. It's a bit hard to know what the words of the Bible mean if we don't even know what the words are! I came to realize that it would have been no more difficult for God to preserve the words of scripture than it would have been for him to inspire them in the first place. If he wanted his people to have his words, surely he would have given them to them (and possibly even given them the words in a language they would understand, rather than Greek and Hebrew). The fact that we don't have the words surely must show, I reasoned, that he did not preserve them for us. And if he didn't perform that miracle, there seems to be no reason to think that he performed the earlier miracle of inspiring those words.[31]

While such views have drawn objections from those who still hold to the idea of an authoritative original and the need to seek it, a growing number of scholars have welcomed the new approach to the NT text as a well-needed breakthrough to the otherwise static and stale discipline of NTTC. They find it refreshing to explore new territories and revitalize an otherwise dying field instead of chasing after a retreating mirage of some authoritative original. They appraise it as ground-breaking and innovative. Other scholars have disavowed the new approach, calling into question the theology and motive of the proponents. Some have exposed the unhistorical nature of the arguments, focusing on matters of church history and canon.

---

30. Ehrman, *Misquoting Jesus*, 10.
31. Ehrman, *Misquoting Jesus*, 11.

Yet others have called into question various factual and methodological inconsistencies in their practice of textual criticism. Full-length monographs have been published, mainly against Ehrman, and many public debates have been held and the results have been published or made available online. The other proponents have not received the same amount of attention but their conclusions are just as harmful.

The goal of the present study is to survey the development of each proponent's view on the goal of NTTC and then provide a critique of their common premises. It is claimed here that the results of the new approach to NTTC are devastating, to say the least. At the heart of the issue is the question of biblical authority, and it is critical that conservative evangelical scholars understand and give an appropriate response. If the new approach in NTTC is correct, then the authority of Scripture is weakened or no longer valid. It will be shown in this study that such is not the case. Furthermore, emphasis will be placed on the need to return to the traditional goalpost of NTTC, i.e., to retrieve the original text. Without a generally definitive text, the door will be left wide open to recreate any desired text of the NT. *An unsettled original text will result in an unsettled biblical theology due to a lack of any authoritative and standard text. Consequently, it will lead to an unsettled Christian faith and practice.*

2

The Traditional Goals And Methods Of NTTC

NTTC experienced a radical shift in its goals within the last quarter of the twentieth century. Formerly, it was commonly assumed the primary goalpost of NTTC was to retrieve the original text and only secondarily to draw inferences regarding the emergence of corrupted readings. A sample of this understanding can be noted in the 1815 preface of Frederick Nolan's work on NTTC, in which he clarified the goal of the discipline as follows: "Various expedients have been, in consequence devised, in order to determine the authentick [sic] readings from the spurious, and to fix the character of those manuscripts which are chiefly deserving of credit, in ascertaining the genuine text of the sacred canon."[1] Less than a century later, Marvin Vincent opened his book, *A History of the Textual Criticism of the New Testament,* with a similar definition: "Textual Criticism is that process by which it is sought to determine the original text of a document or of a collection of documents, and to exhibit it, freed from all the errors, corruptions, and variations which it may have accumulated in the course of its transmission by successive copyings."[2] Much has changed since then, especially in the past few decades, regarding the goals of NTTC. Now, conjecture and speculation about individual corruptions have become the main quest, and recovery of the autographic text has become a secondary, if not

1. Nolan, *Inquiry into the Integrity of the Greek Vulgate,* 2–3.
2. Vincent, *History of Textual Criticism,* 1.

unnecessary, task. This chapter will first provide a basic definition of the term "original text," and then briefly survey how respected scholars of various methodologies within the field considered it to be their main goal in practicing the discipline.

THE GROWING COMPLEXITY OF THE TERM "ORIGINAL TEXT"

In the past three decades, the concept of the original text has become increasingly complex and requires some clarifications.[3] First, the designation "original text" was historically attributed to the text that was penned by the original author. Holger Strutwolf gives a representative definition—"If I speak as a textual critic, I am using the term 'original text' to denote the author's text of a certain writing . . . This is the text that textual criticism can reach by using all the available evidence from manuscripts, early translations, and citations."[4] This original text was generally deemed to be inspired by God and binding for faith and praxis. Procuring this text was the primary goal of NTTC. Recently, these issues were taken up in a compendium of articles edited by D. A. Carson under the heading *The Enduring Authority of the Christian Scriptures*.[5] The authors of the various essays advocated the primacy and necessity of an original text on epistemological and theological grounds, with discussions centering mainly around the themes of inspiration and authority.

Second, based on the conclusions of historical-critical studies, the traditional definition of the original text was challenged. It was claimed it could be one of four chronological texts: preauthorial, authorial, canonical, and postcanonical. These distinctions were first introduced by Epp in his article "The Multivalence of the Term 'Original Text' in New Testament Textual Criticism." He labelled them as "predecessor," "autographic," "canonical," and "interpretive" text-forms.[6] Except for the final category, they are the outworking of the various critical disciplines in NT historical-critical studies: predecessor text-form (derived from form and source criticism); autographic text-form (derived from redaction criticism); and canonical text-form (derived from canonical criticism). The final category

---

3. For a survey of the changing definition of the goal of NTTC, see Holmes, "From 'Original Text' to 'Initial Text,'" 637–88.
4. Strutwolf, "Original Text and Textual History," 39.
5. Carson, *Enduring Authority*.
6. Epp, "Multivalence of the Term 'Original Text,'" 276–77.

of interpretive text-form is represented by the proponents of the new movement in NTTC (Ehrman, Parker, and Epp).

Finally, the original text has received a new taxonomy in recent years with the advent of the CBGM—authorial text, *Ausgangstext* or "initial" text, and archetypal text.[7] The first category of authorial text represents the traditional understanding of the original text, the text as penned by the original biblical author. The second category of *Ausgangstext* is the goal of NTTC under the CBGM. This is distinct from the third category of the archetypal text, which only represents the beginning of the family tree from which all the extant manuscripts descended. It is claimed this initial manuscript is now lost and can only be recreated as a hypothetical ancestor. Conversely, the *Ausgangstext* is deemed to be even more important than the archetypal text since it reaches back closer to the original text. Under the influence of the new movement in NTTC, text-critics are becomingly increasingly hesitant to claim they have the original text and are settling for just the *Ausgangstext* or the initial text.[8] In the same vein, another category has emerged in NTTC—the scribal text. Although it has yet to be included in the above taxonomies, it represents the text that is claimed to have been corrupted by the various scribes through the history of the manuscript tradition to further their agenda and is reflected in the myriad of supposed intentional variants.

The defeatism of ever reaching beyond the initial text is leading to the abandonment of the traditional goal of seeking the original text. It is now commonly assumed that much more benefit can be drawn by hypothesizing regarding the emergence of the scribal texts. Proponents of the new movement tend to depict the text-critics of yesteryear as naïve and out of date due to their penchant for continuing to seek after an original text. A representative definition of this new ideology goes as follows,

> The main goal of earlier textual critics was to establish the original reading of the biblical text. The terminology of "original" text is now seen as problematic because textual critics have recognized the complexity of the writing and "publication" process

---

7. Wachtel and Holmes, *Textual History of the Greek New Testament*, 7. The term *Ausgangstext* was coined by Gerd Mink. See Mink, "Problems of a Highly Contaminated Tradition," 25–27.

8. In the early nineties, William Petersen had even tried to make the case that NTTC needs to reach back beyond what the papyri and the oldest extant uncials allow. He advocated turning to patristic citations wherein readings could be found that were excised from the gospel traditions and never made it into the manuscript tradition but were part of the "original text." See Petersen, "What Text Can New Testament Textual Criticism Ultimately Reach?," 219–35.

in ancient times. However, the goal of establishing the Ausgangstext (the earliest form of the text from which all extant copies descend) is feasible for the New Testament since we have an abundance of manuscripts copied shortly after the autographs themselves were written.[9]

Typically, the blame for the traditional goal is placed upon either the invention of the printing press or the advent of the Reformation. The first, it is claimed, resulted in the concept of the errorless text, an idea that was unknown prior to the printing press.[10] The second, it is claimed, was due to the vacuum left by the absence of the authority of the Roman Catholic Church. The Scriptures became the new *ex cathedra* due to the Reformation.[11] On the surface such claims appear appealing, but on further investigation, they fail to provide any substantial proofs. A major argument against all such theories is the incredible stability of the text throughout its transmissional history. As Tommy Wasserman surmises,

> The optimism in the text-critical task is not only due to the wealth of evidence including the early papyri, but also to what the Alands have termed the 'tenacity' (*Tenazität*) of the New Testament textual tradition, which means that practically every reading that has ever occurred in the textual tradition is stubbornly preserved, even if the result is nonsense.[12]

Contrary to what is being proposed by the new movement in NTTC, the scribes apparently deemed the text important enough to maintain its original state as much as possible.

The major practitioners of NTTC have long held that the goal of the text critic is to reach the original text of the NT. They have commonly asserted that most of the changes in the text are "unintentional"—"errors arising from faulty eyesight," "errors arising from faulty hearing," "errors of the mind," and "errors of judgment."[13] They deemed the "intentional" changes to be relatively few—"changes involving spelling and grammar," "harmonistic corruptions," "additions of natural complements and similar adjuncts," "clearing up historical and geographical difficulties," "conflation of readings," "alterations made because of doctrinal considerations," and "additions

---

9. See Anderson and Widder, *Textual Criticism of the Bible*, 40 (emphasis original).
10. Knust, "In Pursuit of a Singular Text," 188.
11. Holmes, "From 'Original Text' to 'Initial Text,'" 642.
12. Wasserman, "Implications of Textual Criticism," 78.
13. Metzger, *Text of the New Testament*, 186–95.

of miscellaneous details."[14] They considered the task of the textual critic to be one of discarding the majority unintentional errors and focusing on the minority intentional errors. To do textual criticism was to apply the canons of NTTC and one's favored methodology to the harmonistic changes, conflations of readings, and other minor changes to arrive at the original text. Unlike the present proclivity of claiming many notable variants as a doctrinal alteration, the intentional changes for doctrinal purposes were appraised as a minor category. Overall, the text was considered to be intact and trustworthy. Again, Strutwolf represents this sentiment well, saying,

> The reconstruction of the original text of the New Testament is of vital theological and historical interest: we want to know what Paul really wrote to the Romans and what was the original form of the Gospel of Luke. The quest for the original text does not as such involve contradictions and logical impossibilities. The goal may be much harder to achieve than was believed before, but why should we not try to get as far back to the roots as possible?[15]

The following survey will demonstrate that the representative text-critics of the various methodologies were very aware of the complexities of the discipline and the limitations of the data. Nonetheless, they remained optimistic in their individual ability and methodology to reach the original text. The following survey will be divided into three categories based on the three major methods and their practitioners: documentary basis, reasoned eclecticism, and thoroughgoing eclecticism.

DOCUMENTARY THEORISTS ON THE ORIGINAL TEXT

In this category, the external evidence is considered to be the primary factor in determining the NT text. The following are some of the key proponents of this view and their emphasis on the retrievability of the original text. The position of Westcott and Hort will be discussed more than the others under this category since they devoted a considerable amount of their work toward explaining the importance of the external evidence.

Westcott and Hort

The first to give an extensive treatment of the documentary methodology in retrieving the original text of the NT were British scholars Brooke Foss

---

14. Metzger, *Text of the New Testament*, 195–206.
15. Strutwolf, "Original Text and Textual History," 41.

Westcott and Fenton John Anthony Hort. They refined the works of the German text-critics Johann Jakob Griesbach, Karl Lachmann, Constantin von Tischendorf, and others. After a thirty-year collaboration, they published their edition of the NT in 1881.[16] The following year they published their seminal work, titled *The New Testament in the Original Greek: Introduction and Appendix*.[17] Their primary goal was to break the hegemony of the Textus Receptus, which they accomplished quite decisively.[18] Nonetheless, as vehemently as Westcott and Hort rejected the Textus Receptus, they also affirmed the integrity of the NT text. In the introduction, they declared,

> The office of textual criticism, it cannot be too clearly understood at the outset, is always secondary and always negative. It is always secondary, since it comes into play only where the text transmitted by the existing documents appears to be in error, either because they differ from each other in what they read, or for some other sufficient reason. With regard to the great bulk of the words of the New Testament, as of most other ancient writings, there is no variation or other ground of doubt, and therefore no room for textual criticism; and here therefore an editor is merely a transcriber.[19]

Westcott and Hort further clarified the real issue in NTTC is regarding the "eighth" part of the text since the remaining "seven eighths" is "virtually accepted on all hands as raised above doubt."[20] Even this was too much in their estimation since "setting aside differences of orthography, the words in our opinion still subject to doubt only make up about one sixtieth of the whole New Testament."[21] This figure was still too high since the majority of the "one sixtieth" were actually "comparatively trivial," resulting in the "substantial variation" being a scant "thousandth part of the entire text."[22]

It can be plainly seen throughout Westcott and Hort's work that they held to the strong possibility of retrieving the original text of the NT. In the section titled "The Need of Criticism for the Text of the New Testament," they state the ubiquitous premise among text-critics: The originals were lost early and that deviations entered the textual stream in the subsequent

---

16. Westcott and Hort, *New Testament in the Original Greek*.
17. Westcott and Hort, *Introduction and Appendix*.
18. Jongkind, "Text and Lexicography," 288–90.
19. Westcott and Hort, *Introduction and Appendix*, 1–2.
20. Westcott and Hort, *Introduction and Appendix*, 2.
21. Westcott and Hort, *Introduction and Appendix*, 2.
22. Westcott and Hort, *Introduction and Appendix*, 2. It should be pointed out that Westcott and Hort dramatically overstated their case in this 1/1000th estimate.

turbulent period of transmission. As to the early textual laxity evinced in the multiplicity of variants entering the textual stream early in the transmission process, Westcott and Hort attributed it to the late canonical status of the NT text. Scribal proficiency was not a guarantee against corruptions. At times, the standard of transmission was high and at others it was quite low but it was inevitable that "repeated transmission involves multiplication of error."[23] In their view, the surviving manuscripts were not the complete representation of all the material data from the early period of corruption.

In further describing their methodology, Westcott and Hort declared, "There is always an abundance of variations in which no practised scholar can possibly doubt which is the original reading."[24] While internal evidence of readings involving intrinsic and transcriptional probabilities may be inconclusive, the internal evidence of documents or the combination of documents "are the most likely to convey an unadulterated transcript of the original text."[25] They gave the following now-famous maxim for their methodology: "Knowledge of documents should precede final judgement upon readings," along with its corollary,

> Where then one of the documents is found habitually to contain these morally certain or at least strongly preferred readings, and the other habitually to contain their rejected rivals, we can have no doubt, first, that the text of the first has been transmitted in comparative purity, and that the text of the second has suffered comparatively large corruption.[26]

It is obvious from the above discussion that Westcott and Hort not only held to an original text but also had very high hopes of retrieving it.

Westcott and Hort were aware of the various complexities in practicing NTTC. Nonetheless, they continued to affirm a "single universal original" as the ultimate basis for deciphering the common ancestor of a group of documents.[27] They asserted,

> The preservation of a comparatively small number of documents would probably suffice for the complete restoration of an autograph text (the determination of the earliest variations of course excepted) by genealogy alone, without the need of other kinds of evidence, provided that the documents preserved were

---

23. Westcott and Hort, *Introduction and Appendix*, 5.
24. Westcott and Hort, *Introduction and Appendix*, 23.
25. Westcott and Hort, *Introduction and Appendix*, 31.
26. Westcott and Hort, *Introduction and Appendix*, 31–32.
27. Westcott and Hort, *Introduction and Appendix*, 47.

adequately representative of different ages and different lines of transmission.[28]

They were quick to add that "this condition however is never fulfilled."[29] Furthermore, they also acknowledged the limitations of their methodology as follows:

> The utmost result that can be obtained under this condition is the discovery of what is relatively original: whether the readings thus relatively original were also the readings of the autograph is another question, which can never be answered in the affirmative with absolute decision except where the autograph itself is extant.[30]

Overall, it is obvious Westcott and Hort were aware of the same issues and dead ends facing NTTC scholars today, but they continued to hold to the possibility of retrieving the original text of the NT.

Philip Comfort

In an age when reasoned eclecticism has dominated the methodology of NTTC, Comfort has attempted to bring balance by reviving Westcott and Hort's emphasis on external evidence. He draws parallels between his understanding of church history and the transmission process of the NT text. He claims just as the church was initially pure but became corrupt with a handful of remnants carrying on the apostolic faith, so also, "The New Testament text from its inception was pure and untainted, then—generally speaking—went through a long process of textual corruption (during which time there were a few scribes who produced copies that preserved much of the original text), then began to be recovered and restored."[31] Under his methodology, "any early papyrus-supported reading (also having witness from other early manuscripts) is a viable testimony to the original text."[32] He clarifies that the original text can be attained "by consistently employing the practice of adopting the testimony of the earliest manuscripts, where two or more of these manuscripts affirm a particular variant reading."[33] Although many have taken issue with Comfort's view of textual history and praxis,

---

28. Westcott and Hort, *Introduction and Appendix*, 57.
29. Westcott and Hort, *Introduction and Appendix*, 57.
30. Westcott and Hort, *Introduction and Appendix*, 66.
31. Comfort, *Quest for the Original Text*, 127.
32. Comfort, *Quest for the Original Text*, 133.
33. Comfort, *Quest for the Original Text*, 133.

there is no doubt he believes it is possible and imperative "to recover the original text of the Greek New Testament."[34]

Zane C. Hodges and Arthur L. Farstad

Even before they published the first edition of *The Greek New Testament According to the Majority Text* in 1982, Zane C. Hodges and Arthur L. Farstad drew much criticism over their support of the Majority Text, especially Hodges. He distinguished his view from those of the Textus Receptus supporters, who were often regarded as champions of the KJV-only group, a movement which considers the Greek text in the Textus Receptus to be supernaturally preserved.[35] In a series of articles beginning in the 1960s, Hodges offered rebuttals to the common claims against the Majority Text: "The Oldest Manuscripts Do Not Support the Majority Text," "The Majority Text is a Revised, and Hence Secondary, Form of the Greek Text," and "The Readings of the Majority Text are Repeatedly Inferior to Those of the Earlier Manuscripts."[36] He also acknowledges the complexities of NTTC but declares unequivocally, "But to move from the premise that men do not use a perfect text of God's Word to the conclusion that they cannot have one is an egregious *non sequitur*."[37] In the conclusion to their 1985 edition of *The Greek New Testament According to the Majority Text*, Hodges and Farstad declare, "The work can never be final until we are assured of holding a replica of the autographs of the New Testament in our hands."[38] Hence, it should come as no surprise that Hodges and Farstad held to the strong prospect of retrieving the original text of the NT.

Maurice A. Robinson and William G. Pierpont

Although unfairly and naively lumped in the KJV-only or the Textus Receptus camps, Maurice A. Robinson and William Pierpont maintain strict

---

34. See the following reviews of Comfort's works: Petersen, "Review of *The Quest*," 529–31; Robinson, "Review of *The Quest*," 93–99; Elliott, "Review of *The Quest*," 284–87. Also see Comfort, *Quest for the Original Text*, 20.

35. Although Hodges allowed for some preservation argument in his position, he chose mostly to make his case on text-critical grounds. See Hodges, "Modern Textual Criticism," 145–46.

36. Hodges, "Greek Text of the King James Version," 336–45.

37. Hodges, "Rationalism and Contemporary New Testament Textual Criticism," 30.

38. Hodges and Farstad, *Greek New Testament*, xliii.

distinctions between those who prefer the Textus Receptus and their own preference for the Byzantine textform. They cite over 1,800 instances of differences between their text and the early printed editions of the Textus Receptus. Furthermore, they acknowledge much similarity with the text of Hodges and Farstad but point out there are differences regarding methodology, especially the use of stemmatics by the latter in the Pericope Adulterae and the book of Revelation.[39] Robinson and Pierpont call their approach "reasoned transmissionalism," wherein "all pertinent transmissional, transcriptional, external, and internal considerations" are taken into account when evaluating variant readings.[40] They advocate the history of the text can be understood by "carefully considering the effect of scribal habits and accidental and deliberate alteration of the text during the transmissional process."[41] Their resultant text has a history of transmission and a connected sequence of variant readings, unlike the popular eclectic methodology of determining the text on a variant-by-variant basis. While acknowledging "no single manuscript or immediate exemplar can be claimed with certainty to reflect the precise autograph,"[42] they affirm they have a text "that—within the framework of its underlying theory—is considered to reflect the canonical autographs in a highly accurate manner."[43] Repeatedly, Robinson and Pierpont affirm the presence of the original text behind the myriad of manuscripts and the strong likelihood of retrieving it through their methodology.

The above discussion clearly shows those relying on just the external evidence for retrieving the NT text have always worked with the understanding there was an original text behind the myriad of manuscripts and that it was generally possible to retrieve it.

REASONED ECLECTICS ON THE ORIGINAL TEXT

In this category, both the external and internal evidence are deemed important in determining the NT text. Although many have provided a definition of this methodology, Eldon Epp explains it best as follows,

39. Similar distinctions are also maintained regarding Wilbur Pickering's preference for the Family 35 group of manuscripts, a particular subset of von Soden's K^r Byzantine group. See Pickering, *Identity of the New Testament Text*, 159–200.
40. Robinson and Pierpont, *New Testament in the Original Greek*, vii.
41. See Robinson, "Case for Byzantine Priority," 127. It should be pointed out that this essay is a highly abridged version of the longer essay, available either in *TC: A Journal of Biblical Textual Criticism* 6 (2001), or as an appendix in Robinson and Pierpont, *New Testament in the Original Greek*, 533–586.
42. Robinson and Pierpont, *New Testament in the Original Greek*, i.
43. Robinson and Pierpont, *New Testament in the Original Greek*, xvi.

> [W]hen faced with any variation-unit, we would choose the variant reading that appears to be in the earliest chronological group *and* that also makes the best sense when the internal criteria are applied. Moreover, if no one cluster or type of text can be identified unambiguously as the earliest, then we would choose the variant reading in any given case that is in *one* of the earliest clusters *and* that best fits the relevant internal considerations. This method, therefore, utilizes both external and internal criteria and is called "reasoned eclecticism" or "moderate" or "genuine" eclecticism, or simply the "eclectic" method.[44]

Michael Holmes agrees and adds,

> Whether one turns to the introductory discussions or chapters by Metzger, the Alands, Fee, Amphoux, or Holmes, or the more theoretical statements by Colwell, Birdsall, or Greeven, one finds, under the superficial differences of labels, categorization, or arrangement, a virtual unanimity regarding methodology, the key points and aspects of which can all be found in Zuntz. All of these stress the need for a balanced approach that takes into account both external and internal evidence.[45]

Reasoned eclecticism is the most widely adhered-to methodology in NTTC at present. Only select key proponents who hold to the possibility of retrieving the original text will be discussed here.

Léon Vaganay

Vaganay appears to be one of the earliest proponents of the "eclectic" methodology,[46] even though the roots of the methodology go further back.[47] He defines textual criticism as

---

44. Epp, "Decision Points," 35; Epp, *Perspectives on New Testament Textual Criticism*, 267.

45. Holmes, "Reasoned Eclecticism" (1995), 344.

46. Vaganay and Amphoux, *Introduction to New Testament Textual Criticism*, 86–88.

47. Epp rightly points out, "The terms 'eclectic' and 'eclecticism' may have appeared only recently in New Testament textual criticism. Yet in a real sense the eclectic method, taken in its broadest meaning, is as old as the formulation and application of the traditional 'canons of criticism,' such as those promulgated by J. A. Bengel in 1725, by J. J. Griesbach in 1796, by K. Lachmann in 1842, and others" (Epp, "Eclectic Method in New Testament Textual Criticism," 213). Reprinted in Epp, *Perspectives on New Testament Textual Criticism*, 127.

any methodical and objective study which aims to retrieve the original form of a text or at least the form closest to the original.... The goal of textual criticism as applied to the New Testament is thus a very specific one, namely to select from among the many variants transmitted by the manuscript tradition the one which most likely represents the primitive reading.[48]

Although Amphoux, who revised and updated Vaganay's text, is "agnostic about finding the original text,"[49] Vaganay is much more optimistic about reaching the original text of the NT.

Günther Zuntz

Holmes deems Zuntz's *The Text of the Epistles: A Disquisition upon the Text of the Corpus Paulinum*, as "one of the best extended examples of a genuinely balanced reasoned eclectic approach to textual criticism."[50] In his lecture to the British Academy, Zuntz declared, "The purpose and goal of textual criticism is the recovery, within the limits of possibility, of the original text."[51] Contrary to the growing skepticism toward the possibility of recovering the original text, Zuntz remained quite optimistic: "The elucidation of the earliest stage of the textual history should bridge the gap between the originals and the earliest extant evidence and thus afford a basis for inferences about the original text."[52] Inherent in that statement is Zuntz's confidence in the retrievability of the original text of the NT.

Bruce M. Metzger

Often deemed the greatest NT text critic to come out of North America, Bruce Metzger focuses more on documenting data rather than developing methodology. He favors the reasoned eclectic methodology for the following goal:

> The necessity of applying textual criticism to the books of the New Testament arises from two circumstances: (*a*) none of the original documents is extant, and (*b*) the existing copies differ from one another. The textual critic seeks to ascertain from the

---

48. Vaganay and Amphoux, *Introduction to New Testament Textual Criticism*, 1.
49. Elliott, "Foreword," xiv.
50. See Holmes, "Reasoned Eclecticism," 339.
51. Zuntz, *Text of the Epistles*, 1.
52. Zuntz, *Text of the Epistles*, 11.

divergent copies which form of the text should be regarded as most nearly conforming to the original.[53]

It is undeniable that Metzger primarily holds to a singular text of the NT.

Kurt and Barbara Aland

Even though the Alands classify their text-critical praxis as the "local-genealogical method" and are reluctant to be included in the reasoned eclectic camp, others have appraised their methodology as belonging under reasoned eclecticism.[54] In their "twelve basic rules for textual criticism," the first rule declares: "Only *one* reading can be original, however many variant readings there may be. Only in very rare instances does the tenacity of the New Testament tradition present an insoluble tie between two or more alternative readings."[55] The Alands were so optimistic they had reached a text that was as close as it can get to the original text they even declared NA[26] and UBS[3] as the "standard text," for which they were chastised and had to rephrase.[56]

J. Harold Greenlee

In his *Introduction to New Testament Textual Criticism*, Greenlee affirms his high optimism in retrieving the original text of the NT. He declares unequivocally, "Textual Criticism is the study of copies of any written work of which the autograph (the original) is unknown, with the purpose of ascertaining the original text. . . . It is therefore deserving of the acquaintance and

---

53. Metzger, *Text of the New Testament*, v.

54. Michael Holmes takes issue: "Their demurrals notwithstanding, that the Alands use reasoned eclecticism is beyond dispute. . . . [T]he 'twelve basic rules for textual criticism' are basically a restatement of the classic criteria of reasoned eclecticism. Their preference for external evidence over internal reflects a difference of emphasis, not method" (See Holmes, "Reasoned Eclecticism" [2013] 774n10).

55. Aland and Aland, *Text of the New Testament*, 280 (emphasis original).

56. Aland, "Der neue 'Standard Text,'" 257–75. In one of the contra articles, the author warned that "a claim of 'finality' is both sweeping and dangerous" (See Moir, "Can We Risk Another 'Textus Receptus'?," 617). Consequently, the Alands replaced the "standard text" with "new text" in their second edition (Aland and Aland, *Text of the New Testament*, 24, 34–36).

attention of every serious student of the Bible."⁵⁷ Throughout his lifetime Greenlee remained solidly committed to this position.

J. Neville Birdsall

In his 1957 article in the *Baptist Quarterly*, Birdsall emphatically declares,

> The original text is a treasure to be yearned for and prized greatly—yet we cannot be certain today that we have the *ipsissima verba* of the apostles in our printed scriptures.... We must keep on with the search, and leave nothing uninvestigated till certainty be ours. We are nearer today to the original text than our forebears, but there is much still to be done—a colossal volume of work awaits us before our goal be attained.... Our Lord has said that heaven and earth shall pass away but His words never: and in similar vein, that no iota nor tittle shall pass from the Law till all be fulfilled. It would appear that the exact establishment of His words and all the scriptural witness to Him is a prime duty of the Church in every generation. May many within the Church continue to turn their hand to this task.⁵⁸

Later, in his introductory article in *The Cambridge History of the Bible*, Birdsall reaffirms, "In establishing the text we need to resort to an informed and reasoned eclectic approach, since no one strand of tradition has preserved the autograph or its approximation."⁵⁹ Although Birdsall holds to the possibility of retrieving the text of the autographs, it should be qualified that he advocates working with the understanding the "text itself is no autograph but a moving stream."⁶⁰

Gordon D. Fee

In the conclusion to his introductory article on NTTC in *The Expositor's Bible Commentary*, Fee asks, "What difference does all this make to the expositor?" He answers, "Much in every way. On the one hand, it provides him with confidence that for the most part the text he is interpreting, whether it be from a modern Greek text or a contemporary translation, truly represents

---

57. Greenlee, *Introduction to New Testament Textual Criticism*, 1–7.
58. Birdsall, "Current Trends," 109, 114.
59. Birdsall, "New Testament Text," 376.
60. Birdsall, "New Testament Text," 376.

what the biblical author actually wrote."[61] In a separate article, Fee defines the task of NTTC as singular—"to sift through all this material, carefully collating (comparing) each MS with all the others, in order to detect the errors and changes in the text, and thus to decide which variant reading at any given point is more likely to be the original."[62] This belief was clearly reflected in all of Fee's writings.

Michael W. Holmes[63]

In his article "From 'Original Text' to 'Initial Text': The Traditional Goal of New Testament Textual Criticism in Contemporary Discussion,"[64] Holmes charts the evolving goal of the discipline. He begins with his own 1989 essay, "New Testament Textual Criticism" in *Introducing New Testament Interpretation*, wherein he defines it as "the science and art of reconstructing the original text of a document."[65] Holmes now considers this definition to be "inadequate and deficient" due to the growing focus on the history of the transmission of the text as a valid goal in itself and the growing disagreement over the true meaning of the term "original text."[66] Nonetheless, it will suffice to note he still holds to the possibility of retrieving the original text of the NT. He attempts to find a common ground between the two opposite poles of recoverability and irrecoverability of the original text. By appealing to the traditional categories put forth by Lachmann and reintroduced by Paul Maas in the last century of *recensio*, *examinatio*, and *emendatio*, Holmes recasts the understanding of the original text. Whereas in the past, the discipline halted at the *recensio* stage by equating the results with the original text, Holmes proposes a two-step process in which *recensio* is limited to "assessment of all the available witness on a variant-by-variant basis, using the methodology and tools of a reasoned eclecticism." This is followed by *examinatio*, which subjects the most ancient reading to the internal criteria to determine originality.[67] This could be followed by *emendatio*, which will seek to recover the original reading through conjectural emendation in irresolvable cases.

61. Fee, "Textual Criticism of the New Testament," 1:431.
62. Fee, "Textual Criticism," 828.
63. Michael W. Holmes is the editor of *The Greek New Testament: SBL Edition*.
64. Holmes, "From 'Original Text' to 'Initial Text,'" 637–88.
65. Holmes, "New Testament Textual Criticism," 53.
66. Holmes, "From 'Original Text' to 'Initial Text,'" 637–38.
67. Holmes, "From 'Original Text' to 'Initial Text,'" 660–61.

Dirk Jongkind

Dirk Jongkind serves as the academic vice-principal of Tyndale House, the Cambridge-based research institute, which produced a new edition of the Greek NT in 2017. This new edition is unique in that it is based on a "thorough revision" of Samuel Prideaux Tregelles's edition from the nineteenth century, and gives careful attention to scribal habits in transmitting the text.[68] Furthermore, along with associate editor Peter Williams, Jongkind lays out the goal as follows:

> The focus of these sacred scriptures is, of course, on the person of Jesus Christ, presented on page after page as the unique Son of God. No other documents share such a close relationship to him, and this alone is enough reason to encourage all who have the capability and opportunity to devote themselves to the serious study of the New Testament in Greek.[69]

Two years following, Jongkind declared in his introduction to *The Greek New Testament*:

> Textual criticism is a discipline of approximation; it is a discipline that strives to improve further the resolution of the image that is painted by the text. The main message of the text is clear, but we want to have the fine detail too—and evidently, much of the fine detail has been preserved.[70]

Nowhere do the editors claim their text alone contains the "original text," but it appears the editors of the Tyndale House Greek NT are operating under the premise of its attainability through responsible textual criticism.

Conclusion

This brief survey of the select practitioners of reasoned eclecticism reveals they all considered the original text of the NT retrievable and a primary task under their methodology. Although more practitioners could have been included here, this is enough to demonstrate the dominant understanding among reasoned eclectics regarding the original text. Since reasoned eclecticism remains the most popular methodology, the general retrievability of the original text of the NT remains the dominant view among text-critics.

---

68. Jongkind, *Greek New Testament*, vii.
69. Jongkind, *Greek New Testament*, viii.
70. Jongkind, *Introduction to the Greek New Testament*, 23.

THOROUGHGOING ECLECTICS ON THE ORIGINAL TEXT

In this category, the emphasis is on the internal criteria rather than the external evidence or the balance of both (reasoned eclecticism). In the flagship article of the methodology in the *Text of the New Testament in Contemporary Research*, J. Keith Elliott states,

> The thoroughgoing eclectic critic feels able to select freely from among the available fund of variants and choose the one that best fits the internal criteria. This critic is skeptical about the high claims made for the reliability of some manuscripts or about arguments favoring a particular group of manuscripts. For such a critic, no manuscript or group contains the monopoly of original readings.[71]

Elliott elsewhere clarifies some of the misconceptions regarding thoroughgoing eclecticism, saying,

> [We] are not blind to the documentary evidence, as some of our critics might say. We do take account of the quality of the witnesses.... Thoroughgoing textual criticism does not treat documents, that is to say, manuscript witnesses, as mere carriers of variants.... But we do not begin with a predisposed view of the superiority or inferiority of any one manuscript or manuscript grouping.[72]

Nonetheless, the adherents remain strongly confident the original text is extant in the plethora of manuscripts.[73]

Unlike the previous two categories, thoroughgoing eclecticism has the least number of proponents. Elliott acknowledges, "We are seemingly in a minority among text-critics (itself a minority discipline within biblical studies)."[74] Other than George Dunbar Kilpatrick, their chief proponent, Elliott names eminent scholars such as Cuthbert Hamilton Turner, Francis Crawford Burkitt, Burnett Hillman Streeter, Kirsopp Lake, Alfred Edward Housman, Albert C. Clark, and Henry Joel Cadbury as some of the early proponents of the methodology, although it is questionable whether all of

---

71. Elliott, "Thoroughgoing Eclecticism in New Testament Textual Criticism," 745.
72. Elliott, "Case for Thoroughgoing Eclecticism," 103–4.
73. Elliott, "Thoroughgoing Eclecticism in New Testament Textual Criticism," 746.
74. Elliott, "Thoroughgoing Eclecticism," 42. Elliott, *New Testament Textual Criticism*, 42. Originally published in McKendrick and O'Sullivan, *Bible as Book*, 139–45.

these would concur with Elliott's assessment of them.[75] Elliott's protégé, Jeffrey Kloha, is also a proponent of thoroughgoing eclecticism. The following discussion will focus only on those who have provided a significant description of their methodologies, namely Kilpatrick and Elliott.

G. D. Kilpatrick

In his 1957 address to the General Meeting of the Victoria Institute in Croydon titled "The Transmission of the New Testament and its Reliability," Kilpatrick declared the task of retrieving the original text of the NT was vitally important. He claimed,

> The Bible, however, is more than a norm for conduct. For our purposes we may assume that its significance lies, in addition, in its claim to be a vehicle of divine revelation and the archives of a religion whose appeal is to history. For each of these functions it is important that the Bible should have come down to us at least substantially in its original form.[76]

While acknowledging the presence of corruption in the manuscript tradition to the point that no two manuscripts agree totally, Kilpatrick remains confident the availability of early manuscripts made it possible to reach the text close to the time of the original writings. Furthermore, he is optimistic "scholars have evolved criteria which enable us to choose with fair confidence among the variants that manuscripts offer."[77] Kilpatrick produced numerous works investigating the language, style, and theology of the NT authors. He also focused on grammatical issues regarding Atticistic tendencies and the maxim *difficilior lectio potior* among other relevant issues.[78] Nonetheless, his ultimate goal remained to reach the original text of the author.

J. Keith Elliott

Along with Kloha, Elliott appears to be the only major proponent of thoroughgoing eclecticism in recent years.[79] In his 1974 article titled, "Can We

---

75. Elliott, "Thoroughgoing Eclecticism in New Testament Textual Criticism," 748.
76. Kilpatrick, "Transmission of the New Testament," 3.
77. Kilpatrick, "Transmission of the New Testament," 3.
78. Kilpatrick, "Eclecticism and Atticism," 107–12.
79. Kloha, "Textual Commentary." Under Elliott's mentorship, Kloha examined the text of 1 Corinthians using Thoroughgoing Eclecticism.

Recover the Original New Testament?," Elliott was very clear regarding the goal of NTTC, as he declared, "The principle purpose of textual criticism is to establish as far as possible the original text of the books of the New Testament."[80] Since then, Elliott has shifted considerably from his position on the possibility of retrieving the original text. At the 2000 Lille Colloquium in France, Elliott declared his departure, claiming to be "less confident" that an original text can be attained or even "if it is the job of textual criticism to do that."[81] He repeated similar sentiments in a 2003 article, in which he again displayed affinity with other contemporary text-critics such as Ehrman and Parker in abandoning the traditional quest of NTTC.[82] Although more examples of Elliott's shift will be examined later, here it will suffice to say Elliott has abandoned his previous stance on the importance and recoverability of the original text.[83] Nonetheless, going by the traditional understanding, thoroughgoing eclectics also held to the strong probability of retrieving the original text of the NT.

CONCLUSION

This brief survey has demonstrated NT text-critics of the past, as well as major scholars in the field of NTTC even today, have consistently sought to retrieve the original text of the NT. Yet there has been a sea-change in mindset in the past few decades. Over twenty years ago, Jacobus H. Petzer made an insightful prognostication regarding the field of NTTC: "It will be up to twenty-first century textual criticism to solve the two remaining riddles, that of (a) the question of the nature of the earliest transmission of the text, or the second century, and (b) the nature of the original text and its relation to the 'autographs,' or the first century."[84] True to his words, the current focus in NTTC has been on the question of the original text of the NT. Unfortunately, the debate has been marred by extreme skepticism regarding the possibility of retrieving it. It would be understandable if great strides had been made in the accumulation of new data that called for a reassessment of the history of the text or other previously held assumptions. To the contrary, the same basic data are available today that were accessible to the NTTC scholars of yesteryear. It appears the change in goalpost is *not* based on new information but a *new ideology*.

80. Elliott, "Can We Recover the Original New Testament?," 338.
81. Elliot, "Nature of the Evidence," 14–15.
82. Elliott, "Thoroughgoing Eclecticism," 49.
83. Elliott, "Recent Trends," 127.
84. Petzer, "History of the New Testament," 36.

3

Bart D. Ehrman

Bart Ehrman has been the major challenger to the traditional goalpost in NTTC. Since 2005, his bestseller, *Misquoting Jesus: The Story Behind Who Changed the Bible and Why*, has drawn much attention to the relatively unknown discipline of NTTC.[1] Ehrman's appraisal of the state of the NT text continues to challenge the beliefs of the unsuspecting reader with claims such as "We have only error-ridden copies, and the vast majority of these are centuries removed from the originals and different from them, evidently, in thousands of ways"; "There are more variations among our manuscripts than there are words in the New Testament"; and "The more I studied the manuscript tradition of the New Testament, the more I realized just how radically the text had been altered over the years at the hands of scribes, who were not only conserving scripture but also changing it."[2] For someone from an evangelical perspective, it is dumbfounding that a person who attended historic evangelical institutions like Moody Bible Institute and Wheaton College could become an ex-believer after encountering the "truth" regarding NT manuscripts and church history. Concurrently, it has also gratified the skeptical reader that such truth has won over the beliefs and claims of traditional Christianity. Ehrman had aimed *Misquoting Jesus* at the nonscholarly readership and the response was overwhelmingly successful.

1. Ehrman, *Misquoting Jesus*.
2. Ehrman, *Misquoting Jesus*, 7, 90, 207.

SCHOLARLY RESPONSES TO EHRMAN'S THESIS

The reaction among NT scholars was not as sensational. Most had been familiar with Ehrman's 1993 scholarly monograph, *The Orthodox Corruption of Scripture: The Effect of Early Christological Controversies on the Text of the New Testament*.[3] Many had already given positive reviews of the work when it was published.[4] Some had also declared Ehrman's thesis was in the "proper domain of textual criticism" and even applied his methodology in their approach to the text.[5] On the other hand, most evangelical scholars were

---

3. Ehrman, *Orthodox Corruption of Scripture*. This work was released in 2011, with some corrections and an afterword summarizing critical reviews and developments since the first edition.

4. Michael Holmes deemed the work "amply documented" and "transcending the usual categories of 'New Testament' and 'Patristics'" (Holmes, "Review of *The Orthodox Corruption of Scripture*," 237). William Petersen remarked that the book "demonstrates once again that the most reliable guide to the development of Christian theology is the ever-changing text of the New Testament" (Petersen, "Review of *The Orthodox Corruption of Scripture*," 563–64). J. Keith Elliott recognized the scant evidence behind many readings that Ehrman considered to be original but endorsed the book anyway, saying, "The arguments are clearly set out and persuasively presented" (Elliott, "Review of *The Orthodox Corruption of Scripture*," 405–6). David C. Parker declared, "New Testament textual criticism will be changed for the better by this book" (Parker, "Review of *The Orthodox Corruption of Scripture*," 507). Ehrman's *Doktorvater*, Bruce Metzger, happily endorsed *The Orthodox Corruption of Scripture* and made a tongue-in-cheek remark in closing: "Besides learning much concerning the social and intellectual history of early Christianity, readers of Ehrman's book will also understand why the King James Version of the New Testament incorporates each of the three examples of 'orthodox corruptions' mentioned above" (Metzger, "Review of *The Orthodox Corruption of Scripture*," 212). Also, the fifth Birmingham Colloquium (2007) was focused on dealing with the various issues raised in *The Orthodox Corruption of Scripture*. See Houghton and Parker, *Textual Variation*.

5. In 1998, at the NTTC Section of the Society of Biblical Literature Annual Meeting in Orlando, Florida, Eldon J. Epp presented a paper titled, "The Multivalence of the term 'Original Text' in New Testament Textual Criticism," in which he named four text-critics who adopted the new quest of NTTC, among whom Ehrman was chronologically first. Epp listed himself as part of the new movement (Epp, "Multivalence of the Term 'Original Text,'" 245–81). Ironically, he once considered Aland's claim that "the New Testament can have possessed only one text" a truism, which he later recanted in his 2005 anthology of articles (Epp, "Continuing Interlude," 192). Increasingly, Ehrman's thesis has been treated as foundational to the understanding of NT history and text-critical issues. An example of the former may be noted in Frances M. Young's remark in her prelude to volume 1 of the Cambridge History of Christianity: "The gospels were transmitted through a period in which Jesus might have been dissolved into a spiritual visitant, or remained just a good man adopted by God—the gospel texts themselves show traces of the impact of these controversies." Young simply footnoted Ehrman's *The Orthodox Corruption of Scripture* to her remark (Mitchell et al., *Origins to Constantine*, 1:34). Another example of a text-critical work that has followed Ehrman's

slow to respond and disapproved, as expected. Even though *The Orthodox Corruption of Scripture* was written twelve years prior to *Misquoting Jesus*, most of the negative responses came after the publication of the latter. The rebuttals were in the form of blogs, articles, books, reviews, debates, sermons, and even a website. Many of the responses were apologetic in nature.[6] Others took issue with Ehrman's dependence on Walter Bauer's *Orthodoxy and Heresy in Earliest Christianity*, his view of canon formation, and his approval of extracanonical works, mostly gnostic, from early Christianity.[7]

More pertinent to the present study were the many rebuttals that took issue with Ehrman's handling of the text-critical data.[8] A complete survey of every article and review written on this matter is beyond the scope of this discussion.[9] Here it will suffice to highlight just a few. In a ThM thesis, Stratton L. Ladewig uses reasoned eclectic principles to give an alternate explanation of the textual variants in Ehrman's *The Orthodox Corruption of Scripture*.[10] Similarly, Ivo Tamm in his "Magisterarbeit" under Barbara Aland also notes the subjective nature of Ehrman's arguments and adds the early scribes were not as organized and agenda-driven as Ehrman often portrays them. To the contrary, they were everyday people who were making copies for personal use.[11] As to Ehrman's repeated claim the papyri reflect an unstable stage of transmission, Maurice A. Robinson's paper, "The Integrity of the Early New Testament Text: A Collation-Based Comparison Utilizing

---

line of thinking is the book by Kannaday, *Apologetic Discourse and the Scribal Tradition*.

6. One major representative of this approach was the highly publicized debate on January 21, 2009, between Christian apologist James White and Ehrman (See https://ehrmanblog.org/video-bart-ehrman-vs-james-white-debate/). White made a point regarding what he terms the influx of postmodernism in biblical scholarship (although Ehrman does not consider his position to be postmodern, based on a personal email comment to Maurice A. Robinson). White accused Ehrman of bare sensationalism, a point echoed by many others. A similar response was also provided by Timothy Paul Jones in his introductory-level study for the lay audience seeking to find counterpoints to Ehrman's thesis. It focuses more on historical issues than text-critical matters. See Jones, *Misquoting Truth*.

7. See Komoszewski et al., *Reinventing Jesus*; Köstenberger and Kruger, *Heresy of Orthodoxy*; Patzia, *Making of the New Testament*; Bock, *Missing Gospels*.

8. Although the scope is limited (only seventeen selected examples), a good representative of scrupulous text-critical analysis of Ehrman's use of manuscript evidence is Wasserman, "Misquoting Manuscripts?," 325–50.

9. For the latest response to Ehrman, see Marcello, "Myths about Orthodox Corruption," 211–227. A big thanks to Peter Gurry for lending a pre-publication copy of this book.

10. Ladewig, "Examination of the Orthodoxy."

11. Available through http://evangelicaltextualcriticism.blogspot.com/2006/03/theologisch-christologische-varianten.html.

the Papyri of the Second and Third Centuries," shows the papyri remained stable over 90 percent of the time.[12] Similarly, Kim Haines-Eitzen takes on the doubts regarding the state of the text in the first couple of hundred years of Christianity and the fidelity of the scribes. She concludes,

> The scribes who copied Christian literature during the second and third centuries were not 'uncontrolled' nor were the texts that they (re)produced marked by 'wildness.' Rather, the (re)production of texts by early Christian scribes was bounded and constrained by the multifaceted and multilayered discursive practices of the second- and third-century church.[13]

Barbara Aland has also written several articles confirming the earliest papyri (P45, P46, P66, and P75) were copied with utmost care.[14]

The scholar who has interacted the most with Ehrman is Daniel Wallace. In a review article titled "The Gospel According to Bart," Wallace deems *Misquoting Jesus* as nothing more than postmodernism entering NTTC, in which "the Jesus that sells is the one that is palatable to postmodern man."[15] He takes issue with two fundamental theological points in Ehrman's approach: "First . . . it is irrelevant to speak of the Bible's inerrancy because we no longer have the original documents; second, the variants in the manuscripts change the basic theology of the NT."[16] Regarding the former, Wallace disagrees with Ehrman's understanding of inerrancy, whereby the presence of variants suggested an errant text. Instead, he draws a distinction between inspiration and inerrancy where the former "relates to the wording of the Bible" and the latter to the "truth of the statement."[17] Since "we have the text of the New Testament *somewhere* in the manuscripts," there is

---

12. Robinson, "Integrity of the Early New Testament Text."

13. Haines-Eitzen, *Guardians of Letters*, 106. Two other works have contributed much towards a more responsible understanding of the state of the text in the early centuries: Min, *Die früheste Überlieferung des Matthäusevangeliums*, and Bell, *Early Textual Transmission of John*.

14. Aland, "Kriterien zur Beurteilung," 1–13; Aland, "Der textkritische und textgeschichtliche," 19–38; Aland, "Significance of the Chester Beatty Papyri," 108–21; Aland, "New Testament Textual Research," 13–26.

15. Wallace, "Gospel According to Bart," 327–28. He makes an even stronger statement in Wallace, "Challenges in New Testament Textual Criticism," 89. He declares, "At bottom, postmodern textual critics have confused absolute certainty—which we cannot have—with reasonable certainty—which we can. And they are even calling this reasonable certainty a 'blind leap of faith' without recognizing that their own skepticism requires much more faith."

16. Wallace, "Gospel According to Bart," 334.

17. Wallace, "Gospel According to Bart," 334.

no need to think the original text is elusive and hence the NT as we have it is filled with conjectures.[18] Wallace also debated Ehrman in 2008 at the Greer-Heard Point-Counterpoint Forum in Faith and Culture at the New Orleans Baptist Theological Seminary. The forum articles were published as a collection in 2011 under the title *The Reliability of the New Testament: Bart D. Ehrman and Daniel B. Wallace in Dialogue*.[19] This was followed by a second debate on the campus of Southern Methodist University on October 1, 2011, and a third on February 1, 2012, on the campus of UNC-Chapel Hill. Wallace represented a reasoned eclectic position, also held by Bart Ehrman, who made it a point to remind the listeners of their debate that on matters of textual criticism, "Dan Wallace would agree with me on most of this."[20]

Before Ehrman's thesis is surveyed in the following section, it is worth pointing out no efforts to rebut his thesis have changed his mind or diminished his efforts at dispersing his views, as he expressly stated in an interview,

> And there are a lot of websites and blogs and things that attack me. The way I deal with that is by not reading them. I think intelligent people can read what I've written and then can read what people have said in response and then decide for themselves who's got the better argument. I don't feel a need to respond to my critics or anything like that.[21]

In the following section, attention will be given to Ehrman's *The Orthodox Corruption of Scripture* rather than *Misquoting Jesus* because it is a critical work and represents his thesis far more comprehensively than his popular work.

EHRMAN'S DEPENDENCE ON WALTER BAUER

In the introduction to *The Orthodox Corruption of Scripture* Ehrman declares, "Scribes occasionally altered the words of their sacred texts to make them more patently orthodox and to prevent their misuse by Christians who espoused aberrant views."[22] He claims this tendency was far more prevalent

---

18. Wallace, "Gospel According to Bart," 334 (emphasis original).
19. Stewart, *Reliability of the New Testament*.
20. In 2011, a collection of articles by Wallace's former academic interns and ThM students was published through Kregel. See Wallace, ed., *Revisiting the Corruption of the New Testament*. A recent example of a nontext-critical response is Köstenberger et al., *Truth in a Culture of Doubt*. Also see Chatraw, "Disunity and Diversity," 449–65.
21. Morgan, "Complete Interview with Bart Ehrman."
22. Ehrman, *Orthodox Corruption of Scripture* (1993), xi.

in the first couple of centuries of Christianity than any other period because it was rife with struggles between "social structures, religious practices, or ideologies" in the church.[23] To bolster his thesis, Ehrman appeals to Walter Bauer's theory of early church history in his *Orthodoxy and Heresy in Early Christianity*.[24] In a nutshell, Bauer had challenged the traditional view that early Christianity was a monolith wherein (1) orthodoxy came first, was widespread, and normative; (2) heresy came later and was a distortion of the truth and marginal; and (3) orthodoxy confronted and successfully repudiated heresy.

The traditional view was unchallenged since the days of Eusebius, who held to the divine superiority and dominance of the "catholic and only true church" over the occasional objections by heretics.[25] It was contested in the mid-nineteenth century by F. C. Baur, who proposed that earliest Christianity was an uncomfortable mix of Jewish and gentile Christianities, which were later combined to form the orthodox church. A key premise for his view was "the Paul of the Acts is manifestly quite a different person from the Paul of the Epistles."[26] In other words, early Christianity displayed a conflict between Petrine and Pauline forms of Christianity. The former was Jewish, the latter gentile, and the two were later synthesized in the second century and the centuries following into a catholic Christianity. In his view, the canonical book of Acts betrayed the attempts to cover up and smooth over some of these conflicts. A major weakness of Baur's proposal was he lumped Peter completely in the anti-Pauline camp, implying Jewish and gentile Christianity were completely at odds with each other. These lines were too artificial when examined in light of the biblical data and historical facts.

Even though Baur's view was not without its detractors, it opened wide the door to nontraditional understandings of early church history. Several attempts were made to advance Baur's thesis, but the most significant came in the early part of the twentieth century through Walter Bauer. His *Orthodoxy and Heresy in Early Christianity* challenged all previous discussions of early church history, orthodoxy, and NT studies. Contrary to Eusebius's one-sided account and Baur's rigid classification, Bauer proposed the following thesis,

23. Ehrman, *Orthodox Corruption of Scripture* (1993), 3.
24. Bauer, *Rechtgläubigkeit und Ketzerei*. For the English translation, see Bauer, *Orthodoxy and Heresy*.
25. Grant, *Eusebius as Church Historian*, 1.
26. Baur, *Paul*, 1:11. For a comprehensive treatment of the subject, see Baur and Menzies, *Church History*.

> Certain manifestations of Christian life that the authors of the church renounce as "heresies" originally had not been such at all, but, at least here and there, were the only form of the new religion—that is, for those regions they were simply "Christianity." The possibility also exists that their adherents constituted the majority, and they looked down with hatred and scorn on the orthodox, who for them were the false believers.[27]

He therefore challenged Origen's dictum: "All heretics at first are believers, then later they swerve from the rule of faith."[28] He declared this view to be untenable and a reflection of the view of one party only. To the contrary, he held that the early church was an assortment of many competing heretical minorities that were brought to unity by the clever ecclesiastical maneuverings of Roman Christianity, which utilized traditions, financial lures, organization, interference in the affairs of other churches, and other effective methods to gain this control.[29] Bauer set out to prove his thesis by examining the world of early second-century Christianity, beginning with the fringe regions of Syria, heretical Christianity, and concluding with Antioch—the bastion of orthodox Christianity.

Numerous rebuttals and critiques have been offered against various aspects of Bauer's theory, as noted in the introduction.[30] Many claimed the tone of Bauer's arguments was far from objective. James Moffat notes Bauer seemed to "take the position of the barrister rather than of the judge."[31] Similarly, Desjardins remarks "his professed impartiality shifts at times to an apologist on behalf of the 'heretics.'"[32] Another common complaint is Bauer's thesis was not as original as was often portrayed. Desjardins points to the Tübingen critics' use of Hegelian dialectic as the progenitor of Bauer's hypothesis.[33] Overall, the reviews have proven his methodology was fraught with *non sequiturs* due to hasty generalization, argument from silence, exaggeration, and oversimplification. Henry Ernest William Turner concludes,

> His fatal weakness appears to be a persistent tendency to oversimplify problems, combined with the ruthless treatment of such

---

27. Bauer, *Orthodoxy and Heresy*, xxi.
28. As quoted by Bauer in *Orthodoxy and Heresy*, xxiii. Taken from Origen, *Commentary on the Song of Songs*, 3 (to Cant. 2.2): *omnes enim haeretici primo ad credulitatem veniunt, et post haec ab itinere fidei et dogmatum veritate declinant*.
29. Bauer, *Orthodoxy and Heresy*, 89.
30. Parker, *Living Text of the Gospels*, 212.
31. Moffatt, "Review of Professor Bauer's *Rechtgläubigkeit und Ketzerei*," 475.
32. Desjardins, "Bauer and Beyond," 68n9.
33. Desjardins, "Bauer and Beyond," 67–68.

evidence as fails to support his case. It is very doubtful whether all sources of trouble in the early Church can be reduced to a set of variations on a single theme. Nor is it likely that orthodoxy itself evolved in a uniform pattern, though at different speeds in the main centres of the Universal Church. The formula . . . represents an historical generalization too neat to fit the facts. History seldom unfolds itself in so orderly a fashion.[34]

Similarly, Thomas A. Robinson cautions,

The failure of the Bauer Thesis in western Asia Minor is not merely one flaw in an otherwise coherent reconstruction. The failure of the thesis in the only area where it can be adequately tested casts suspicion on the other areas of Bauer's investigation. Extreme caution should be exercised in granting to the Bauer Thesis insight into those areas for which inventive theses appear credible only because evidence is either too scarce or too mute to put anything to test.[35]

Even though Bauer forever changed the discussion of early Christianity, orthodoxy, and NT writings, his thesis did not gain universal acceptance. It only served to challenge long-held views regarding the development of early Christianity.

FROM BAUER TO ORTHODOX CORRUPTION

Ehrman agrees with Bauer that the traditional view of the early church or apostolic church was a misrepresentation of earliest Christianity and needed to be abandoned. He concurs with Bauer that the historical evidence proved that at various points in the history of Christianity there have been pluralities of movements that have differed on key theological issues, that inevitably led to a period of struggle, and, in time, the dominant group emerged victorious.[36] Ehrman is aware of the weaknesses in Bauer's thesis. Nonetheless, he maintains "despite the clear shortcomings of his study, Bauer's intuitions were right *in nuce:* if anything, early Christianity was even less tidy and more diversified than he realized, and contrary to his opinion, we do not need to wait for the second century to begin painting this picture."[37] In other words, Bauer's thesis could be salvaged if the period of discussion

---

34. Turner, *Pattern of Christian Truth*, 79.
35. Robinson, *Bauer Thesis Examined*, 204.
36. Ehrman, *Orthodox Corruption of Scripture* (1993), 7.
37. Ehrman, *Orthodox Corruption of Scripture* (1993), 8.

were stretched beyond the second century into the silent years of earliest Christianity where the lines between "acceptable" and "aberrant" beliefs in early Christianity were blurred.[38]

Ehrman even questions the legitimacy of using the terms "orthodoxy" and "heresy" prior to the fourth century, since the struggle in the early period regarded power more than beliefs. Even so, he continues to use the established designations and even concocted the title "proto-orthodox" to designate the group that was victorious in the struggle for dominance and was later claimed by the orthodox as their predecessor in the struggle for right belief. The proto-orthodox group was not monolithic because several contradictory views existed in the overall movement. He further extends Bauer's thesis to claim such groups, with their newly acquired power, set out to rewrite church history in their own favor in order to legitimize their authority and maintain control.

Ehrman claims the proto-orthodox altered the NT text in their favor. Their presence may be detected in what they rejected rather than what they affirmed in the NT text. They rejected what they perceived in their opponents to be out of line with the central thesis of the orthodox faith. Most of the battle seemed to have been in the realm of Christology, a hotbed issue in the early church. Many of the christological beliefs of the proto-orthodox were "paradoxical" in nature, which, according to Ehrman, was a by-product of the polemics of that period.[39] He turns to the discipline of NTTC to demonstrate the traces of these skirmishes since the "scribes modified their texts of Scripture in light of the polemical contexts within which they worked, altering the manuscripts they reproduced to make them more orthodox on the one hand and less susceptible to heretical misuse on the other."[40] In other words, the evidence of the struggle for dominance in earliest Christianity and the proto-orthodox attempts to maintain such paradoxical views on Christology in the second and third centuries can be noticed in the many variants in the NT manuscripts. Ehrman even utilizes the writings of the early fathers and the apologists to reinforce his thesis.

Moreover, Ehrman accuses the orthodox of masterminding the canon to preserve and elevate writings that favored their position. Although he affirms the criteria of apostolicity for canonicity, he contends "Decisions concerning 'apostolicity' were ultimately based not on claims of authorship per se, but on a book's essential conformity to the *regula fidei*, that is, to the apostolic doctrine that orthodox Christians claimed as their own unique

---

38. Ehrman, *Orthodox Corruption of Scripture* (1993), 10–11.
39. Ehrman, *Orthodox Corruption of Scripture* (1993), 13.
40. Ehrman, *Orthodox Corruption of Scripture* (1993), 15.

possession."⁴¹ He even includes the various hermeneutical debates between literal and allegorical interpretations of the NT writings as part of the struggle. He deems writings such as the Pastoral Epistles and 2 Peter as simply forgeries by the orthodox church to further their agenda, being cautious to point out these writings were not forged by the orthodox, since according to Ehrman the orthodox party did not appear on the scene until the fourth century.⁴² Nonetheless, both the Pastoral Epistles and 2 Peter were useful to the "incipient orthodoxy" of the early period.⁴³ In essence, Ehrman turns the traditional view on its head that heretics tampered with the Scriptures. Instead, he alleges the orthodox were just as guilty for their part in corrupting the NT text. In essence, this reflects Ehrman's previously stated maxim, "winners not only write the history, they also reproduce the texts."⁴⁴

Not only does Ehrman build his proposal upon Bauer's shaky thesis, but he goes far beyond the latter's claims and supporting evidence. First, under Bauer's thesis, the significant heresies appeared at the end of the second century, and Bauer used the writings of the early church fathers to make his case. Under Ehrman's thesis, these heresies are expected to be fully developed and vying for dominance in a much earlier period, and Ehrman uses the NT text itself as his primary source since not much else is available from the early period. While the doctrinal stances of the church fathers are documented, most of the NT manuscripts do not provide any information regarding the theological stance of the owners or the scribes. All of his arguments are speculative at best.

Unlike Bauer, who focused on caricatures of orthodox and heretical figures and events without dealing with any particular stream of doctrine, Ehrman deals much more with different streams of doctrine. While Bauer's attempt at connecting the streams of doctrine with the various figures and events of orthodoxy and heresy is vague at best, Ehrman specifically fails to connect the various leaders and events with the thousands of NT manuscripts, particularly when the latter are utilized in a highly selective and often contradictory manner. Another major difference between Bauer and Ehrman's theses is the former's thesis is based on the geographical location of the various churches and the supposed diversity and priority of heretical Christianity in those parts of Christendom. To the contrary, NT manuscripts reveal very little with regards to their geographical provenance or destination. Hence, what may work as a premise for Bauer is only remotely

---

41. Ehrman, *Orthodox Corruption of Scripture* (1993), 18.
42. Ehrman, *Orthodox Corruption of Scripture* (1993), 22–23.
43. Ehrman, *Orthodox Corruption of Scripture* (1993), 23.
44. Ehrman, *Orthodox Corruption of Scripture* (1993), 27.

possible for Ehrman. Bauer's attempt to engage in regional historical studies seems to be much different from what Ehrman attempts, since there are no clearly regional manuscripts. Whereas Bauer argued the different heresies were simply geographical variants of early Christianity, Ehrman is attempting to examine the different textual variants in order to retrace their history and thereby to establish the presence of variant Christianities underlying the NT text. It appears identical words are being used but with entirely different implications, ones even Bauer had declared unworkable:

> As we turn to our task, *the New Testament seems to be both too unproductive and too much disputed to be able to serve as a point of departure.* The majority of its anti-heretical writings *cannot* be arranged with confidence either chronologically or geographically; nor can the more precise circumstances of their origin be determined with sufficient precision. It is advisable, therefore, first of all to interrogate other sources concerning the relationship of orthodoxy and heresy, so that, with the insights that may be gained there, we may try to determine the time and place of their origins.[45]

This should have been a major counterincentive for Ehrman to claim Bauer's thesis as his starting point but such has not been the case.

Ehrman's thesis also faces a major problem with regard to the time required for the struggle to end in early Christianity and the victorious party to declare their hegemony. While Bauer's thesis proposed a movement toward catholicity over a period of 400 years, Ehrman's thesis allows for substantially less time for the changes to be made and smoothed over into the NT text. Ehrman has backed himself into an even tighter spot by proposing it was the proto-orthodox who made the changes. As it is commonly accepted most of these changes came about in the first couple centuries, it allows only a period of little over 150 years for the changes to be made and solidified as an authoritative text to some particular community. Also, Bauer argued in his thesis that Rome played some role in mandating a certain doctrinal system as it gained control leading up to the councils. Although this view has been contested in the various works challenging Bauer, the dominance of the church in Rome is evident by the end of the fourth century. This same argument cannot be used in Ehrman's thesis since there is no evidence of an ecclesiologically dominant Rome in the first couple centuries of the early church. There remains no ecclesiastical power that compelled the scribes uniformly to alter the text to fit a proto-orthodox agenda.

---

45. Bauer, *Orthodoxy and Heresy*, xxv (emphasis added).

Finally, there is a major difference between Bauer's and Ehrman's uses of the term "orthodoxy." Everett Fergusson insightfully points out "Bauer weighted the case in his favor by a narrow definition of 'orthodoxy' in institutional terms to the neglect of normative elements of belief in the early preaching."[46] Ehrman, on the other hand, is not dealing with this "institutional" use of the term "orthodoxy," but is delving into actual doctrines that made up right and wrong beliefs in the early church. The focus of Bauer's approach is more on the triumph of a particular geographic see, namely Rome, while Ehrman's thesis seeks to make it a more prevalent movement anywhere and everywhere.

This brief discussion demonstrates even though Ehrman claims dependence on Bauer's thesis, his approach goes far beyond, and in a very different direction from, what Bauer intended.

BRIEF ANALYSIS OF EHRMAN'S THESIS

In Ehrman's thesis, the original text is essential but retrieving it is no longer critical or even possible.[47] Instead, the goal is to identify and appreciate the subsequent forms of texts through the centuries following the period of the original text.[48] Ehrman even finds an affinity between focusing on the later forms of text and reader-response criticism where any variant could be worthy in the eye of the beholder. He identifies four qualifying categories represented in separate chapters of his *The Orthodox Corruption of Scripture*.

---

46. Ferguson, *Backgrounds of Early Christianity*, 612.

47. In the updated edition of *The Orthodox Corruption of Scripture* in 2011, Ehrman keeps the content of the book unchanged except for corrections and adds an afterword to summarize the state of the field since the release of the first edition in 1993. Curiously, he remarks, "the book does not represent the field as it would if it were written de novo today. In the book, for example, I continue to talk about the original text . . . if I were to write the book now I would use a different term and employ a different conception." He claims "it would ultimately have no bearing on my analysis if, instead of the 'original' text, I referred to 'the earliest attainable form of the text,' or simply to 'an earlier form of the text.' With any of these formulations we have the same result: scribes inherited a form of the text and changed it. They may have inherited five forms of the text and changed it to a sixth, and it still would not affect the basic argument" (Ehrman, *Orthodox Corruption of Scripture* [1993], 334, 342).

48. Ultimately, Ehrman's entire thesis is based on some type of definite "original text" that serves as a baseline to compare any deviation. Without such a baseline 'original text,' there is no longer any evidence that the text has been altered to fit the agenda of a scribe. Whether one terms the baseline 'original text,' 'earliest form of the text,' or 'initial text,' a lengthy iterative process and much testing will still be required before any specific claims can be made regarding supposed 'original' alteration.

Anti-Adoptionistic Corruptions of Scripture

Ehrman begins this chapter by noting the early Christians were not quite sure about the actual meaning of the phrase "Son of God." In struggling with the concept of Jesus' nature, they leaned toward adoptionism, which he defines as follows,

> Christ was a flesh and blood human being without remainder, a man who had been adopted by God to be his Son and to bring about the salvation of the world. To be sure, these representatives of adoptionism construed no monolith; they differed among themselves, for example, concerning the moment at which Jesus' adoption had taken place. But by the second century, most believed that it had occurred at his baptism, when the Spirit of God descended upon him.[49]

Ehrman is quick to admit "for the vast majority of believers, whether heretical or orthodox, this form of Christianity represented an error of the most egregious kind."[50] Nevertheless, he goes on to claim it was probably an original view of the first Christians, even more so than the orthodox views that have been passed down through the centuries.[51] He identifies the Ebionites, Theodotus, Paul of Samosata, and Artemon as some of those who held to adoptionist views and were descendants of the early proto-heterodox. The tone and the amount of discussion given to adoptionism as an early form of Christianity leaves one with the impression it was not a minor offshoot but a major branch of Christianity that was strategically eradicated by the proto-orthodox. In his work, *Lost Christianities: The Battles for Scripture and the Faiths We Never Knew*—a later, more popular, and less technical work than his *The Orthodox Corruption of Scripture*—Ehrman adds: "Roman 'adoptionists' were eventually weeded out and their views castigated by those who insisted that even though Jesus Christ was a man, he was not a 'mere man'; he was also God."[52] Although Ehrman declares such a struggle took place between the proto-orthodox and the proto-heterodox, he fails to list any sources for his conclusion.

According to Ehrman, evidence for the struggle to define and propagate the orthodox view can be noticed in the NT text. He lists many examples of such orthodox corruptions that were supposedly created to suppress and eradicate any adoptionist claims for the sonship of Christ. He divides them

---

49. Ehrman, *Orthodox Corruption of Scripture* (1993), 47.
50. Ehrman, *Orthodox Corruption of Scripture* (1993), 47.
51. Ehrman, *Orthodox Corruption of Scripture* (1993), 48.
52. Ehrman, *Lost Christianities*, 153.

under various subheadings: "Jesus the Unique Son of God: The Orthodox Affirmation of the Virgin Birth,"[53] "More than Chosen: The Orthodox Opposition to an Adopted Jesus,"[54] "Jesus, Son of God before His Baptism,"[55] "The Orthodox Opposition to a Low Christology,"[56] "Christ as Divine: The Exchange of Predicates,"[57] and "Christ: No Ordinary Human."[58]

For example, Ehrman alleges the presumed addition of the phrase υιου θεου in Mark 1:1 demonstrates a scribal attempt to counteract the heretics since the adoptionists held to the view that Jesus's sonship began at his baptism. The longer reading, Ιησου Χριστου υιου θεου is supported by ℵ¹ B D L W *pc* (*sed* του q. A f1 f13 33 𝔐) latt sy co; Ir^lat. On the other hand, the shorter reading without υιου θεου is found in ℵ* Θ 28^c 1555, syr^p arm geo, and Origen. Ehrman refuses to dismiss the latter few witnesses, primarily because of the antiquity of ℵ*. For those who might suggest a homoioteleuton due to parablepsis, Ehrman points to the wide range of manuscript evidence for the omission. He also points out "the slate of witnesses is diverse in terms of textual consanguinity and geography."[59] He insists it was odd that scribes would make an accidental omission at the beginning of a book.

Ehrman's argument fails to allow for a simple and obvious explanation of the variant. The omission is most probably a case of homoioteleuton where four genitives could be listed as *nomina sacra*.[60] It is very likely the scribe accidently jumped from one ending to another. Furthermore, Mark's Christology in 5:7, 9:7, 14:61, 15:39, and other passages strengthens the presence of υιου θεου in the passage.

Anti-Separationist Corruptions of Scripture

Ehrman lists the separationists in the category of Gnostic Christians who "comprised a plethora of divergent groups that manifested a wild array of

53. The passages are listed in the order Ehrman discusses them in his work: Matt 1:16, 25; Luke 2:33, 48; 3:23; 4:22; John 6:41–51; 1 John 5:6; Acts 2:30.

54. Luke 3:22; 9:35; Acts 10:38; 1 John 5:18.

55. Mark 1:1; Luke 2:43; 3:21; Matt 1:18; Eph 4:9.

56. 1 Tim 3:16; John 1:18; Mark 1:3; Matt 3:3; Luke 3:5; John 1:23; John 19:40; 1 John 3:23; John 10:33; 12:41; Luke 1–2; 9:20; Mark 3:11; Luke 7:9; 8:28, 40; 20:42; 2 Pet 1:2; Gal 2:20; 1 Tim 1:1; 2 Tim 1:10; Titus 3:6; Heb 13:20.

57. Acts 20:28; 1 Pet 5:1; 1 Cor 10:5; Rom 14:10; 2 Cor 5:10.

58. Matt 24:36; Luke 2:40; John 19:5; 1 Cor 15:47; Heb 2:18; 10:29; Col 1:22.

59. Ehrman, *Orthodox Corruption of Scripture* (1993), 73.

60. It needs to be acknowledged here that υιου is typically not reduced as a *nominum sacrum*. This does not affect the possibility of a homoioteleuton leap from to within the string of various abbreviations.

mythologies, beliefs, and cultic practices. These groups nonetheless appeared to have shared some basic notions about the nature of the world and of human existence within it."[61] Ehrman narrows the heading to focus on one figure, the arch-heretic Cerinthus, who demonstrated the belief the divine Christ came upon Jesus at the time of the baptism. He descended upon him in the form of a dove, remained in him throughout the duration of his ministry, and empowered him to do his ministry and perform miracles. After this, the Christ left him right before the passion and Jesus had to suffer his crucifixion alone. According to Ehrman, the scribes made many attempts to make sure those who believed in the Separationist Christology would not find support in the biblical text. Under this understanding, he claims the following to be such examples: pronouncement of an anathema on anyone who would try to separate the natures of Christ,[62] Jesus was Christ before his baptism,[63] Christ did not enter into Jesus at the time of the baptism but was already there,[64] Christ did not leave him before his passion,[65] Christ actually died and was resurrected,[66] explicit references to Jesus as Christ,[67] and, the introduction of the phrase "our Lord Jesus Christ."[68]

For example, in Galatians 6:17 Ehrman finds "stigmata of Jesus" to be the only plausible reading because the remaining variants have an underlying agenda. The shorter reading with simply τα στιγματα του Ιησου is supported by P46 A B C* 33. 629. 1241^s *pc* f t vgst sa^{ms}. Manuscript evidence exists for other readings that have vied for acceptance. For example, the reading τα στιγματα του Χριστου is supported by P Y 0278 81 365 1175 2464 *pc* bo; also, the reading τα στιγματα του κυριου Ιησου is supported by C³ D² (1739) 1881 𝔐 vg^{cl} sy$^{(p)}$; and τα στιγματα κυρ. ημων (-ℵ D¹) Ιης. Χρ. is supported by a D* F G it (sa^{mss}); Ambst Pel. According to Ehrman, the

---

61. Ehrman, *Orthodox Corruption of Scripture* (1993), 163.

62. 1 John 4:3; Matt 12:30; Luke 11:23; 2 Cor 11:4.

63. Matt 1:16, 18; Luke 1:35.

64. Mark 1:11; Matt 3:16; Luke 3:22.

65. Mark 15:34; Heb 1:3; 2:9; Rom 8:34; 1 John 1:7; John 1:36; Matt 16:21, and other minor examples.

66. Acts 3:13; 4:33; 13:32–33; 1 Cor 9:1; Mark 16:19; Matt 28:4, 17. Although Ehrman claims in his updated edition that he corrected mistakes, "some of them real howlers," he acknowledges they still remain. True to his statement, incorrect scriptural references continue in the updated edition. One such is the repetition of 1 John 1:17 (1 John 1 ends at verse 10) in the conclusion of the chapter. See Ehrman, *Orthodox Corruption of Scripture* (1993), vii, 193.

67. Mark 1:34, 3:11; Acts 8:36; 1 John 4:15, 5:5; John 1:49; Rom 15:8; 2 Cor 4:10; Heb 3:1.

68. Luke 5:19; Matt 4:18, 9:27, 20:30; Mark 10:51; Gal 6:17; Acts 2:38, 7:59; Rom 6:11, 10:9, 16:8; Rev 22:21.

reading "stigmata of Christ" is an attempt to show that Christ suffered too. He also claims the reading "stigmata of our Lord Jesus" is to show Jesus was also Lord, and the reading "the stigmata of our Lord" is a scribal attempt to show Jesus was also *the* Lord.

Anti-Docetic Corruptions of Scripture

The term "docetism" comes from the Greek word δοκειν, which means "to seem" or "to appear." The adherents of docetism tended to diminish the humanity of Jesus. They argued Jesus did not actually feel all the suffering and pain. Eusebius noted one of the first to mention this heresy was Serapion of Antioch.[69] J. N. D. Kelly also points out this heresy helped to spur Marcionism and Gnosticism.[70] Ehrman remarks, "Docetism was not the view of one particular social group, but a christological tendency that characterized several groups, some of them unrelated," and points to Hippolytus for possible evidence in his writings.[71] He contends some docetists were from the Johannine community and others from among the unknown opponents of Ignatius and Marcion of Pontus. Ehrman charges the following texts with possible corruption: passages that speak of the physical reality of Christ's passion[72] or its salvific necessity and redemptive effect[73]; passages about Jesus's bodily ascension into heaven[74] and his coming in judgment[75]; and passages dealing with the physical dimension of Christ's presence,[76] that stress his humanity,[77] that speak of his real, physical birth,[78] or that would point to the Old Testament to prove Christ was truly God.[79]

Another example is Luke 24:51. In this passage Luke records the departure of Jesus from his disciples: "Now it happened, while He blessed

---

69. Eusebius, *Ecclesiastical History*, 6.12.6. See Crusé, *Eusebius' Ecclesiastical History*, 202.

70. Kelly, *Early Christian Doctrines*, 141.

71. Ehrman, *Orthodox Corruption of Scripture* (1993), 181. See also Hippolytus, in Litwa, *Refutation of All Heresies*, 581, 720–24.

72. Luke 22:43–44; John 19:28; Matt 20:22, 23; 27:49; Mark 9:12.

73. Luke 22:19–20; 1 Cor 11:23; Col 1:14; Mark 14:22, 24; 1 Cor 15:50.

74. Luke 24:51–52; Mark 16:4, 19.

75. 1 John 2:28; Acts 20:31; Luke 23:42.

76. 1 John 5:9, 20; Heb 2:14; Eph 5:30.

77. John 19:5; 7:46; Matt 8:27.

78. Gal 4:4; Rom 1:3.

79. Ehrman, *Orthodox Corruption of Scripture* (1993), 242. See John 10:8; Rom 9:5; Gal 5:16, 17.

them, that He was separated from them and taken up into heaven."[80] Some Western manuscripts, D a B d e ff² l (syˢ), along with ℵ and geo¹ omit και ανεφερετο εις τον ουρανον. Ehrman deems the inclusion of this phrase in P75 and the remaining manuscripts to be simply a proto-orthodox attempt to emphasize the actual bodily ascension of Jesus. The lack of ανεφερετο εις τον ουρανον can be explained by homoioarcton, where the scribe accidently skipped to the beginning of an identical word (KAIA . . . KAIA) Metzger notes the majority of the UBS Committee sided with the longer reading in this case. Along with homoioarcton, Metzger alleges the omission might be a "deliberate excision" to reconcile the possible dispute concerning the ascension date between Luke 24:51 and Acts 1:3–11.[81] Ehrman does not take into account the introduction to Acts: "The former account I made, O Theophilus, of all that Jesus began both to do and teach, until the day in which he was taken up" (Acts 1:1–2a). The longer reading at the end of Luke's Gospel thus serves as a fitting introduction to his second composition. Ehrman appears to ignore some of these important arguments and hastily sets out to prove his thesis.[82]

Anti-Patripassianistic Corruptions of Scripture

The final chapter is barely twelve pages, reflective of what Ehrman admits: "The controversy was relatively limited in scope and generated far fewer textual corruptions than the adoptionistic, separationistic, and docetic heresies."[83] Another aspect of this controversial doctrine presumed the Father also suffered at the time of the crucifixion, a view that may have arisen due to the Jewish desire to maintain the unity of God.

As an example of a possible corruption, Ehrman points to Acts 20:28. There are two possible variants in this verse. The first, την εκκλησιαν του

---

80. My translation.

81. Metzger, *Textual Commentary on the Greek New Testament*, 162–63, suggests this was done "to relieve the apparent contradiction between this account (which seemingly places the ascension late Easter night) and the account in Acts 1:3–11 (which dates the ascension forty days after Easter)."

82. A similar example can also be noted in Mark 16:4. Here the Old Latin manuscript Codex Bobiensis (itᵏ) gives the description of the actual resurrection of Jesus Christ, translated as follows: "But suddenly at the third hour of the day there was darkness over the whole circle of the earth, and angels descended from the heavens, and as he [the Lord] was rising [reading *surgente eo*] in the glory of the living God, at the same time they ascended with him; and immediately it was light. Then the women went to the tomb" (See Metzger, *Textual Commentary on the Greek New Testament*, 101–2).

83. Ehrman, *Orthodox Corruption of Scripture* (1993), 262.

θεου, is supported by ℵ B 614 1175 1505 *al* vg sy bo^{ms}; Cyr, and the second, την εκκλησιαν του κυριου, is supported by P74 A C* D E Y 33 36 453 945 1739 1891 *al* gig p sy^{hmg} co; Ir^{lat} Lcf. Also, a third possibility exists (unmentioned by Ehrman) with την εκκλησιαν του κυριου και (του *pm*) θεου, supported by C¹ 𝔐. Ehrman considers the reading with the "Lord" to be an emendation by the orthodox scribes who were trying to replace "the church of God, which he purchased with his own blood" with "the church of the Lord, which he purchased with his own blood." He finds the variant to be a deliberate attempt to prevent any Patripassianistic idea from emerging from the Scripture.[84]

PUBLICATIONS SUPPORTING THE THESIS OF ORTHODOX CORRUPTION

Ehrman followed *The Orthodox Corruption of Scripture* with many works in support of his thesis. He has published books directed toward three different groups whom he identified in an interview as scholars, college-level students (textbooks), and the popular audience.[85] In the past twenty-plus years, issues that were the subject of symposia, theological journals, and invitation-only online groups have become the topic of discussion in introductory seminary classes, Sunday schools, and book clubs. It is obvious Ehrman has succeeded in reviving the otherwise boring field of textual criticism. Furthermore, he has managed to intertwine the text-critical threads with many other disciplines such as patristics, historical-critical methods, gnostic apocryphal gospels, historical Jesus studies, and even theodicy. Ehrman's impact on the field of biblical scholarship cannot be understated or merely rebuffed by ignoring his claims.

In the late 1990s, Ehrman published several texts that focused on background issues in NT studies.[86] Unlike the typical NT introductory author, Ehrman presents himself as the objective historian who is on a mission to lay out the facts. In the introductory chapter of *The New Testament: A Historical Introduction*, he declares,

---

84. Ehrman, *Orthodox Corruption of Scripture* (1993), 264.

85. Witherington, "Bart Ehrman's on *Did Jesus Exist?*" This is the correct title of Witherington's blog in spite of the improper use of the possessive.

86. Ehrman co-edited two editions of a very important volume on NTTC with Michael Holmes. Since those volumes are mostly a compilation of articles by other scholars, they are not as significant for the present study. See Ehrman and Holmes, *Text of the New Testament in Contemporary Research*. The second edition has retained the title, but it is expanded and included in the New Testament Tools, Studies, and Documents Series.

> I should be clear at the outset, though, that as the author of this book, I will neither tell you how to resolve this issue nor urge you to adopt any particular set of theological convictions. My approach instead will be strictly historical, trying to understand the writings of the early Christians from the standpoint of the professional historian who uses whatever evidence happens to survive in order to reconstruct what happened in the past.
>
> That is to say, I am not going to convince you either to believe or to disbelieve the Gospel of John; I will describe how it probably came into existence and discuss what its message was. I am not going to persuade you that Jesus really was or was not the Son of God; I will try to establish what he said and did based on the historical data that are available. I am not going to discuss whether the Bible is or is not the inspired word of God; I will show how we got this collection of books and indicate what they say and reflect on how scholars have interpreted them.[87]

Contrary to his claim of remaining strictly historical rather than theological or literary, Ehrman, in his conversational style, repeatedly mocks commonly held Christian beliefs and passes theological judgments throughout the book. For example, he declares the following on the veracity of the gospels' claims regarding Jesus: "Even though we as twentieth-century persons tend to think that something cannot be true unless it happened, ancient Christians, along with a lot of other ancient people, did not think this way. For them, something could be true whether or not it happened."[88] Again, challenging the Pauline authorship of Ephesians, Ehrman asks, "According to Ephesians 2, believers are seated with Christ in the heavenly places, above everything else. Can this be the same author who castigated the Corinthians for maintaining that they had already come to be exalted with Christ and were therefore already ruling with him?"[89] Many more examples could be cited but these should suffice to prove Ehrman is far from being historically objective. Instead, his goal appears to be to dismantle every element of traditional belief in the authority of the NT.

A year later in 1998, Oxford University Press published *The New Testament and Other Early Christian Writings*.[90] The most interesting feature of

---

87. Ehrman, *New Testament*, 16. Second (2000), third (2004), and fourth editions (2007) have subsequently been released.

88. Ehrman, *New Testament*, 44–45.

89. Ehrman, *New Testament*, 331.

90. Ehrman, *New Testament and Other Early Christian Writings*, v. The book was released as a second edition in 2004. Another work of significance is Ehrman, *After the New Testament*.

the book is the table of contents, where gnostic gospels are listed along with the canonical Gospels under the heading "Early Christian Gospels." So also, the Acts of Paul and Thecla and the Martyrdom of Polycarp are listed along with the Acts of the Apostles, letters of the apostolic fathers along with the General Epistles, and the Shepherd of Hermas and the Apocalypse of Peter along with the Revelation of John. Ehrman's rationale for grouping later works along with the canonical writings was to provide an "inexpensive collection of *all* of the earliest Christian writings from the ancient world" for his students and other interested readers.[91] Ehrman extends the chronological boundary to 130 CE, with 2 Peter dated around 120 CE. Although Ehrman admits many of the writings "can be dated with only proximate accuracy," he opens the gate for many later and chronologically uncertain writings to be included along with early canonical writings.[92] Furthermore, "for the sake of convenience," he chooses to use the genre categories provided by the NT. Quite interesting is the inclusion of the Acts of Paul and Thecla and the Martyrdom of Polycarp along with the Acts of the Apostles. Although Ehrman admits they did not fit the chronological limits, he includes them nonetheless.

Next to follow was Ehrman's *Jesus: Apocalyptic Prophet of the New Millennium*. Again, claiming to use the scalpel of the historian, Ehrman proceeds to remove every layer of presumed tradition and myth imposed upon the historical Jesus. He remarks,

> The Jesus of history, contrary to a modern "common sense" (at least in large chunks of American Christianity), was not a proponent of "family values." He urged his followers to abandon their homes and forsake families for the sake of the Kingdom that was soon to arrive. He didn't encourage people to pursue fulfilling careers, make a good living, and work for a just society for the long haul; for him, there wasn't going to *be* a long haul. The end of the world as we know it was already at hand. The Son of Man would soon arrive, bringing condemnation and judgment against those who prospered in this age, but salvation and justice to the poor, downtrodden, and oppressed.[93]

Ehrman acknowledges Albert Schweitzer as the source of his portraiture of Jesus as the apocalyptic prophet.

---

91. Ehrman, *New Testament and Other Early Christian Writings*, 1–4 (emphasis original).

92. Ehrman, *New Testament and Other Early Christian Writings*, 5.

93. Ehrman, *Jesus, Apocalyptic Prophet*, 244.

In 2003, Ehrman released *Lost Scriptures: Books That Did Not Make it into the New Testament*. While maintaining the genre categories found in the NT, Ehrman brings together forty-seven different extracanonical texts. The naïve reader is sure to be shocked at the sight of forty-seven more writings other than the typical twenty-seven, especially with statements such as the following introduction to the gospel section: "There were many Gospels available to early Christians—not just the Matthew, Mark, Luke, and John familiar to readers of the New Testament today. Even though most of these other Gospels have become lost from public view, some were highly influential within orthodox circles throughout the Middle Ages."[94] The above statement misleads the uninformed into thinking (à la Dan Brown, as noted below) the church leaders have been intentionally concealing the rest of the story in order to control the masses and maintain their hegemony.[95]

Later that year, Ehrman also published *Lost Christianities: The Battles for Scripture and the Faiths We Never Knew*, wherein he claims, "As historians have come to realize, during the first three Christian centuries, the practices and beliefs found among people who called themselves Christian were so varied that the differences between Roman Catholics, Primitive Baptists, and Seventh-Day Adventists pale by comparison."[96] He recommended *Lost Christianities* as "my best book for [the Barnes and Noble's] crowd."[97] Such statements are presented with very few citations.

Soon to follow was *Christianity in Late Antiquity 300–450 CE: A Reader*. Interestingly, Ehrman chooses Peter Brown's category of "Late Antiquity" to describe the fourth and fifth centuries instead of the traditional categories of "Nicene Christianity" or "Chalcedonian Christianity."[98] It appears to be a deliberate attempt to move away from the presumption of a monolithic period to one of a growing Christian population marked by creativity and diversity, as Ehrman remarks: "Despite the highly rhetorical presentation of Christian apologists and historians from these early centuries, Christianity was characterized by diversity and marginalization."[99] Using the designation "Late Antiquity" is a clear attempt to detach early Christianity from its traditional categories and cast it in the framework of a secular dating system. The readings included in the collection range from Athanasius to Arius.

---

94. Ehrman, *Lost Scriptures*, 8.
95. Brown, *Da Vinci Code*.
96. Ehrman, *Lost Christianities*, 1.
97. Morgan, "Complete Interview with Bart Ehrman," para. 13.
98. Brown, *World of Late Antiquity*, 7.
99. Ehrman and Jacobs, *Christianity in Late Antiquity*, 3.

The same year (2004) was marked by the remarkable success of Dan Brown's *The Da Vinci Code*.[100] Needless to say, the fiction was filled with historical errors and fabrications. Ehrman wrote *Truth and Fiction in the Da Vinci Code: A Historian Reveals What We Can Really Know about Jesus, Mary, and Constantine* to examine the truth claims made by the characters regarding Jesus, canonicity, and early Christianity.[101] Ehrman almost appears to be on the evangelical side as he exposes many of the historical blunders and the misinformation by Brown. Nonetheless, Ehrman holds to his previous understandings regarding early church history and NT text.

The following year (2005) Ehrman became the joint author of the revised fourth edition of Metzger's *The Text of the New Testament*, and in the process presented some of his altered views regarding NTTC.[102] While the overall text of Metzger mostly remained the same, Ehrman added a section titled, "The Use of Textual Data for the Social History of Early Christianity," wherein he includes subsections titled, "Doctrinal Disputes of Early Christianity," "Jewish-Christian Relations, Oppression of Women in Early Christianity," "Christian Apologia," "Christian Asceticism," and "The Use of Magic and Fortune-Telling in Early Christianity."[103]

In 2005, Ehrman released *Misquoting Jesus*—the book in which he turns his attention from academia to the lay audience.[104] The tone of the book is far from academic. He begins by relating his journey of personal enlightenment after years of struggle regarding the assertions of the Bible. He claims scholarship opened his eyes to the truth that not only was his faith misplaced, but also that the NT text was less reliable than he had originally thought. The book shocked and shook the faith of countless individuals, especially those who were unfamiliar with text-critical matters. On the other hand, even on a casual reading, NTTC matters have been oversimplified, complicated examples have been presented as the normal state of things, and logical fallacies are ignored. Overall, the book is a diluted form of *The Orthodox Corruption of Scripture*, but without enough qualifications to warn the unacquainted reader. Nevertheless, the book not only made the best-seller list in 2005 but also managed to take NTTC from the academicians to the average person.

The following year (2006) was a banner year for Ehrman, with three publications—one from Brill and two from Oxford University Press.

---

100. Brown, *Da Vinci Code*.
101. Ehrman, *Truth and Fiction*.
102. Metzger and Ehrman, *Text of the New Testament*.
103. Metzger and Ehrman, *Text of the New Testament*, 280–99.
104. Ehrman, *Misquoting Jesus*.

Ehrman's twenty-one collected articles were released through Brill as *Studies in the Textual Criticism of the New Testament* and are quite insightful in revealing his evolving understanding of the NT text, even though they are not in chronological order.[105] The publications from Oxford include Ehrman's take on some recently popularized apocryphal works—*Peter, Paul, and Mary Magdalene: The Followers of Jesus in History and Legend* and *The Lost Gospel of Judas Iscariot: A New Look at Betrayer and Betrayed*.[106] Although Ehrman admits in the former that "none of these stories about Peter, Paul, and Mary is historically accurate," he gives credence to them as important in the understanding of the people who retold them.[107] Using canonical and extracanonical literature, he creates a composite of all three as Jewish apocalypticists. His purpose is twofold: first, to go to the facts of history regarding the characters, and, second, to appreciate the tales that were created about them.[108]

Ehrman's involvement with the *Gospel of Judas Iscariot* came by invitation of the National Geographic Society to help authenticate the Tchacos manuscript. Needless to say, it is a gnostic Gospel wherein Jesus supposedly revealed the secrets of the other world. Ehrman concludes correctly that it was not from the historical Judas and it did not give any true account of the historical Jesus. Nonetheless, he attempts to demonstrates its usefulness to understand the lost Christian community that created and espoused it.[109]

Two years later Ehrman published *God's Problem: How the Bible Fails to Answer Our Most Important Question—Why We Suffer*.[110] The book begins in the same vein as *Misquoting Truth*, wherein Ehrman chronicles his journey from faith to agnosticism—this time it was due to all the suffering in the world, especially toward children. He baldly states, "I don't 'know' if there is a God; but I think that if there is one, he certainly isn't the one proclaimed by the Judeo-Christian tradition, the one who is actively and powerfully involved in this world. And so I stopped going to church."[111] After highlighting the "inconsistencies" of all the classical reasons proposed for theodicy, Ehrman once again declares his aversion to the biblical concept of a good and powerful God in an evil world.

---

105. Ehrman, *Studies in the Textual Criticism*.

106. Ehrman, *Peter, Paul, and Mary Magdalene*; Ehrman, *Lost Gospel of Judas Iscariot*.

107. Ehrman, *Peter, Paul, and Mary Magdalene*, xiii.

108. Ehrman, *Peter, Paul, and Mary Magdalene*, 259.

109. Ehrman, *Lost Gospel of Judas Iscariot*, 171–80.

110. Ehrman, *God's Problem*.

111. Ehrman, *God's Problem*, 4.

The following year, again through Harper Collins,[112] Ehrman published *Jesus Interrupted: Revealing the Hidden Contradictions in the Bible (And Why We Don't Know About Them)*.[113] He lays out his basic assumptions and motivations regarding his life and work more than ever before. Repeatedly, he expresses his frustration with pastors who choose to focus only on the devotional approach to the Bible and refuse to enlighten their parishioners regarding the innumerable inconsistencies in it. He advocates for the rehabilitation of the historical-critical method, which he assures the reader does not "necessarily [lead] to a loss of faith."[114] Ironically, he espouses the very method when he faces the issue of the lack of the original text of the NT, which led to his loss of faith. Ultimately, for Ehrman, everything from the Christian canon to doctrines regarding "the divinity of Christ, the Trinity, and the existence of heaven and hell" were later creations of the church.[115]

In 2011, Ehrman released yet another book directed toward the lay audience titled *Forged: Writing in the Name of God—Why the Bible's Authors are Not Who We Think They are.*[116] It is an expansion of his opening chapters from *Lost Christianities*. The questions were provocative to say the least:

> Is it possible that any of the early Christian forgeries made it into the New Testament? That some of the books of the New Testament were not written by the apostles whose names are attached to them? That some of Paul's letters were not written by Paul, but by someone claiming to be Paul? That Peter's letters were not written by Peter? That James and Jude did not write the books that bear their names? Or—a somewhat different case, as we will see—that the Gospels of Matthew, Mark, Luke, and John were not actually written by Matthew, Mark, Luke, and John?[117]

One can see that, for Ehrman, everything from the Acts of Paul and Thecla to the Pastoral letters was fair game in deciding how much of Paul's writings are actually forgeries.

In the same year, Ehrman partnered with UNC-Chapel Hill colleague Zlatko Pleše (Associate Professor of Ancient Mediterranean Religions) to

---

112. One anonymous source has called both HarperCollins and its parallel HarperOne "probably the leading publisher of non-Christian anti-orthodox material, and this to such a degree that a particular agenda is more than suspect."
113. Ehrman, *Jesus Interrupted*.
114. Ehrman, *Jesus, Interrupted*, 17.
115. Ehrman, *Jesus, Interrupted*, 275.
116. Ehrman, *Forged*.
117. Ehrman, *Forged*, 357.

release a compendium titled *Apocryphal Gospels: Texts and Translations*.[118] Included in it are over forty different extracanonical "gospels," divided into four subheadings: Infancy Gospels; Ministry Gospels; Sayings, Gospels, and Agrapha; and Passion, Resurrection, and Post-Resurrection Gospels.

In 2012, Ehrman published *Did Jesus Exist?: The Historical Argument for Jesus of Nazareth*.[119] He once again puts on the hat of the supposedly unbiased historian and takes on those who decry the existence of the historical Jesus, especially the mythicists. Ehrman appears to be fighting on the side of those who would take a conservative viewpoint, even though his own personal view aligns with that of Albert Schweitzer, who considered Jesus to be an apocalyptic Messiah. In a similar tone, Ehrman deals with the issue of forgeries from the early Christian era in his more scholarly work *Forgery and Counterforgery: The Use of Literary Deceit in Early Christian Polemics*.[120]

In 2013 and 2014, Ehrman released two significant works: first, an introduction to the Bible for students in introductory-level college classes, a fifteen-chapter introduction of the entire Bible—Jewish Scripture (Old Testament) and NT, Genesis to Revelation (including Apocrypha);[121] second, *The Other Gospels: Accounts of Jesus from Outside the New Testament* with Zlatko Pleše, where the authors claimed to give an account of Jesus from forty ancient gospel texts and textual fragments that are not found in the NT.[122]

The following year, Ehrman's controversial work, *How Jesus Became God: The Exaltation of a Jewish Preacher from Galilee*, was released.[123] Ehrman claims in his blog he had long awaited the opportunity to write it but was distracted by other projects. As can be expected, his premise is Jesus was raised to the position of deity much later by the proto-orthodox and orthodox. The work has drawn much attention, again due to its highly nonorthodox claims. In 2016, another controversial work was released, titled *Jesus Before the Gospels: How the Earliest Christians Remembered, Changed, and Invented Their Stories of the Savior*.[124] The phrase "Earliest Christians" in the title proves yet again that Ehrman still views the history of early

---

118. Ehrman and Pleše, *Apocryphal Gospels*.
119. Ehrman, *Did Jesus Exist?*
120. Ehrman, *Forgery and Counterforgery*.
121. This work was expanded to twenty-six chapters in the second edition (Ehrman, *Bible*).
122. Ehrman and Pleše, *Other Gospels*. This work includes only the English translation, unlike the editors' previous *Apocryphal Gospels*, which includes the Greek text as well.
123. Ehrman, *How Jesus Became God*.
124. Ehrman, *Jesus before the Gospels*.

Christianity and the NT text through his particular "historian" lenses. The latest publication by Ehrman is titled *The Triumph of Christianity: How a Forbidden Religion Swept the World*.[125] Once again, Ehrman sets early Christianity in the cradle of sociopolitical struggle between what became the dominant orthodox and the eventually weakened heterodox. The final two books are both aimed at the popular audience.

CONCLUSION

Ehrman has popularized the new approach to the NT text more than any other proponent. His *Orthodox Corruption* has played a key role in changing the traditional goal of NTTC. Furthermore, his numerous popular books have continued to disseminate his view to the lay audience who are not aware of the intricacies involved in the NT text or early church history.

---

125. Ehrman, *Triumph of Christianity*.

4

David C. Parker

Unlike Ehrman, who is well known among academicians as well as the average person interested in the matters of the NT text, David Parker is mostly known in scholarly circles. He is a leading proponent of the new approach to the NT text, and is a well-known figure in the field of NTTC. Along with his professorship in NT and Greek at the University of Birmingham, he serves as the director of the Institute for the Textual Scholarship and Electronic Editing at the university's theology and religion department. Under his leadership, the institute has made various contributions to digital methodologies and tools in the field, pride of place going to the online editions of codices Sinaiticus and Bezae. Since 1987, Parker has served as the Executive Editor of the International Greek New Testament Project and continues to hold several editorial roles. All these accomplishments, coupled with his books and numerous articles in the field, have resulted in some very important accolades.[1]

PARKER'S THESIS IN THE LIVING TEXT OF THE GOSPELS

In 1997, Parker published *The Living Text of the Gospels*, in which he made the ambitious claim the book is written "with the growing conviction that, once

---

1. In 2015, the Queen of England honored Parker with the appointment as an Officer of the Order of the British Empire (OBE).

the present approach has been adopted, much else in our understanding of the Gospels requires revision."[2] True to his promise, Parker's definition of NTTC is atypical compared to those found in the introductory works to the field—"in essence the act of understanding what another person means by the words that are laid before me."[3] Inherent in that definition is the impression that the reader, whether expert or novice, can enter the world of NT manuscripts without any intimidation typically associated with the discipline of NTTC. In fact, Parker bemoans the fact that textual criticism has been treated as the exclusive right of the experts. According to him, this has created a two-part focus for the current field.[4] First, it has led to the belief that the experts have determined the original text. Consequently, it is wrongly assumed whatever has been relegated to the foot of the page can be safely discarded as being a viable variant. Second, the purpose of NTTC was simply to recover the original text, but Parker deems such optimism to be far-fetched.

To make his case, Parker presents the various forms of Shakespeare's plays and asks the reader if the version Shakespeare first penned should be called the original, or the one that was altered through the rehearsals. In a similar example from Mozart, Parker questions whether the original is what the composer first wrote or what he edited to accommodate the singer's voices. After arousing suspicion over the use of the phrase "original text," Parker concludes, "The task of textual criticism and the role of textual critics have changed. Instead of eliminating material in order to recover a single original text, the editor analyses all the developments of the material in order to demonstrate the process to which they owe their origin."[5] In essence, just like Shakespeare's plays or Mozart's concertos, the Gospels could also have many different originals rather than just one.

Although Parker's analogy appears appealing at first, it is far from convincing when studied closely. Shakespeare and Mozart no doubt have written inspiring works, but their material was never deemed inspired or theological. To the contrary, very early in the history of the church, the NT writings took on the status of being on par with the Old Testament Scriptures. They were given the same care as that accorded to the Hebrew writings. While some have claimed the presence of variants in the early stages of the transmission of the text negates any high view of the NT writings, a careful study of the matter proves the contrary and will be discussed in the later sections of this study.

2. Parker, *Living Text of the Gospels*, xi.
3. Parker, *Living Text of the Gospels*, 1.
4. Parker, *Living Text of the Gospels*, 2–3.
5. Parker, *Living Text of the Gospels*, 6.

As with Bart Ehrman in his *The Orthodox Corruption of Scripture*, Parker also seems to rely on Walter Bauer's view of early church history. He claims:

> It is important to remember that the later concept of orthodoxy is in some respects an anachronism, for no one group in the church was in that position of power necessary if other groups are to be outlawed or prohibited. Instead, Christianity of this age consisted of a number of competing groups, approving and condemning one another as they saw fit.[6]

Much issue can be taken with the above statement. Here it will suffice to note many of Bauer's conclusions, as well as Ehrman's, have been proven to be far-fetched and without evidence, and they have been examined in the previous section. In the following section, the scholarly responses against Parker's thesis will be briefly surveyed. It will be shown that Parker's thesis fits into the same goalpost-changing camp of NTTC as seen in Ehrman.

SCHOLARLY RESPONSES TO PARKER'S THESIS

The initial reaction to *The Living Text of the Gospels* was similar to the one Ehrman received for his *The Orthodox Corruption of Scripture*. The responses came only from the scholarly circles and most of them were favorable; thus Metzger, who in *The Princeton Seminary Bulletin*, put forth a rather vapid 340-word summary with no deep assessment of the work.[7] To the contrary, a favorable and yet substantial review came from J. Keith Elliott. He begins by comparing *The Living Text of the Gospels* to Parker's earlier work on Codex Bezae and points out "the maverick text of Codex Bezae is regularly in evidence."[8] Furthermore,

> His beloved Codex Bezae is merely one example of a particular set of Christians' attitudes to the tradition—Bezae is not itself (nor is any MS, or printed edition) that tradition. Christianity did try to produce controlled texts—the Syriac Peshitta, or the Latin Vulgate are examples.[9]

Peter Head notices the same tendency: "It sometimes appears that Parker takes the freedom of the Bezan tradition as the paradigm for the

---

6. Parker, *Living Text of the Gospels*, 22.
7. Metzger, "Review of *The Living Text*," 231–32.
8. Elliott, "Review of *The Living Text*," 176.
9. Elliott, "Review of *The Living Text*," 179.

whole textual tradition. We might say that it is precisely because not all scribes acted in a free manner that we are now able to study those which did."[10] Anthony Ernest Harvey also calls into question Parker's tendency to generalize. He points out the "implicit circularity" in the latter's arguments and remarks: "A certain addition was made to the text of Luke's Gospel by an editor (or copyist?) seeking to meet the threat of Docetism. How do we know that there was such a threat? Because of variants such as this in the text of Luke's Gospel."[11] As can be noticed in the above reviews, most scholars remain cautiously favorable to Parker's thesis, but not all.

The most trenchant review came from J. Neville Birdsall, who admits, "He has found it extremely difficult to follow, its gist hard to grasp or, if grasped, to précis."[12] He begins by taking Parker to task for giving the impression his study is groundbreaking, in showing the Gospels need to be read with the understanding that they existed first as manuscripts. He remarks, "It is a pity however that the impression is given that this is the first time that anyone has done this."[13] The same thesis had been propagated in several works beginning in the 1920s. He rightly challenges Parker's comparison of the development of the NT manuscripts to Shakespeare and Mozart or Wordsworth and James Joyce. He attempts to clarify and determine Parker's position by asking, "Does he either consider that no one of the gospels had a definable literary beginning or that from a set of shared materials the ancestors of any particular one of our gospels came together into different entities, like and yet unlike, the *Urtexte* of the earliest textual forms which we can discern?"[14] Birdsall further chastises Parker in "his tendency to choose dramatic examples in his discussion."[15] Of course, all the chosen passages are *cruces interpretum*. Birdsall's chastisement continues:

> Almost every mention of a manuscript gives excuse for a digression about it, its discovery, appearance, importance, relevance, irrelevance. There is a kind of naïve excitement about it, like a child opening Christmas presents. Like that experience, it gives us first a taste of shared rapture, and then a sobering awareness that it all badly needs tidying up and some of the wrapping thrown away, or we shall never be able to live in the place again.[16]

10. Head, "Review of *The Living Text*," 360.
11. Harvey, "Review of *The Living Text*," 142.
12. Birdsall, "Review of *The Living Text*," 275.
13. Birdsall, "Review of *The Living Text*," 276.
14. Birdsall, "Review of *The Living Text*," 279.
15. Birdsall, "Review of *The Living Text*," 280.
16. Birdsall, "Review of *The Living Text*," 282.

In his concluding paragraph, Birdsall points out Parker's work on Codex Bezae is much different in standard and quality than *The Living Text of the Gospels*. In short, in Birdsall's estimation, Parker's thesis falls short of academic and literary standards, not to mention text-critical standards, since it shows "dire pessimism"[17] regarding reaching the earliest strata of the text. Neither does it offer any history of the text.

Other scholars wholeheartedly endorsed Parker's thesis in *The Living Text of the Gospels* as a breakthrough in the otherwise stagnated field of NTTC. In his epochal article "The Multivalence of the Term 'Original Text' in New Testament Textual Criticism," Epp includes Parker's thesis as a tributary in the new movement in NTTC. He adds, "Textual critics are encouraged to permit the New Testament's fluid and living text of the past to sustain its free, vital, unbroken, multifaceted tradition in the present and into the future."[18] In other words, Parker is squarely in line with the new movement's penchant for rejecting a firm original text and creating a text that fits the reader. In a later article, Epp categorizes Parker's work as a form of "narrative textual criticism."[19]

Similarly, Paul Ellingworth explains Parker's position by listing three competing texts: chronological priority (what is "original" in Parker's strict sense), authenticity (what the author would recognize as his own work), and authority (what is accepted in a wider community).[20] He acknowledges the complexity of the term "original text" and concedes it is unattainable, per Parker. But he also counterbalances by affirming "some texts in the New Testament are firmer than others; that some readings are more probable than others."[21]

Moisés Silva offers a negative review of Parker's *The Living Text of the Gospels*, calling into question his jumbling of text-critical information and historical facts. He notes that "text-critical data—like data from a variety of other sources—may well throw light on the historical question (and vice versa). But the two issues are *quite* distinct."[22] Silva also questions Parker's motives, noting,

> Any reader of this book must wonder, at various points, whether theological and philosophical perspectives may have motivated or affected the theses presented here . . . one would be naïve to

---

17. Birdsall, "Review of *The Living Text*," 287.
18. Epp, "Multivalence of the Term 'Original Text,'" 266.
19. Epp, "It's All about Variants," 289.
20. Ellingworth, "Text, Translation, and Theology," 66.
21. Ellingworth, "Text, Translation, and Theology," 73.
22. Silva, "Review of *The Living Text*," 297 (emphasis original).

suppose that the author's philosophical commitments have not had an effect on the selection and description of the data—to say nothing of the inferences drawn from the material. Whether by design or not, Parker's strategy has been to erode, little by little, the reader's confidence in the stability of the NT text.[23]

Silva surmises that Parker's *The Living Text of the Gospels* belongs in the postmodern camp,

> Like much so-called postmodernist writing these days, this book is riddled by a fundamentalist incoherence: throughout his argument, the author must assume the reality of the very thing he seeks to disprove (and one doubts Parker is enough of a deconstructionist to respond that his own assertions may be freely understood in ways he did not intend).[24]

For Silva, the book would have been enlightening had the concept of the original text been upheld instead of the notion of a living, multiple, and even nonexistent authoritative text. Daniel B. Wallace, in his article "Challenges in New Testament Textual Criticism," also places Parker under the subheading "Postmodern Intrusions into New Testament Textual Criticism."[25] He derides Parker, noting, "If he were some pseudo-scholar putting this idea out on the internet, no one would take him seriously. But David Parker is probably Great Britain's best NT textual critic today."[26]

In an insightful article titled "From 'Original Text' to 'Initial Text': The Traditional Goal of New Testament Textual Criticism in Contemporary Discussion," Michael Holmes weighs in that "Parker and others are raising questions not just about methodology but also about epistemology."[27] In other words, the current discussion in NTTC is no longer just about comparing manuscripts, evaluating variants, and applying canons of textual criticisms, but about rehashing well-worn questions of historical criticism. As Holmes pointedly comments,

> It will not do to dismiss their concerns by saying that they are bringing ideological perspectives into the discipline; their perspectives are no more ideological than the assumptions that have shaped the traditional view of the discipline and definition of its goal. Rather, their concerns challenge colleagues in the

---

23. Silva, "Review of *The Living Text*," 299.
24. Silva, "Review of *The Living Text*," 301.
25. Wallace, "Challenges in New Testament Textual Criticism," 80.
26. Wallace, "Challenges in New Testament Textual Criticism," 82.
27. Holmes, "From 'Original Text' to 'Initial Text,'" 678.

discipline to recognize and acknowledge the intrinsically and unavoidable hermeneutical nature of our work, no matter how or from what perspective we practice it.[28]

In essence, textual critics will have to reexamine all previously held assumptions before making any definite claim about the text. Under Parker's thesis, NTTC has become more of an artistic enterprise than a scientific discipline.

SUMMARY OF PARKER'S THESIS

Under Parker's thesis, the original text of the NT is not important or even retrievable. To make his case, he devotes a chapter to significant text-critical passages that have multiple solutions. He identifies eight such cases.

"As our Savior taught us . . .": The Lord's Prayer

Parker begins this chapter by cautioning the reader against assuming we actually have the Lord's Prayer in its original form. He warns, "We shall certainly be mistaken if we believe ourselves to be uttering Jesus' words *verbatim*. As a matter of fact, this prayer contains within its short compass every conceivable problem that could afflict a Gospel saying."[29] To prove his case, Parker offers the premise that the form of the Lord's Prayer in the Byzantine text in Luke is actually a harmonized form of the prayer from Matthew. Hence, in Parker's opinion, as valiant as Tyndale's, the Geneva Bible's, and the Authorized Version's efforts were to utilize a text based on the available Greek manuscripts of the time, they failed to reach the earliest form of the Gospel text. Even though the Roman Catholic Douai translation was based on the Latin versions and was not conducive for reading by the average person, it nevertheless contained a text that supposedly was closer to the earliest form. Parker's reasoning is the Vulgate contained a text that was edited by Jerome based on the earliest available manuscripts at the time. In other words, "The humanists were not always right when they preferred the Greek manuscripts they studied, and the traditionalists were not always wrong in favoring the Latin Vulgate."[30] Parker argues the principle of dissimilarity

---

28. Holmes, "From 'Original Text' to 'Initial Text,'" 679.
29. Parker, *Living Text of the Gospels*, 49.
30. Parker, *Living Text of the Gospels*, 53.

proves the form of the text that has the least evidence of harmonization is more authentic. Hence, the Alexandrian reading of Luke is the earliest form.

To further complicate matters, Parker points out Matthew has one textual problem and Luke has three major forms of the text. The Matthean issue, according to Parker, involves the doxology with seven possible readings of the text:

1. The shortest ending at "evil."
2. Adding "Amen" after "evil."
3. Adding the doxology "Because thine is the kingdom and the power and the glory for ever. Amen."
4. Adding "of the Father and of the Son and of the Holy Spirit" after "glory."
5. Omitting "the kingdom and" in the doxology.
6. Omitting "Amen" in the doxology.
7. Omitting "for thine is the power for ever and ever" in the doxology.

The first and the third readings are the only ones that deserve any consideration. The former finds support in ℵ B D Z 0170 f1 1582 lat mae bo Cyr Or Cyp.[31] The latter is found in the majority of the manuscripts with K L W D Θ f13 33 288ᶜ 565 579 700 892 1241 1424 *l*-844 𝔐 f q syʰ boᵖᵗ (g¹ k syᶜ·ᵖ sa). Parker includes another possible reading from the Didache, which is similar to the fifth possibility. It does not appear to be a major contender since it is found only in an eleventh-century Greek manuscript. Parker favors the shortest reading (number 1) and concludes the doxology was a later interpolation in Matthew. He further concludes the variation in the doxology is proof the interpolation arose from the insuppressible desire to add some form of praise in conclusion. On the other hand, the Lucan issue involves four main forms of the text.

1. The short text
2. The long form of the text in Codex Bezae
3. The long Byzantine form of the text
4. A different form of the clause "Thy kingdom come."

The first and the third forms are the major contenders here. The first is supported by P75 B 1192 1210 1342 and manuscripts 1 and 1582 of f1. Origen also appears to have been acquainted with the shorter text along with syˢ

---

31. Although Parker lists Family 13, it is Family 1 according to the NA²⁷ apparatus.

vg. The third form is supported by C A and a majority of the witnesses. The textual evidence is complicated with many variations.[32]

While Parker allows that the shorter forms of the prayer in Matthew and Luke are probably the earliest forms of the text, he claims all the other forms contribute to our understanding of the tradition. He further claims each of the variants had a "wide circulation at different times, even though several of them are now known only in a very few witnesses."[33] He points to the early stage of textual chaos in the first two centuries as the point of inception of all the extant readings, no matter how late the witnesses appear to be. There does not appear to be any clear-cut classification of manuscripts in favor of the overall text. Ultimately, Parker's goal is not resolution. Instead, he leaves the reader in a convolution of data to the point of despair regarding ever reaching the original text of the NT.

The sayings on marriage and divorce

Parker agrees with Bart Ehrman's *The Orthodox Corruption of Scripture* in alleging that because the sayings of Jesus were so important, they were constantly altered "to bring out the meaning which the scribes believed to be correct."[34] Although Ehrman attributes the reason for the changes to the christological debates, Parker attributes them to the changing interpretation of the words of Christ in the lives of the believers. Supposedly, a major area of contention was the sayings of Jesus on marriage, divorce, and remarriage in Matthew 5:27–32, 19:3–9, Mark 10:2–12, and Luke 16:18.[35] Parker's premise is as follows: "Generally, debate has centered on the meaning of a single authoritative text. But it will soon become plain that such a text does not exist today, and never has existed, and that therefore the theological arguments built on such a text are castles in the air."[36] Parker discounts the typical arguments that simply take the critical text of a Greek edition as authoritative and proceed to decide which evangelist was more authentic and authoritative. Instead, he claims a myriad of differences exists between the manuscripts of

---

32. Codex Sinaiticus (ℵ) in this passage reflects a mixture of variant readings that do not regularly correspond to either the short or long forms of the text.

33. Parker, *Living Text of the Gospels*, 70.

34. Parker, *Living Text of the Gospels*, 75.

35. Parker did not include John 7:53—8:11 and 1 Cor 7:12–16 in this section. The former is treated in a separate chapter later and the latter comes from the Pauline corpus and carries a different textual character than the Gospels. See Parker, *Living Text of the Gospels*, 77.

36. Parker, *Living Text of the Gospels*, 76.

an individual passage in discussion. The following is a summary of Parker's interpretation of the textual data of the five marriage passages.

Mark 10:2–12

Here Jesus clarifies his answer to the Pharisees' question to the disciples, saying, "Is it lawful for a man to divorce his wife?" Parker identifies seven different forms of the text at this point. He finds a commonality in all seven forms of a "woman divorcing her husband" and proposed this phrase could not have been original to Jesus since it would have been unnecessary to mention such a statement in a Jewish society where women do not have the right to divorce their husband. Hence, Parker argues it was more than likely an adaptation to a situation in the Roman society wherein the woman had to be warned of the need to remain in marriage. Furthermore, under the Markan-priority hypothesis it appears the alteration to the text took place rather early in the history of transmission. Although issue could be taken with such conjectures, it will suffice to note Parker fails to allow for the possibility that the Jewish society of the time may have been much more open to the rights of women than is often assumed.

Matthew 5:27–32

This passage does not have a direct parallel in either Mark or Luke. Unlike Mark 10:2–12, where remarriage amounts to adultery, the point here is the woman who has been divorced is now an adulteress. Parker identifies five different forms of the text. He claims the circumstances facing the development of Mark 10 are quite different than those facing Matthew 5. The exception clause, "except for the cause of *porneia*," is more in line with the original setting of Jesus than the various adaptations of Mark 10. Parker admits all this is "very complicated."[37] It is hard to follow Parker's arguments because of their subjective tone. Without much historical basis for his conclusions, everything appears to be a guesswork.

Matthew 19:3–9

Parker admits the textual evidence for Matthew 19:3–9 is also "extremely complex."[38] Unlike its Markan parallel, where the adultery was the result of

---

37. Parker, *Living Text of the Gospels*, 85.
38. Parker, *Living Text of the Gospels*, 85.

divorcing one's spouse and remarrying another, here adultery is the result of marrying a divorced person. Parker attributes some of the exceptions to cases of harmonization between Matthew and Mark. He also ascribes the other forms to cases of harmonization. Again, it becomes very hard to follow where harmonization ends and the true text begins. Parker also acknowledges, "As with the Lord's Prayer, the pattern of change and preservation is unpredictable."[39] Overall, this represents the most complicated combination involving harmonization and source criticism Parker suggests when resolving text-critical matters.

Luke 16:18

In Luke 16:18, the text focuses on the adultery of the man. It exists in one form with some minor variations. Parker concludes from all the passages: "We have seen that to compare the Gospels with a view to establishing the priority of one form is to presuppose that each Gospel has a definite form. The investigations of this chapter have found no evidence that either the evangelists or their successors believed such a form to exist."[40] Furthermore, Parker claims there was no set law regarding divorce and remarriage. Instead, much had to be reinterpreted through the centuries, even after the coming of the ecclesiastic Byzantine text. He claims the discipline of NTTC safeguards against any attempts to legitimize any particular viewpoint of any particular period or person. Such understanding will lead to the abandonment of any favorite versions in favor of the mass of textual evidence, giving us an ecumenical insight into the development of the church.

As well-meaning as the above hope is regarding the neutrality of versions, it fails to deal seriously with the importance of the external evidence of the manuscripts. Manuscripts cannot be discarded in such a haphazard manner. To raise them all to the same level is to discard any objective decision regarding any portion of the text. The result is sheer chaos, which fits well under current prevailing methodologies.

The story of the woman taken in adultery

Even though the *Pericope Adulterae* is a major battleground in textual criticism, Parker relegates a very brief chapter to it. He declares it is "not part

---

39. Parker, *Living Text of the Gospels*, 89.
40. Parker, *Living Text of the Gospels*, 91.

of the supposed authoritative and original text."[41] He lists the various locations where it is found in the manuscript tradition to emphasize its spurious nature and concludes, "It is regularly the case that passages whose inclusion is in doubt come at different places in different groups of witnesses."[42] He postulates it is nothing more than an inauthentic oral tradition that made its way into the manuscript tradition.

The major weakness of the chapter is the lack of discussion on the weight of each manuscript. When Parker discusses the various locations of the pericope, he treats every manuscript or family of manuscripts with equal weight. Although Parker's view regarding the inauthenticity of the text is common among most textual scholars, he lays out the external evidence based on the importance of each manuscript, which fails to bring any resolution.

Secrets and hypotheses

In this section, Parker deals with a prominent theme of Mark's Gospel known as "The Messianic Secret" as it relates to NTTC. He focuses on the minor agreements between Matthew and Luke against Mark. A passage in contention is Mark 4:11: "To you has been given the secret of the kingdom of God." Matthew and Luke deviate slightly, but importantly for Parker, Matthew 13:11 states, "To you it has been given to know the secrets of the kingdom of heaven" and Luke 8:10 states, "To you it has been given to know the secrets of the kingdom of God."

Parker discounts the solution of both Streeter and Koester at this point. The former contends for the authenticity of the singular "secret" by Matthew (Old Syriac, Old Latin, Clement of Alexandria, and the Latin translation of Irenaeus of Lyons) and Luke (Latin witnesses) over the plural "secrets." The latter contends Matthew and Luke, with their plural "secrets," were authentic over Mark's singular "secret." Parker rightly exposes the verbal dependence gymnastics Koester employs to make his case. He concludes the arguments from the Two-Document Hypothesis are far from convincing and "suspicion must arise when the text is emended to conform with a particular solution to the Synoptic Problem."[43] Parker's case appears to be very convincing.

---

41. Parker, *Living Text of the Gospels*, 95.

42. Parker, *Living Text of the Gospels*, 100. It should be pointed out here that the claim regarding differing Pericope Adulterae locations has been refuted (Keith, "Initial Location," 209–31). All noted relocations are tenth century or later.

43. Parker, *Living Text of the Gospels*, 112.

Parker even brings up other examples of minor agreements that have led some scholars to invoke conjectural emendation. Although Parker considers conjectural emendation a necessity since there is a possibility the original text has not survived in any extant manuscript, he does not find it applicable in the cases under discussion. He settles with the conclusion that the text, in the period from which we do not have any extant manuscript evidence, saw much harmonization and cross-contamination, so as to render useless source criticism's attempts at "separation of the several strands into their constituent threads."[44] Again, Parker does not discount the documentary solution completely, but he does not find the arguments from it to be foolproof.

Parker proposes a complicated scenario where there is not just a single point of contact between the texts, but multiple points:

> Matthew copies bits out of Mark in reproducing a tradition; then a later copy of Mark is enriched by some of Matthew's alterations; and next a copy of Matthew (already different from the one we begin with) is influenced by something from the also changed Mark. Add in Luke, and oral tradition, and any other sources that might have been available, at any points in the development that you please, and you have a process a good deal less recoverable than any documentary hypothesis. It is not at all the orderly business we had hoped, and looks instead like molecules bouncing around and off each other in bewildering fashion.[45]

In conclusion, Parker makes no attempts at giving any resolution to the differences between the Synoptic Gospels. Instead, he simply wants his readers to accept the fact the text has been corrupted beyond recovery and what can best be recovered is the surviving corrupted text. His appeal to the proponents of the various theories of the Synoptic problem is to become aware of the fact the text in the published editions is not the original text, but just a surviving, altered, harmonized, and cross-contaminated tradition. In conclusion, the reader is left in despair regarding ever reaching the original text of the NT.

The endings of Mark's Gospel

Parker lists six possible endings in his discussion of the endings of Mark's Gospel, one of the most debated passages in NT textual criticism:

---

44. Parker, *Living Text of the Gospels*, 120.
45. Parker, *Living Text of the Gospels*, 121.

1. The Short Ending: Reaches only to verse 8 of Mark 16 and is found in only three Greek manuscripts—ℵ B 304 (twelfth century)—with some isolated versional support. There is also patristic support from Clement of Alexandria, Origen, Eusebius, and Jerome.

2. The Intermediate Ending: Found alone only in the African Old Latin witness *Codex Bobbiensis.*

3. The Long Ending: Found in all remaining continuous text manuscripts, especially A C D W Θ f13. It is also found in the lectionaries and most versional witnesses.

4. The Long Ending with either a critical symbol or a note on the problem between verses 8 and 9: It is found in three various forms in 1 20 22 209^{mg} 137 138 1528.

5. The All-Inclusive Reading: Including all the various alternatives together, found in three forms in L Ψ 0112 (099 *l*1602 cop$^{sa\ mss\ bo\ mss}$ 274^{mg} 579 syr$^{h\ mg}$.

6. The Extended Reading at the end of verse 14: The Freer Logion found only in W.

In discussing this variant segment, Parker blames the conservatives for rejecting "historical observations" and "self-critical scholarship" and clinging to the long ending due to their erroneous belief in the divine preservation of Scripture.[46] Although he acknowledges "both the Short and the Long Ending are second century," he concludes "the oldest form of the Gospel is the Short Ending."[47] Parker takes the typical response of the reasoned eclectic position by placing emphasis on the codices Sinaiticus and Vaticanus and explaining the long ending as the creation of scribes looking to compensate for an otherwise bland ending to Mark's Gospel.

Ultimately, Parker's goal is not to advocate for the short reading over the other five alternatives. Instead, he wants to reiterate his thesis that the church has chosen different endings of Mark to support their changing preferences regarding doctrine and belief.

The last three chapters of Luke

Unlike the previous cases that deal mostly in major or minor variations, this chapter focuses on the matter of several variants scattered throughout a long passage. The prime examples of such are the final three chapters of

---

46. Parker, *Living Text of the Gospels*, 129.
47. Parker, *Living Text of the Gospels*, 137, 143.

Luke. Parker very well could have titled this chapter with Hort's designation of "Western noninterpolations" since this is truly the heart of the matter here—readings that are found in the Alexandrian text but are absent from the Western text, or, more specifically, readings found in the codices Sinaiticus and Vaticanus but lacking in Codex Bezae.[48] The following are some of the Western noninterpolations along with other variants discussed by Parker in this chapter.

The Last Supper

Luke 22:14

Even though the text seems to be very secure in mentioning Judas as part of the "twelve apostles," some manuscripts seem hesitant and reluctant to include him by changing "apostles" to "disciples" or omitting the number "twelve." The paucity of manuscript support for the alternative readings makes this hypothesis far-fetched.

Luke 22:16

Marcion omitted it, as deduced from the writings of Tertullian and Epiphanius.

Luke 22:19–20

This is the most familiar Western noninterpolation. While Codex Bezae, along with e a B ff² i l, preserves the shorter text, codices ℵ and B uncharacteristically have the longer text and agree with the majority of the manuscripts. Parker compared the longer reading with other eucharistic passages—Matt 26:26–29; Mark 14:22–25; 1 Cor 11:23–25—John necessarily excluded. He concludes the longer reading is an example of harmonization to the other parallel passages and remarks, "Harmonisation is primarily a matter of sense and theology, and only secondarily of wording."[49] He claims the wording of the longer text has been harmonized to 1 Corinthians and the sense to Mark. Parker again finds common ground with Ehrman—a "doughty champion"—who even claims that, in Luke's understanding, Jesus's death was not atoning.[50] Hence, Irenaeus and Tertullian took upon themselves the task of making the

---

48. See Westcott and Hort, *Introduction and Appendix*, 175–77. Such "Western non-interpolations" are found beyond Luke. For a discussion regarding one such in Matt 27:49, see Shah, "Alexandrian Presumption of Authenticity," 92–99.
49. Parker, *Living Text of the Gospels*, 155.
50. Parker, *Living Text of the Gospels*, 155.

text more orthodox. One would have hoped the long-established verdict that D carries an unrestrained text would have been a safeguard against such hypotheses, but Parker knowingly disregards this tendency.

Luke 22:35-37

Omitted by Marcion.

The Agony in the Garden (Luke 22:43-44)

While Parker again argues his case that the shorter text without the mention of the great sweat drops of blood is original, the manuscript evidence is now on the opposite side. Now, it is the Alexandrian text that is shorter and the Western that is longer. He subdivides the data into five readings. Again, Parker aligns his arguments with Ehrman's claim that scribes intentionally added to the text in order to avoid any docetic misunderstanding of Jesus.

The Servant's Ear (Luke 22:49-51)

Omitted by Marcion.

Peter's Remorse (Luke 22:62)

Omitted by 0171^{vid} and Old Latin.

Jesus before Pilate (Luke 23:1-5)

Parker claims Marcion's addition of Jesus corrupting the nation was taken into some Old Latin manuscripts–e b c ff² i l q.

The need to release one at the feast (Luke 23:17)

Parker regards this as more of an interpolation rather than a harmonization, but characteristically opts for the shorter text without the verse.

The Crucifixion of Jesus

Luke 23:32

It is only a switch in the word order of κακουργοι δυο. Parker assumes the switch was to avoid the embarrassment of mistakenly implying Jesus was also a criminal.

Luke 23:34

Parker suggests the absence of "And Jesus said, 'Father, forgive them; for they know not what they do'" (omitted in P75 ℵ¹ B D* W Θ 0124 579 1241 Lvt (a b^c d) Syr^s Cop^{sah} Cop$^{boh\ mss}$) is due to Christian anti-Semitism.

Luke 23:35

The absence or presence of certain derogatory remarks by passersby are chalked up to "developments in the exegetical and theological issues at stake in exegesis" without any discussion or documentation of the manuscripts involved.[51]

Luke 23:37

D c (sy$^{s.c}$) add the putting of the crown of thorns in various words. This is suggested to be a harmonization to the other three gospels.

Luke 23:39, 44–45, 46, 48

The variants in these passages display minor changes by individual manuscripts.

The main counterpoint once again is that there is no distinct stream or continuity of the manuscript evidence. Instead, random manuscripts are strung together in support for the shorter text to claim that the text was flexible in the early period of transmission.

The Burial of Jesus

Luke 23:52, 53; 24:1, 2

Minor variants.

---

51. Parker, *Living Text of the Gospels*, 162.

The Resurrection

Luke 24:3

In this second Western noninterpolation, Parker again agrees with Ehrman that the words "of the Lord Jesus" were added in order to avoid any heretical confusion that the body was indeed of Jesus or that it was not just the Christ who was risen. He even raises the question whether the text could have grown in three stages: "'And entering they did not find the body' through 'And entering they did not find the body of Jesus' to 'And entering they did not find the body of the Lord Jesus'?"[52] There is no trail of manuscript evidence that could piece together any firm answer. It will have to remain an interesting question at best.

Luke 24:6

In this third Western noninterpolation, the words "He is not here, but is risen" are missing. Parker considers the addition to be a case of "free harmonization" since the words are not identical.[53]

Luke 24:12

Parker favors this fourth Western noninterpolation, especially since it has non-Lukan features.

On the Road to Emmaus (Luke 24:23–35)

Parker points to the disagreement over the distance from Jerusalem, between a few manuscripts, and the inclusion of names of the two disciples in some manuscripts of the Latin tradition, as evidence of tampering with the text. Although Parker's point is well taken, the majority of manuscripts are very stable in both cases.

In the Upper Room

Luke 24:36

Here is another case of the Western noninterpolation omitting "Peace to you" that Parker regards as a later harmonization.

---

52. Parker, *Living Text of the Gospels*, 166.
53. Parker, *Living Text of the Gospels*, 167.

Luke 24:40

A Western noninterpolation and not to be considered original.

Luke 24:43

Although not a case of Western noninterpolation, Parker deems it to be a harmonization to John 21:13.

Luke 24:51

Parker considers this to be the penultimate Western noninterpolation. He acknowledges the support of the original hand of Sinaiticus for the omission is not very substantive since the scribe is known to mistakenly omit phrases. Nonetheless, he finds the longer reading, "and carried up into heaven," to be an effort to inject orthodoxy regarding the physical ascension of Jesus into the Lucan text. Parker points out some have argued the shorter text could have been a heretical corruption and reminds the reader "the debate illustrates how seriously theological issues must be taken in studying the history of the text."[54]

Luke 24:52

In the final Western noninterpolation, Parker opts for the view that the addition, "worshiping Him," was an indication that the focus was shifting from having worshiped him at the temple to worshiping Jesus.

Parker concludes the chapter by noting, "The sum total provides incontrovertible evidence the text of these chapters was not fixed, and indeed continued to grow for centuries after its composition."[55] He claims no text type was immune to the need to add to the text, especially the Western noninterpolations that betray an anti-docetic bias. Consequently, the resultant Lucan text lost its unique non-Markan understanding of Jesus. As noted throughout the discussion, issue can be taken with Parker over many of his arguments throughout the chapter.

The development and transmission of the Fourth Gospel

Unlike the previous chapters that focus on the Synoptic Gospels, except for the *Pericope Adulterae*, this chapter focuses on the methodological question

---

54. Parker, *Living Text of the Gospels*, 171.
55. Parker, *Living Text of the Gospels*, 172.

of conjectural emendation arising out of the Fourth Gospel. Parker begins by using the accretion of additional information in the account of the angel at the pool in the pericope of John 5:1–15 as an illustration of the process of conjectural emendation. He takes the traditional understanding of conjectural emendation to a new level by bringing up the case of John 19:29, where Jesus is given a sponge full of vinegar on hyssop. Some have argued it is highly unlikely a small bushy herb like hyssop was used to hold the sponge.[56] Nonetheless, the lack of any solid external evidence, except for the reading υσσω (lance) in two late medieval Old Latin manuscripts, has prevented any possibility of claiming conjectural emendation. Parker finds the paucity of textual evidence to be made up by literary criticism, by which he makes a case for the later addition of chapter 21 and the switching of chapters 5 and 6. He concludes, "There is no difference between conjectural emendation and literary theories about the development of the Fourth Gospel."[57] He deems the difference between conjectural emendation and literary theory to be an "artificial one."[58] Ultimately, Parker's argument from textual evidence to literary criticism and back again is circular and weak, to say the least.

From codex to disk

Parker's key argument in this chapter is the idea of an authoritative text did not emerge until after the coming of the printing press, since prior to the press the text was not stable. As appealing as this argument may seem against the doctrine of inerrancy, the support or lack thereof for the authority of Scripture needs much sturdier support than just the above argument. The frailty of scribal competency and weakness cannot be the deciding factor for a belief that requires historical evidence. In fact, the belief of the church regarding the NT Scripture was based more on the Jewish belief regarding the Old Testament.

According to Parker, the introduction of computers in the study of the NT text has opened a newer vista than before in NTTC. Individuals can not only access the text on their own, but also alter it to suit their own purpose. He finds a parallel to the early stage of manuscript production where the "electronic text may be more similar to the manuscript than to the printed book."[59] In the concluding chapter Parker makes the following bold statement: "There is a sense in which there is no such thing as either the New

---

56. O'Day and Hylen, *John*, 188.
57. Parker, *Living Text of the Gospels*, 178.
58. Parker, *Living Text of the Gospels*, 179.
59. Parker, *Living Text of the Gospels*, 191.

Testament or the Gospels. What is available to us is a number of reconstructions of some or all of the documents classified as belonging to the New Testament."[60] Overall, Parker decries any effort to claim the text is definitive. Instead, under the guise of "the presence of the Spirit is not limited to the inspiration of the written word," he has attempted to erode any confidence in the authority of a single original text of the NT.[61] Under Parker's text-critical understanding, one is left with no authoritative biblical text, but only those exhibits that give a glimpse of the various stages of church history.

PUBLICATIONS SUPPORTING THE THESIS OF THE LIVING TEXT

In 2008, Parker published *An Introduction to the New Testament Manuscripts and Their Texts*. In the introduction he declares:

> The first ports of call, the natural books to go on a student reading list, tend to present "business as usual," describing things very much as they have been for several generations but are no longer. This book offers an account of textual criticism today. I have tried to write a book with as original a shape and as fresh a content as possible. I am more interested in explaining the questions than in providing the answers, with the result that I have regularly become distracted into various exciting forays.[62]

Parker challenges all previous notions of "the textual criticism of the New Testament" as he states baldly:

> There is no longer such a thing, unless as a useful definition of a field of research, as opposed to the textual criticism of Homer or Shakespeare. It is true that some aspects of the study of these twenty-seven books are very similar. But so would textual criticism of the New Testament have similarities of approach to the textual criticism of any early Christian writer, such as Origen or Augustine, as well as differences from it.[63]

In other words, the NT is no different than any early text of the first few centuries of Christianity. Parker repeatedly claims his purpose is not as much to resolve any difficulties or reach any solutions to text-critical

---

60. Parker, *Living Text of the Gospels*, 204.
61. Parker, *Living Text of the Gospels*, 211.
62. Parker, *Introduction to the New Testament Manuscripts*, 2.
63. Parker, *Introduction to the New Testament Manuscripts*, 6.

problems but to "imitate the skilled host in performing introductions between its readers and its topics, and then leaving them together."[64] True to his word, Parker raises many issues throughout the book that more than challenge the credibility of the original text of the NT. A common idiosyncrasy that shows up again is Parker's aversion to footnotes, as observed by the present writer.

A year later, Parker's essays from 1977 to 2007 were published as *Manuscripts, Texts, Theology*.[65] They are invaluable in tracing Parker's thought development over the years. There are three that are particularly important for the subject at hand. The first, "Scripture is Tradition," from 1991, contains in germ form Parker's thesis in *The Living Text*.[66] In it, he admits, "The basis for the history of the text that is about to be offered is the study of a particular New Testament manuscript, one that represents a remarkably free form of text. This manuscript, Codex Bezae, now consists of the Gospels and Acts, in parallel Greek and Latin columns."[67] In conclusion, he remarks,

> There is a sense in which there is no such thing as the New Testament. What is available to us is a number of reconstructions of some or all the documents classified as belonging to the New Testament. . . . Textual criticism makes it clear that the text is in a sense inaccessible to us. The fact that the recovery of the original text is a task that remains beyond all of us sets a question mark against any claim that we can in any sense "possess" the text—literally or metaphorically.[68]

In his second article, "Et Incarnatus Est," Parker further develops his thesis in *The Living Text*.[69] He expresses the following confidence:

> The blanket hermeneutics and the specifically Christian interpretations will be in need of revising. For already the textual critics are producing the kinds of texts that they are able to make and want to create, and the users will find that the forgotten

---

64. Parker, *Introduction to the New Testament Manuscripts*, 9.

65. Parker, *Manuscripts, Texts, Theology*.

66. Parker, "Scripture is Tradition," 11–17. Also found in Parker, *Manuscripts, Texts, Theology*, 265–72.

67. Parker, "Scripture is Tradition," 12. Also see Parker, *Manuscripts, Texts, Theology*, 267.

68. Parker, "Scripture is Tradition," 12. Also see Parker, *Manuscripts, Texts, Theology*, 267.

69. Parker, "Et Incarnatus Est," 330–43. Also see Parker, *Manuscripts, Texts, Theology*, 311–22.

lower critics are calling the tune. Assuredly, theology will be at the mercy of historical vicissitudes.[70]

The third article of significance for the present study is "Textual Criticism and Theology."[71] Here Parker challenges the view that theology developed linearly. He claims instead if the text was not settled in the early period of the transmission, then neither was theology. He challenges any high view of Scripture, which he considers to be superimposed on the textual tradition. After all, how can there be an authoritative text "when the text has survived for us as a number of competing and equal forms?"[72]

The story of Codex Sinaiticus has long fascinated both the academic and the layperson. Parker's *Codex Sinaiticus: The Story of the World's Oldest Bible* is the story retold with some up-to-date information.[73] It is a byproduct of the recent collaboration between the Archbishop of Sinai, the Chief Executive of the British Library, the Director of Leipzig University Library, and the Deputy Director of the National Library of Russia, St. Petersburg. In describing the textual world of the manuscript until the Renaissance, Parker considers the present world of identical print editions to be "one of textual poverty."[74]

Parker's 2011 Lyell Lectures at Oxford University are expanded in his book *Textual Scholarship and the Making of the New Testament*.[75] Although slightly shorter than *The Living Text*, it comes as Parker's manifesto of NTTC. In characteristic fashion he challenges previous categories regarding the goal of textual criticism, manuscript classification, and even dependence on the standard critical texts. Interestingly, he distinguishes between works (e.g., Gospel of John), documents (manuscripts), and texts (form of the work in a manuscript). He also offers an introduction to the CBGM as the cutting-edge tool of doing textual criticism. Parker envisions a day when "the user will potentially be able to select any witness as the base text, and to see how the rest of the tradition looks from a new point of view. From that we can imagine future online editions where users will be able to build their

---

70. Parker, "Et Incarnatus Est," 343. Also see Parker, *Manuscripts, Texts, Theology*, 321–22.

71. Parker, "Textual Criticism and Theology," 583–89. Also see Parker, *Manuscripts, Texts, Theology*, 323–33.

72. Parker, "Textual Criticism and Theology," 588. Also see Parker, *Manuscripts, Texts, Theology*, 331.

73. Parker, *Codex Sinaiticus*.

74. Parker, *Codex Sinaiticus*, 114.

75. Parker, *Textual Scholarship*.

own text."[76] Parker has also been involved in many additional text-critical projects that do not involve expression of his views, such as the massive *International Greek New Testament Project* on the Gospel of John.

CONCLUSION

Parker's thesis undermines the concept of a single original text. Under his methodology, NTTC is about creating various texts suitable for readers of all backgrounds and various needs rather than any attempt to retrieve an original authoritative text. Parker has made a significant contribution toward the shifting of the goalpost of NTTC.

---

76. Parker, *Textual Scholarship*, 137.

5

Eldon J. Epp

Unlike Ehrman, but similar to Parker, Eldon Epp is not well known outside NT and NTTC circles. He belongs to the category of text-critics who focus more on theorizing and philosophizing regarding the discipline, rather than on counting and classifying the material. This is not to say he is deficient in the latter in any way but that his writings are mostly focused on construing the ideology behind the progress and various shifts in the discipline and prognosticating the future of NTTC. It may be said, without hesitation, that apprehending and communicating the abstract about the complicated field of NTTC is in some ways more tedious and intricate than examining and cataloging (collating) the evidence. Epp's impact on shifting the goalpost of NTTC cannot be overstated.

SCHOLARLY RESPONSES TO EPP'S THESIS

Epp has been a key figure in the changing quest of NTTC. In fact, he could very well be deemed the father of the new movement in NTTC. His evolution toward his present position of multiple originals seems to have begun decades ago with his published 1961 dissertation, *The Theological Tendency of Codex Bezae Cantabrigiensis in Acts*, wherein he declares, "The recovery of the original text and the historical reconstruction of the transmission of the text do not exhaust the tasks or the value of textual criticism."[1] It appears

---

1. Epp, *Theological Tendency*, 14.

even back then he was implying that seeking the original text might not be the only desirable enterprise, since it may not be attainable. He hints at this idea throughout the dissertation. Even so, through the years, Epp still operated under the assumption of the original text, as can also be noticed in the dissertation: "Perhaps D *d* alone have preserved the original Lucan text here" or, where he "would hardly suggest that the D-version is original here."[2] In other words, in theory Epp appears to be hinting toward the abandonment of the original text, but in practice he still operates under the parameters of the traditional quest of the discipline. Epp denies this disparity in the introduction of his 2004 anthology, saying he had "made no attempt to determine the 'original' text of Acts—whether the B-text or D-text. Rather, given the difficulty (then and now) in deciding on the priority of the B-text or D-text, I remained neutral on the issue."[3] He regrettably remarks,

> Though my 1966 volume received some fifty reviews and was cited rather widely for its general theme, as well as in discussions of individual variants, at the time it too failed to foster a groundswell of fresh studies in the same mode, and I published only one further study on this approach to theological tendency. Indeed, only some thirty years later was *Theological Tendency* acknowledged to have provided a stimulus for views that carried the method forward in impressive new directions.[4]

Although issue may be taken with Epp's retrospective recasting of his dissertation, one can fairly deduce Epp began his career with hints of his present view regarding the quest of NTTC, albeit in germ form.

In recent decades, Epp returned to the topic of the goals of NTTC. He attributes his rekindling of interest to three new emphases between the late 1990s and the early twenty-first century: first, a new assessment of the Oxyrhynchus papyri in their larger contexts; second, a new interest in the meaning and implications of the original text; and third, the relationship between textual criticism and canon.[5] He further elaborates on the changing philosophical landscape, saying,

> In simple terms, our world has changed, and not least the world of scholarship. It is clear to me that we in our diverse intellectual world—if at times pulled and dragged—have moved beyond the "certainties" of historism and even beyond the comforts of

---

2. Epp, *Theological Tendency*, 79, 92.
3. Epp, "Introduction," xxviiin4.
4. Epp, "Introduction," xxix–xxx.
5. Epp, "Introduction," xxxiv.

modernism to a recognition that the notion of "multiple truths" is more than a novel fad or a passing fancy. I believe that we now must acknowledge that claims to a single interpretation are increasingly difficult to justify in our multicultural and pluralist world—both secular and religious.[6]

In this new world of increasing possibilities, Epp appraises the traditional goal of NTTC as outdated and restrictive toward the growth and potential of the discipline. Now, determining the baseline text is no longer the desired or even achievable goal. Instead, the baseline text serves to enhance the understanding of the variants and vice versa. The text has now become a "virtual museum, with its variation units comprising exhibits of narratives and interpretations located, whenever possible, contextually in time and place."[7] Overall, in Epp's understanding, textual criticism has moved "farther away from 'science' and more closely toward 'art.'"[8] In this new world of possibilities, the growth of the field is in direct proportion to the text critic's imagination as he/she seeks to open the window on the history of the variants rather than to determine something like the original text—an outmoded, impossible, and fruitless task.

Unlike the responses to Ehrman and Parker, not many individual reviews have been directed toward Epp's works on textual criticism. Most responses must be gleaned from articles and essays recapping the progress of the discipline. The main reason for this paucity is the nature of Epp's writings. While the previous proponents have produced monographs directed toward the subject, Epp has contributed primarily through essays. Michael Holmes rightly remarks, "Epp, one of North America's leading textual critics, is a master of the essay genre."[9] Peter J. Williams concurs: "Epp's career shows how a scholar can rise to the top of a discipline predominantly on the basis of writing critical essays."[10] Epp indeed continues to write incisive essays.

The reviews are generally favorable, with appellations such as "world-class scholar"[11] and "big beast" in NTTC.[12] In his review in *Novum Testamentum*, Peter R. Rodgers proclaims the publication of Epp's collected essays as "an important event in the study of the text of the New Testament."[13] In an

6. Epp, "Introduction," xxxv.
7. Epp, "Introduction," xxxvii.
8. Epp, "Introduction," xxxviii.
9. Holmes, "Review of *Perspectives*," 192.
10. Williams, "Review of *Perspectives*," 146.
11. Thiselton, "Review of *Junia*," 266.
12. Hurtado, "In Gratitude," para. 1.
13. Rodgers, "Review of *Perspectives*," 292.

earlier encomium of Epp, Larry Hurtado praises his teacher's contribution to the field in two major emphases: "The history of the discipline as the necessary context in which to view particular developments, and a persistent concern for progress in the history and theory of the NT text."[14] Hurtado admits, "His approach requires a lot of investigation and assimilation of information, and the results for the development of a theory and history of the earliest transmission of the NT writings are not as immediate as one could wish."[15] In concluding the otherwise positive tribute, Hurtado points out Epp's contributions have been "exploratory and provisional."[16] J. Keith Elliott also credits Epp for exposing "the unclarity in previous writings about what the vainly sought *original* text may be, and show[ing] it to be a weasel word."[17]

Contrarily, Wallace accuses Epp, along with Ehrman and Parker, of being postmodern in his approach. He warns, "They are three extremely influential voices. And those who get involved in textual criticism need to be wary of the pitfalls of their agenda."[18] Wallace further adjudicates,

> Concomitant with the new definition of textual criticism is a frontal attack on any kind of certainty. This is in keeping with postmodernism's focus on relativism and of seeing all views as equally possible with none more probable than the others.[19]

Epp was perturbed at such charges of postmodernism. In reflecting back to "The Multivalence of the 'Original Text,'" he bemoans that the "responses, to be sure, [are] extended from acceptance to charges of postmodernism."[20] This is bewildering since, as discussed earlier, Epp considered his articles to be pioneering in moving the discipline of NTTC beyond modernism.[21] If so, then Wallace's charges of postmodernism against Epp are befitting.

Although Ehrman, Parker, and Epp share commonalities in their overall approach to the text of the NT, there are wide differences between them. For example, in Epp's approach, the NT text was readily available and easily transported all over the known world, but in Ehrman's approach, based on Bauer, Christianity took on certain local tendencies and beliefs due to lack

---

14. Hurtado, "Going for the Bigger Picture," 1. The article was originally presented at a special session of the SBL NTTC annual meeting program unit in honor of Eldon Jay Epp at his 80th birthday, in Atlanta, November 2010.
15. Hurtado, "Going for the Bigger Picture," 6.
16. Hurtado, "Going for the Bigger Picture," 8.
17. Elliott, "Recent Trends," 127 (emphasis original).
18. Wallace, "Challenges in New Testament Textual Criticism," 85.
19. Wallace, "Challenges in New Testament Textual Criticism," 85.
20. Epp, "In the Beginning," 35.
21. Epp, "Introduction," xxxv.

of interaction with other communities. The difference might appear subtle at first, but it is critical. Holmes, in his article chronicling the development of the new trend, credits Epp along with Parker for giving a "substantial and sustained attention to the topic."[22] Nonetheless, he questions Epp's ambivalence regarding what he means by the "earliest" text, since at times it appears he is implying "chronological" priority, but at others "logical" priority.[23] Holmes also challenges some of Epp's presumptions regarding the state of the text. While Ehrman has aimed his works primarily toward the popular audience and Parker has aimed his toward the academy, Epp has directed his thesis toward the upper echelons of the discipline.

This survey of Epp's contribution to the repositioning of the goal of NTTC demonstrates he is not just a player in the field, but an effectual captain due to his influence on NTTC. The mild responses to his writings further show most text-critics are either reluctant, or feel inadequate, to respond to his thesis. Many probably accept his writings at face value, probably reading into them much more than what Epp had intended his theories to be.

SHIFT IN EPP'S VIEW

At the 1960 SBL Annual Meeting in New York City, Epp delivered a paper suggesting his present view on the original text, albeit in an embryonic form.[24] He advocated the view of Hans Conzelmann as a starting point in examining "tendentious readings"[25] in the text of Acts. Conzelmann, in his seminal work on redaction criticism entitled *The Theology of St Luke*, had argued Luke placed the blame for Christ's crucifixion on the Jewish people. However, the blame is stronger in the Gospel than in Acts. In Acts, the Jewish people are excused on the ground of ignorance, which he referred to as the "motif of 'ignorance.'"[26] The reason for this was probably the missionary goal of the church, which would be hindered by blaming the Jewish people. Epp expanded upon Conzelmann's thesis in his own detailed dissertation by suggesting the D-text in Acts actually reverses the "ignorance motif" and reinstates the guilt on the Jewish people, while in the process extolling the value of seeking the history behind the variants rather than just distinguishing right from

---

22. Holmes, "From 'Original Text' to 'Initial Text,'" 640–41.
23. Holmes, "From 'Original Text' to 'Initial Text,'" 649–50.
24. Epp, "'Ignorance Motif,'" 51–62.
25. Epp, "'Ignorance Motif,'" 53.
26. Conzelmann, *Theology of St Luke*, 89. It should be pointed out that in his later German editions Conzelmann became hesitant in proposing that Luke tailored his source for Acts to soften the accusation against the Jewish people.

wrong readings. The following are three samples from Epp's dissertation, each taken from the three subheadings of "Anti-Judaic Tendencies in Acts."

The Jews and Jesus—Acts 3:17

In Acts 3, Peter gives a message to those who were amazed at the healing of the lame man who sat by the Beautiful Gate in Jerusalem. Both the Alexandrian and Western texts carry the reading that reminded the Jewish listeners of their guilt in crucifying Christ, but softened the blow by adding they and their rulers "acted in ignorance." However, the variants in the D-text bring out certain elements that appear to hesitate in exonerating the Jewish people for their actions.

B	D
και νυν αδελφοι,	και νυν ανδρες αδελφοι,
οιδα	επισταμεθα
οτι	οτι υμεις μεν
κατα αγνοιαν	κατα αγνοιαν
επραξατε,	επραξατε πονηρον,
ωσπερ και οι αρχοντες υμων.	ωσπερ και οι αρχοντες υμων.

The first difference is the sharpening of the community lines between the Jews and the Christians, with the use of the first-person plural επισταμεθα ("we know") in D versus the first-person singular οιδα ("I know") in B. This is further emphasized by the use of υμεις ("you all") in D. Furthermore, the presence of a μεν-δε construction between verses 17 (υμεις μεν) and 18 (ο δε θεος) sets the works of the Jewish people against the sovereign plan of God. But the final clincher is the addition of πονηρον ("evil") in D. This, according to Epp, leaves no doubt D considers the act of the Jewish people in crucifying Jesus as evil. He even refers back to D's omission of Jesus's prayer of forgiveness from the cross in Luke 23:34 as further support for his argument. Epp acknowledges that although "these textual variants, like so many others in D, are small—there is, after all, a basic conservatism in all New Testament texts."[27]

The Jews, Gentiles, and Christianity—Acts 1:2

Anti-Judaic tendencies in D can be noted among the additional words in the D-text.

---

27. Epp, *Theological Tendency*, 44.

B	D
αχρι ης ημερας	αχρι ης ημερας
	ανελημφθη
εντειλαμενος τοις αποστολοις	εντειλαμενος τοις αποστολοις
δια πνευματος αγιου	δια πνευματος αγιου
ους εξελεξατο	ους εξελεξατο
ανελημφθη·	
	και εκελευσε κηρυσσειν το ευαγγελιον·

Epp notes the similarity between this passage and Luke 24:43–53: both are an account of the final instructions of Jesus to his disciples before he ascended. Epp considers κηρυσσειν ("to preach") in the D-text in Acts 1:2 an allusion to κηρυχθηναι ("should be preached") in Luke 24:47. Based on this assumption, he postulates παντα τα εθνη ("to all nations") in Luke 24:47 is the background for κηρυσσειν το ευαγγελιον ("to preach the gospel") in Acts 1:2 of the D-text. Hence, according to the D-text, Acts 1:2 anticipates the widening of the church's mission to the gentiles much earlier than commonly assumed in Acts 10 with Cornelius. Epp refers to this as "intense universalism," wherein the church's focus is no longer on just the Jewish people but all people, especially in light of the former's actions toward Jesus.[28]

The Jews and the Apostles—Acts 4:8b–9

Although Epp acknowledges many of the examples here had been covered under previous headings, he differentiates them as Jews *versus* the apostles rather than "Jews *and* the Apostles."[29]

B	D
Αρχοντες του λαου	Αρχοντες του λαου
και πρεσβυτεροι,	και πρεσβυτεροι του Ισραηλ
ει ημεις σημερον	ει ημεις σημερον
ανακρεινομεθα	ανακρεινομεθα αφ υμων
επι ευεργεσια	επ ευεργεσεια
ανθρωπου ασθενους	ανθρωπου ασθενους

28. Epp, *Theological Tendency*, 66.
29. Epp, *Theological Tendency*, 120.

D, along with the other Western witnesses, emphasizes αφ υμων ("by you"), pointing back to Αρχοντες του λαου και πρεσβυτεροι ("Rulers of the people and Elders"). Epp contends that the association is not as strong in the B-text. Furthermore, the D-text adds του Ισραηλ ("of Israel") so "as if to leave no doubt as to who these rulers and elders were."[30]

Epp provides many other examples of similar subtle changes to draw the conclusion many Anti-Judaic tendencies mark Codex Bezae Cantabrigiensis in Acts. The primary point of the study is to demonstrate the early scribes corrupted the text to fit their sociopolitical and theological agendas. It becomes apparent in view of later developments that the secondary point of the study was to advocate the setting aside of the old goal of NTTC and embark upon similar exploratory studies of early manuscripts. Once again, it should be reiterated Epp never suggested abandoning the quest for the original text altogether in his dissertation. To the contrary, he operates within the parameters that presume such an original text.

After his dissertation, Epp appeared to have lost interest in the subject of theological corruptions in the NT text for the next thirty years or so. Although he wrote voluminously in the field of NTTC, he did not bring up the issue again until recently. His renewed interest can be gleaned from a host of his recent essays in theological journals, *Festschriften*, and special studies. Only those relevant for the present discussion will be examined below.

Through the years, Epp has written several salient articles challenging the status quo of NTTC in which he decries the impasse facing the discipline and the lack of progress reflected in the popular critical editions.[31] He repeatedly has called for new and fresh approaches that would open new vistas for future studies. Unfortunately, many of his cries have fallen on deaf ears. Beginning in the late 1980s, Epp devoted several articles to the study of the NT papyri. His goal was to prove the state of the papyri in Egypt, specifically Oxyrhynchus, represented the state of the text in the rest of the Mediterranean. In other words, the unsettled and chaotic nature of the NT text in Oxyrhynchus was a sample of the NT text throughout Christendom in the early centuries.

In his first papyrus-related article, "The New Testament Papyrus Manuscripts in Historical Perspective," Epp asks, "If the New Testament papyri

---

30. Epp, *Theological Tendency*, 120.

31. Epp, "Twentieth Century Interlude," 386–414. This essay has been reprinted in Epp and Fee, *Studies in the Theory and Method*, 83–108. Epp's second article is "Continuing Interlude" (131–51). A revised version of that essay also appears in Epp and Fee, *Studies in the Theory and Method*, 109–23. See also his "Decision Points" (17–44). Also see Epp's concluding article on the matter, "New Testament Textual Criticism in America," 94–98.

are considered to be so extraordinarily important by virtually all textual critics, then why was their importance really not recognized—or at least not widely recognized—for something like fifty or sixty years after the first discoveries?"[32] As is commonly known, he reiterates that the NT papyri were found mostly on rubbish heaps and survived "only when protected from moisture, either by placement in protective caves, buildings, or jars, or when buried in ordinary ground in the virtually rain-free areas of Egypt, Palestine, and Mesopotamia."[33] Added to the natural elements, the "human hazards" were no less destructive.[34] While acknowledging the survival of the papyri was a miracle in itself, Epp still attempts to deduce the state of the text in the early period of transmission from the available evidence. For example, regarding the discovery of P52 in Egypt, Epp opines it was very interesting because it could prove "John's Gospel was written recently enough to have been transferred to Egypt and to have been copied and circulated there at that early period."[35]

Epp's insights on the early NT papyri offer a couple of benefits: they can demonstrate that letter-carrying in the early period was much more expeditious than commonly assumed, and the Alexandrian text may not be as late as some have claimed. But they also raise certain questions: In a world of such "vibrant Christianity," perhaps the papyri were consigned to the rubbish heap due to damage or (as even Epp acknowledges) by following the practice of their Jewish predecessors, particularly by burying defective or fragmentary manuscripts near a cemetery.[36] Perhaps text-critics from the late nineteenth and early twentieth century did not place much emphasis on the papyri because of such reasons and not just due to ignorance or bias.

In his second article on the papyri, Epp acknowledges at the outset, "This is largely an exercise in *historical-critical imagination*. It is an attempt to discover some things we do not know about the earliest stages of New Testament textual transmission by applying *creative imagination* to what we do not know."[37] Unlike the previous article on the papyri that offered general observations, Epp's goal now is to challenge the traditional view of static texts or local texts and propose a hypothetical dynamic text that was circulating at a faster rate across the NT world than previously inferred. By admittedly

---

32. Epp, "NT Papyrus Manuscripts," 261–62.
33. Epp, "NT Papyrus Manuscripts," 263.
34. Epp, "NT Papyrus Manuscripts," 263.
35. Epp, "NT Papyrus Manuscripts," 264.
36. Epp, "NT Papyrus Manuscripts," 265. Also see Roberts, *Manuscript, Society and Belief*, 6–7.
37. Epp, "Significance of the Papyri," 71 (emphasis added).

conducting a "hasty and quite inadequate survey of activities and movements in the first few centuries of Christianity," Epp concludes the NT text was not as fixed in the early period as is commonly assumed.[38] To make his case, he focuses on Egypt since the "forty-five earliest [papyri] virtually all come from Egypt and that twenty of these (as well as seven others) were unearthed at Oxyrhynchus."[39] It is commonly understood the early centuries of Egyptian Christianity are hazy at best and so, according to Epp, not much can be asserted with confidence about the origins of the papyri or even the uncials א and B. To fill in the gaps, Epp turns to the non-Christian Egyptian papyri and suggests two factors previously neglected in determining the history of the Christian papyri in Egypt: "First, the papyri attest extensive and lively interaction between Alexandria and the outlying areas, and also between the outlying areas and other parts of the Roman world, including Rome itself; and, second, they provide evidence of the wide circulation of documents in this early period."[40] These suggested factors can prove helpful in understanding the spread of the NT manuscripts in earliest Christianity.

Based on the arguments above, Epp calls for the abandonment of the practice of judging the earlier papyri by the later fourth-century witnesses. Instead, he proposes the papyri be studied in their own right against the background of non-Christian Egyptian papyri. As can be seen, his ultimate goal is to prove the papyri in Egypt represent not just the state of the text in Egypt, but in the entire Mediterranean world of the time. Epp garners further support for his theory from the presence of the *nomina sacra* that are found in the earliest Christian manuscripts in Egypt, as well as the use of the codex. He concludes the resultant text of the NT throughout the Roman Empire was unsettled at best.

Much issue may be taken with the above arguments, as even Epp acknowledges. Granted, the world of the papyri in Egypt was active and vibrant, but this understanding still does not apply *carte blanche* to the NT papyri themselves. First, the NT papyri were the religious literature of the Christians and held sacred value, unlike the non-Christian papyri. Second, unlike letters and government documents that were frequently transmitted from one place to another, the sacred Scriptures did not require the same frequency of transmission since such texts would meet a primarily local need and were used in that particular sociological context. Third, the fragmentary nature of the biblical papyri limits greatly any sweeping verdict regarding the state of the overall text of the NT.

38. Epp, "Significance of the Papyri," 74–75.
39. Epp, "Significance of the Papyri," 76.
40. Epp, "Significance of the Papyri," 80.

In a follow-up article linking NT papyri and letter-carrying in the Greco-Roman period, Epp furthers his case that early Christian Egypt was far from being static and isolated. He concludes, "If papyrus was needed, it could be sent; if forwarding was required, that could be arranged; if detailed delivery instructions were essential, they could be provided; if a reply was urgent, a return letter carrier might be designated."[41] Based on the above claim, Epp submits the theory the state of the text in Egypt could represent the state of the text across the Mediterranean area or vice versa. As innovative as Epp is in his thesis and as compelling as the evidence is of the well-developed and efficient governmental postal system in Egypt, he underestimates the control local communities and their leaders exercised over their sacred texts. It seems doubtful the conclusions regarding the sending and receiving of governmental documents and personal dispatches can be applied wholesale to the transfer of sacred documents in the ancient world. The reluctance of present-day denominations, churches, and individuals to change Bible versions is a good reminder people do not readily or hastily switch between favored and established readings, texts, or versions.

In a later article, Epp concentrates his attention on Oxyrhynchus, the location of as much as 46 percent of the early biblical papyri.[42] Using the works of Eric Gardner Turner and others on Oxyrhynchus, Epp asks, "What does it mean for the New Testament papyri at Oxyrhynchus when it is recognized that they were found in a city where vast numbers of literary texts were in use and were subjected to scholarly analysis and editing?"[43] Furthermore, there is evidence of other noncanonical Christian literature in Oxyrhynchus, which led Colin H. Roberts to conclude there could very well be a Christian *scriptorium* there.[44] Nonetheless, Epp is unable to locate any evidence of scribal activity, whether an

> editor's or scholar's notations or critical marks, such as *glosses* or *scholia* (marginal notes, respectively, for explanation and illustration or for elucidating the meaning of difficult passages); *onomastica* (glosses explaining the meaning of names and places); notes of *commentary*, pointers to a commentary, or indications of a need for a commentary to a portion of text; and very specific

---

41. Epp, "New Testament Papyrus Manuscripts and Letter Carrying," 51.

42. Epp, "New Testament Papyri at Oxyrhynchus," 52–53.

43. Epp, "New Testament Papyri at Oxyrhynchus," 59. Cf., Turner, "Roman Oxyrhynchus," 78–93. Also see Turner, *Greek Papyri*; Turner, *Greek Manuscripts of the Ancient World*.

44. Roberts, *Manuscript, Society and Belief*, 24. See also Epp, "New Testament Papyri at Oxyrhynchus," 62–63.

critical marks or signs, most commonly the χ sign and the > or diple (διπλη), but also the obelus and antisigma, and others.[45]

Epp concludes this lack of evidence of scribal activity could be because at this stage the NT text was still in an evolutionary process. Contrarily, this could also be because the community was not competent in editing the text, did not feel they had the authority to alter the text, did not consider the copies either sufficient for general use, or possibly considered them to be faulty and thus cast them on the rubbish heap.

The present section concludes[46] with Epp's final comments on the subjects of papyri, letter-carrying, and Oxyrhynchus, which Epp presented in his Presidential Address at the 2003 annual meeting of SBL.[47] He summarized his previous articles on the papyri in Oxyrhynchus and extended the discussion as it impacted canonicity.[48] In his introductory remarks, he said,

> At last New Testament textual criticism has lost its innocence and has learned to tolerate ambiguity—one of the sure signs of maturity.... Our discipline, to be sure, has its technical aspects, but it remains primarily an art, and therefore it is for neither the perfunctory, nor the inflexible, nor the unimaginative, nor the tender-minded; and above all it is not the safe harbor that for so long and by so many it has been perceived to be. And "this"—as the saying goes—"is not your father's" textual criticism, but an entrance into a brave new world, with provocative challenges and captivating promises![49]

Although Epp admits the papyri are fragmentary and random in their survival, he attempts to recreate the setting of the Oxyrhynchus papyri.[50] By considering the presence of extracanonical works (e.g., *Shepherd of Hermas*) side by side with the canonical NT manuscripts without any claims of canonicity, Epp concludes the idea of canonicity is later and should be abandoned. He proposes, "There is no basis for assigning preference to one group

---

45. Epp, "New Testament Papyrus Manuscripts and Letter Carrying," 64 (emphasis original).

46. Chronologically, another article by Epp critical to the "new quest" for the NT text intervenes at this point; discussion of that article is postponed until the next section of this dissertation.

47. Epp, "Oxyrhynchus New Testament Papyri," 5–55.

48. Although another article by Epp applies Gamble's conclusion to the Oxyrhynchus context, the conclusions do not apply directly to the issue at hand. See Epp, "Codex and Literacy," 15–37.

49. Epp, "Oxyrhynchus New Testament Papyri," 9–10.

50. Epp, "Oxyrhynchus New Testament Papyri," 10.

over the other, or even for claiming that they were separable groups. . . . [O]ne is tempted to remark, 'Why should the third and fourth centuries be any different from the twentieth and twenty-first?'"[51] Although much of Epp's discussion in this article is hypothetical, it reveals his continuing effort to erase the idea of an original text by liberating it from any constraints due to canonicity.

Thus, Epp attempts to revise the quest of the original text through conclusions drawn from the state of the early NT papyri, letter-carrying in ancient times, and the discoveries at Oxyrhynchus. Although much can be learned from these articles, they fail to provide convincing evidence against seeking for a single, original text behind all the NT manuscripts. They do demonstrate the erudition of a creative scholar, but fail to support his underlying thesis.

EPP'S APPROACH TO THE NT TEXT

The first published statement of Epp's clear shift on the goalpost of NTTC appears in his chapter "Textual Criticism in the Exegesis of the New Testament, with an Excursus on Canon" in Stanley Porter's *Handbook to Exegesis of the New Testament*.[52] In the excursus, he attributes Helmut Koester's presentation at the 1988 conference on "Gospel Traditions in the Second Century" as the catalyst to his shift.[53] In his opening remarks, Koester had said: "The oldest known manuscript archetypes are separated from the autographs by more than a century. Textual critics of classical texts know that the first century of their transmission is the period in which the most serious corruptions occur. Textual critics of the New Testament writings have been surprisingly naïve in this respect."[54] Epp extends Koester's discussion with a couple of well-known examples of textual variants from the Gospels and the Pauline corpus to draw the following conclusion:

> Whereas traditional textual criticism has contributed much by moving its textual investigations ever closer to the time that the New Testament authors wrote, more recently its tasks have become more intriguing and more challenging as the discipline turns its attention away from the search for merely one 'original'

51. Epp, "Oxyrhynchus New Testament Papyri," 54–55.
52. Epp, "Textual Criticism in the Exegesis of the New Testament," 45–97. It also appears in Epp, *Perspectives on New Testament Textual Criticism*, 461–95. The excursus is not included in the latter compendium.
53. Koester, in Petersen, *Gospel Traditions in the Second Century*, 19–37.
54. Koester, "Text of the Synoptic Gospels," 19.

text to an understanding of earlier stages of composition and to earlier 'texts'—earlier 'originals'—that lie behind what we have become accustomed to consider the autographs of our 'canonical' New Testament writings.[55]

For Epp, the state of the NT text in the first few centuries is inseparable from the complexities regarding the NT canon. On this basis, he identifies four "various" originals: (1) precanonical original, (2) author's autograph, (3) canonical original, and (4) interpretive original.[56]

Epp's programmatic treatment of the subject came first as a paper delivered in 1998 at the NTTC Section of the Society of Biblical Literature Annual Meeting, and later was published as an article in 1999 in the *Harvard Theological Review*.[57] He deems burdensome the common practice of putting the words "original text" in quotation marks, implying their limitation in reaching "the" original text and asks, "Why, then, should textual critics be expected to define and to disclose their purposes in fine detail when already they are overwhelmed by data and are struggling to find the way out of this textual morass? . . . Is it not time that textual critics scrutinize those aims and intentions, evaluate them realistically, and then articulate them as clearly as possible?"[58] Epp took it upon himself to accomplish the task once and for all, laying out the obvious and clarifying the ambiguous goals of NTTC. After surveying the many handbooks on NTTC and finding very meager discussion of the subject, Epp names four textual critics who "departed decisively from the notion of a single 'original text' and that favor the multivalence of the term": Bart Ehrman, William L. Petersen, Epp himself, and David C. Parker.[59]

Epp offers the following definition of what he calls the "legitimate sphere" of the new approach to NTTC:

> Any search for textual *pre*formulations or *re*formulations of a literary nature, such as *prior* compositional levels, versions, or formulations, or *later* textual alteration, revision, division, combination, rearrangement, interpolation, or forming a collection of writings, legitimately falls within the sphere of text-critical

---

55. Epp, "Textual Criticism in the Exegesis of the New Testament," 87.
56. Epp, "Textual Criticism in the Exegesis of the New Testament," 89.
57. Epp, "Multivalence of the Term 'Original Text,'" 245–81.
58. Epp, "Multivalence of the Term 'Original Text,'" 247.
59. Epp, "Multivalence of the Term 'Original Text,'" 258–66. Petersen's statements on this matter do not involve a sufficiently significant body of literature to warrant a chapter-length discussion.

activity *if such an exploration is initiated on the basis of some appropriate textual variation or other manuscript evidence.*[60]

He even extends this definition to canonicity by asking, "If 'original' is multivalent, can 'canon' escape multivalence?"[61] He also questions the traditional definition of canon in the following words:

> What does "canon" or "canonical" mean? Just as each of the 5,300 Greek New Testament manuscripts and the perhaps 9,000 versional manuscripts is an "original," so each of these thousands of manuscripts likely was considered "canonical" when used in the worship and teaching of individual churches—and yet no two are exactly alike. . . . So "canon" and "canonical" which inherently involve authority, have varying dimensions of meaning at various times and in diverse places, and "canon" is no less polyvalent than "original text."[62]

Epp's proposal goes beyond the question of the open or closed status of the canon to a total abandonment of the idea of canon.[63] In the past few decades, much interest has developed on issues relating to the canon due to the discovery of the Qumran library and the Nag Hammadi discoveries containing the Gospel of Thomas and other gnostic documents. Attention has been given to extracanonical writings and some such as Koester have argued for a complete disbandment of any canonical boundaries.[64] Ebeling conveys a similar view and argues when the canon is considered to be a "strictly dogmatic reality, that is, when not only the boundaries of the canon but also the meaning of its canonicity are considered as beyond all discussion, Protestantism has already become Catholic in principle, for it is then founded upon the infallibility of a doctrinal decision of early Catholicism."[65] Likewise, Kurt Aland proposes the church consider a briefer and more unified canon that would serve the entire church and even bring about general

---

60. Epp, "Multivalence of the Term 'Original Text,'" 268 (emphasis original).

61. Epp, "Multivalence of the Term 'Original Text,'" 271.

62. Epp, "Multivalence of the Term 'Original Text,'" 275.

63. The past two centuries have seen a varying interest in the canon of the NT. In the late nineteenth and the early twentieth centuries, scholars like Zahn, Harnack, Lietzmann, and Leipoldt took interest in the history and development of the canon. In the 1930s, a brief revival of interest was seen in the works of Goodspeed and Lagrange. For a brief survey of the history of study in the NT Canon, see Gamble, *New Testament Canon*.

64. Koester, "New Testament Introduction," 1–20. Also see Koester, "Apocryphal and Canonical Gospels," 105–30.

65. Ebeling, *Problem of Historicity in the Church*, 63.

unity.⁶⁶ Epp's proposal seems to build on such claims, and thus completely disregards traditional arguments for an early canon.

In dealing with the causes of corruption and their relation to the canonization process, Frederik Wisse has argued if there were a marked difference in the transmission between the pre and postcanonical stage, there would be some indication of it in the text. Writings that did not gain immediate canonical acceptance should actually have more variations than those that were immediately part of the canon. Since this is not the case, it could very well be that the NT books attained their canonical status relatively soon. He further adds, "It is only when a text is considered authoritative that its teachings become problematic if they no longer conform to current beliefs and practices."⁶⁷ Earlier Ernest Cadman Colwell had also remarked, "Pious devotion to the Scriptures is not in and of itself a guaranty of accuracy. The enthusiastic, uneducated, and undisciplined clergyman of today yields to no one in the degree of his devotion to the Sacred Book, but he will misquote it from memory in the pulpit or in his letters without realizing that he is doing so."⁶⁸ Claims to extend, shorten, or abandon the canon fail to understand the true meaning of the NT. Metzger analyzed the problem well, as he states,

> Suggestions that the canon might be enlarged by the inclusion of other "inspirational" literature, ancient or modern, arise from a failure to recognize what the New Testament actually is. It is not an anthology of inspirational literature; it is a collection of writings that bear witness to what God has wrought through the life and work, the death and resurrection of Jesus Christ, and through the founding of his church by his Spirit.⁶⁹

Epp, like other proponents of the new approach in NTTC, seems to disregard all such arguments that bring any idea of theological or religious authority into the text-critical or canonical discussion of the NT text.

The following year (April 6–7, 2000), at the "Symposium on New Testament Studies: A Time for Reappraisal" that dealt with NTTC, held on the campus of Southeastern Baptist Theological Seminary, Epp concluded his lecture with a section entitled "Textual Criticism and Early Church History" in the following words:

> We see now how Parker's analysis and his bold statements and Ehrman's creative position reconnect us with the views of Lake,

---

66. Aland, *Problem of the New Testament Canon*, 33.
67. Wisse, "Nature and Purpose," 45.
68. Colwell, *What is the Best New Testament?*, 54.
69. Metzger, *Canon of the New Testament*, 271.

Harris, and the Chicago school and—it should be noted—meet the complaint of the Alands that "New Testament textual criticism has traditionally neglected the findings of early Church history, but only to its own injury." Now we have new possibilities in this important arena, with the goals of textual criticism properly expanded as well.[70]

Epp attempts to garner support for his theory by appealing, as also in his previous "Multivalence" article, to the Chicago school of NT scholars (Donald Riddle, M. M. Parvis, and Kenneth Clark), whom he considered to be the progenitors of this approach. Although each of these text-critics called for an approach beyond simply recovering the "original text," they never advocated a complete abandonment of the latter. Epp quotes Riddle as follows: "The legitimate task of textual criticism is not limited to the recovery of approximately the original form of the documents, to the establishment of the 'best' text, nor to the 'elimination of spurious readings.'"[71] It should be clarified that the phrase "not limited" in Riddle's above statement is a reminder Riddle is not discounting the value of the original text. He is simply calling for wider applications and deeper inroads in previously ignored territories in NTTC. As Riddle admits in the article, "Of course the New Testament writers wrote something," but promptly adds, "But what is the use of picturing this original copy? It had no status as a sacred document; no reverence for it as Scripture was accorded it until a century after its writing."[72] Parvis makes a similar proposal that values the place of the autographs but calls upon the textual critic to "value the readings of his late manuscripts just as he does those of his early manuscripts."[73] Even Kenneth Clark, who made the case that some textual variants do "affect," "alter," or "modify" doctrine, warns these variations are "willful and deliberate, yes. But not tampering, falsification, and fraud. Alteration, yes; but not corruption. Emendation, yes; but not in bad faith."[74] Granted, some of the above-mentioned proposals betray a weak view of NT canonization and textual authority, yet they still affirm the importance and validity of an original text.

In the compendium of articles on the canon titled *The Canon Debate: On the Origins and Formation of the Bible*, Epp contributed a chapter titled "Issues in the Interrelation of New Testament Textual Criticism and

---

70. Epp, "Issues in New Testament Textual Criticism," 61. For Epp's quote of Aland, see Aland and Aland, *Text of the New Testament*, 49.
71. Riddle, "Textual Criticism as a Historical Discipline," 221.
72. Riddle, "Textual Criticism as a Historical Discipline," 227.
73. Parvis, "Nature and Tasks," 172.
74. Clark, "Theological Relevance of Textual Variation," 5.

Canon."[75] He extends some of the points he had introduced in his earlier article "Textual Criticism in the Exegesis of the New Testament, with an Excursus on Canon" in *Handbook to Exegesis of the New Testament*.[76] Epp then examines three major issues: the presence of unexpected books in what are considered New Testament manuscripts, the absence of expected books in some of those New Testament manuscripts, and the varying order of books in the New Testament manuscripts themselves. He relies heavily on the newly discovered papyri to prove the text of the NT was in a state of flux in the early centuries of Christianity and consequently the canon was far from being settled. He attempts to dismantle many of the previous assumptions of what may or may not have been in a papyrus that had disintegrated or was missing leaves. For example, Epp argues the assumption the scribe of P46 "intended to include 1–2 Timothy and Titus" is far from conclusive.[77] After all, the scribe of P46 seemed to be sophisticated and even attempted to save space by compressing the text, but then did not include the Pastorals. While one may argue he glued in more pages to include some missing books, Epp plays the devil's advocate by suggesting, "For a scribe to compress the text and still leave some nine blank pages does not make sense either."[78] Epp does not choose a side on the matter but simply challenges the reader to question everything that does not have rock-solid evidence and is thus open to speculation.

In "Anti-Judaic Tendencies in the D-text of Acts: Forty Years of Conversation," Epp revisits a familiar topic from his 1961 dissertation and a 1962 article, where he attempted to prove Codex Bezae was marred by anti-Judaic tendencies.[79] The former received mixed reviews, as Epp himself acknowledged. While some referred to it as an "epoch-making thesis," others questioned whether "occasional alterations . . . really constitute a tendency."[80] The article gave the impression of being Epp's apology for his earlier thesis on anti-Judaic tendencies in Codex Bezae. He clarifies his original intent:

75. Epp, "Issues in the Interrelation," 485–515.
76. Epp, "Textual Criticism in the Exegesis of the New Testament," 45–97.
77. Epp, "Issues in the Interrelation," 501–2.
78. Epp, "Issues in the Interrelation," 502. It should be clarified that P46 does *not* actually have 9 blank pages at the end. Epp is simply making a hypothetical statement, assuming the need for a full extra quire to allow for the Pastorals, even though their text would not have needed all pages supplied by a full quire. Epp also rejects Jeremy Duff's claim that only "a small, four-page quire" might have been needed. See Duff, "P46 and the Pastorals," 578–90.
79. Epp, "Anti-Judaic Tendencies," 111–46; Epp, *Theological Tendency*; Epp, "'Ignorance Motif.'"
80. Delobel, "Focus on the 'Western' Text," 401. Also see Hanson, "Review of *The Theological Tendency*," 283.

"It soon became clear to me that the title of the monograph had invited some needless misunderstanding and that it should have been *The Theological Tendency of the So-Called 'Western' Text of Acts*."[81] He also attempts to shift away from any comparison between the B-text and D-text that would imply priority to one over the other or temporal antecedence. Regardless of Epp's claim of attempting to treat Codex D or the Western text on its own merit, it is an illusion at best to try to prove theological bias without having any "standard" to compare with, which Epp also reluctantly admits.[82] In the article, Epp continues to push back the existence of the Western text (as primarily found in Codex Bezae) to the first century since it bolstered his thesis of anti-Judaic bias. If, on the other hand, the text was later, then any proposal for anti-Judaic bias becomes superfluous as there was much less interaction between the church and the Jewish nonbelievers as time went by and not much motivation to alter the text.[83] Nevertheless, there are overall too many unprovable assumptions in Epp's thesis.

In 2007, Epp revisited the subject of multivalence in an article in the *Harvard Theological Review* titled "It's All about Variants: A Variant-Conscious Approach to New Testament Textual Criticism," wherein he emphasizes again "the very notion of 'the original text' is elusive and that 'original' must be recognized as multilayered and multivalent."[84] He again blurs the distinction between author and scribe, claiming "multiple variants in a passage reveal various 'authorial' presentations of a text."[85] Instead, he prefers the goal of the earliest attainable text since the original text is not only elusive but also "most likely illusive and mythical."[86] In this revised approach, using an analogy from the world of film editing, he remarks, "It is not only the scenes in the edited film that have value, but also the rejected snippets left on the cutting room floor, which we now rush back to rescue lest we lose some significant elements in the story."[87] Overall, he advocates seeking only the "earliest attainable text."

In an article analyzing the various canons of NTTC, which Epp prefers to rename "criteria" or "probabilities," he tips the scale for the earliest

---

81. Epp, "Anti-Judaic Tendencies," 123.

82. Epp, "Anti-Judaic Tendencies," 131.

83. It of course is possible that the Western text has late first-century origins, since Irenaeus utilized a similar form of text in the second century with no suggestion that the readings before him were recent.

84. Epp, "It's All about Variants," 279.

85. Epp, "It's All about Variants," 280.

86. Epp, "It's All about Variants," 287.

87. Epp, "It's All about Variants," 288. Epp is quoting an analogy that he used previously in the introduction to *Perspectives on New Testament Textual Criticism* (xxxviii).

attainable text in favor of the exegete rather than the text critic. He remarks, "The exegete is the arbiter in textual-critical decisions."[88] He also gives a revised and extended definition of the goal of NTTC as follows:

> New Testament textual criticism, employing aspects of both science and art, studies the transmission of the New Testament text and the manuscripts that facilitate its transmission, with the unitary goal of establishing the earliest attainable text (which serves as a baseline) and, at the same time, of assessing the textual variants that emerge from the baseline text so as to hear the narratives of early Christian thought and life that inhere in the array of meaningful variants.[89]

Epp goes on to clarify:

> Our discipline functions somewhat like a kaleidoscope—the numerous texts with their many variants are translucent gems. With each turn of the kaleidoscope, the light shining through it reveals differing but ever-vivid images of some aspects of early Christianity. But a single view, as through a telescope or a microscope—analogous to seeking only the original or the earliest attainable text—provides merely a partial vision of the whole.[90]

In the same year, Epp published another article, "Are Early New Testament Manuscripts Truly Abundant?," in which he suspends all prejudgments and theories, and deals with actual numbers of the extant manuscripts of the NT text through the centuries.[91] This study by Epp is helpful for understanding his shift, to say the least. It is filled with charts and tables laying out the distribution of the thousands of manuscripts. Here were some of his conclusions:

> First, that it is impossible to know how many manuscripts of New Testament writings, in addition to those that have survived, were actually in existence in any given period. Second, though our statistics cover all areas of Christianity, there is no way to know, specifically or generally, the proportions in which manuscripts existed in various locations in these periods, except that common sense would dictate that the great Christian centers (for example, Antioch, Caesarea, Alexandria, Constantinople) would possess significant quantities. Third,

---

88. Epp, "Traditional 'Canons,'" 125.
89. Epp, "Traditional 'Canons,'" 127.
90. Epp, "Traditional 'Canons,'" 127.
91. Epp, "Are Early New Testament Manuscripts Truly Abundant?"

> our knowledge of the surviving manuscripts is skewed by the fact that all the earliest ones were found in Egypt or regions of similar climate, namely, dry areas where papyrus survives well unless subjected to repeated wetness and drying. . . . Fourth, and finally, the quantity of early manuscripts, whether surviving or not, was affected by another factor. It is obvious that copies of Christian writings multiplied rapidly as scriptoria . . . increased and as more and more congregations required more and more copies.[92]

Later, he remarks,

> Prior to the influx of minuscule manuscripts in the ninth century and following, there are some 370 papyri and majuscules now extant with the New Testament content, with 166, or 45 percent of them, available around 500 CE, and the 63 mentioned earlier (that is, 17 percent) already in use around 300 CE All, of course, survive in varying degrees of completeness.
>
> To describe this complex situation in terms of a metaphor, the textual transmission of the New Testament is a forest, thick with trees at the later stages, but with trees thinning as we move backward toward the beginning of the process. In fact, only a few trees stand there, but the ground is randomly scattered with hundreds of leaves, and in many cases it is difficult to identify even the kinds of trees from which they have come.[93]

As astute and insightful as the article is, it leaves a sense of hopelessness regarding any efforts at retrieving the original text of the NT.

In his introductory article on the NT papyri, Epp emphasizes their significance in the study of the NT text.[94] He homed in on Oxyrhynchus since many of the NT papyri were found there and it happened to be bustling with Christian activity around the fourth/fifth centuries. Since the papyri are dated from the third/fourth centuries, Epp considers them valuable in providing important information regarding the development of the text in Egypt and beyond in that early period. In the past, the papyri evidence had been considered as indicative of the textual situation in Egypt of that period.

---

92. Epp, "Are Early New Testament Manuscripts Truly Abundant?," 89.

93. Epp, "Are Early New Testament Manuscripts Truly Abundant?," 104. Epp's "varying degrees of completeness" is a (intentionally?) gross understatement, since nearly all of the 370 papyri and uncials noted are mere fragments or only a page or so in length.

94. Epp, "Papyrus Manuscripts of the New Testament," 3–21. This was later reprinted with many updates in Epp, *Perspectives on New Testament Textual Criticism*, 411–35, and in the 2013 edition of Ehrman and Holmes, *Text of the New Testament in Contemporary Research*, 1–39.

Now Epp extends it to the rest of Christendom. He bases this argument on the evidence regarding mobility of people and letters in the period, noting,

> The several differing textual complexions contained in the NT papyri did not necessarily have to originate in Egypt, nor would they necessarily have remained in or been confined to Egypt once they arrived there. By the same token, mss that had originated in Egypt—that is, had been copied there—need not represent texts native or exclusive to Egypt. In fact, these dynamic interchanges of people, letters, and books to and from Egypt, as well as within Egypt, could allow the extreme assertion—though no one would wish to make it—that *none* of the NT textual complexions represented in our papyri necessarily had to originate in Egypt. They could have been carried there relatively quickly from anywhere in the Mediterranean world.[95]

He concludes,

> This analysis, moreover, permits another assertion—though one that cannot be proved: the intellectual commerce demonstrable in the Mediterranean area, particularly to and from Egypt, supports the strong possibility—if not probability—that the various textual complexions evident in our Egyptian papyri represent texts from that *entire Mediterranean region* (including, of course, texts that might have originated in Egypt itself). Thus, in contrast to the common view that the papyri represent "only" the text of "provincial Egypt," it is much more likely that they represent an extensive if not the full textual spectrum of earliest Christianity.[96]

Such a line of reasoning that uses scant evidence and hasty conclusions raises more questions than provides answers, as already noted earlier.

In his 2014 article, "In the Beginning was the New Testament Text, but Which Text? A Consideration of 'Ausgangstext' and 'Initial Text,'" Epp surveys the terminology of the original text used from the early sixteenth century until the present day.[97] Out of the several different usages of *Ausgangstext*, he prefers the one that defines it as "a starting point or beginning phase of some broad or significant event, situation, or entity."[98] The concept

---

95. Epp, "Papyrus Manuscripts of the New Testament," 13 (emphasis original).

96. Epp, *Perspectives* on New Testament Textual Criticism, 421, (emphasis original). The quote is revised with minor changes in the 2013 edition article in Ehrman and Holmes, *Text of the New Testament in Contemporary Research*, 14–15. The revision does not impact the main object of the discussion.

97. Epp, "In the Beginning," 35–51.

98. Epp, "In the Beginning," 66–67.

of "initial text" carries with it an ambiguity which Epp considers virtuous. Epp says, "for each term is open to several interpretations by the user of the *ECM*. The designation 'Initial Text' may commend the printed text-line to a wider audience and some among those users may be initiated thereby into the 'mysteries' of textual criticism and seek to learn its inner workings."[99] Epp is aware that some (e.g., Holger Strutwolf) would try to equate the initial text with the original text, but he is willing to take that chance if it would promote the dialogue further.

Again in 2014, Epp's article, "Why Does New Testament Textual Criticism Matter? Refined Definitions and Fresh Directions," appeared in *Expository Times*.[100] It is directed toward the lay audience and hence lacks the typical depth evinced in his other writings. Nonetheless, it is ideal for capturing the essence of Epp's understanding of the current state of NTTC. He distills the complexities of the discipline under the following two realities: (1) The plethora of manuscripts and other witnesses to the NT text, along with the myriad textual variations they contain; and (2) the perceived complications in the goals and methods employed in making text-critical decisions.[101] Epp admits there is "no reliable estimate of the total number of variants found in our extant witnesses" but then proposes a "wild guess" of somewhere between "two fifths to perhaps three quarters of a million" variants in the NT manuscript traditions.[102] He whittles down the number to about 30,000 more significant variants, then to about 12,000 most significant variants and admits "the problem is not nearly as large as first appears, though it also guarantees that more than enough variants are available to occupy textual critics for decades."[103]

Further on, Epp asks the title question "Why does textual criticism matter?," and then presents the following answer:

> Because scholars, students, clergy, and others wish to access the earliest attainable text of the churches' authoritative writings as they engage in interpretation and exegesis. Textual criticism, however, is important beyond achieving the earliest recoverable text, for it remains to explore what insights into early Christianities might be gleaned from the textual variants that were cast aside and not selected for the earliest text-form.[104]

---

99. Epp, "In the Beginning," 70.
100. Epp, "Why Does New Testament Textual Criticism Matter?," 417–31.
101. Epp, "Why Does New Testament Textual Criticism Matter?," 418.
102. Epp, "Why Does New Testament Textual Criticism Matter?," 419.
103. Epp, "Why Does New Testament Textual Criticism Matter?," 420.
104. Epp, "Why Does New Testament Textual Criticism Matter?," 424.

Previously, Epp had divided the practice of textual criticism as an equal mixture of science and art, but now he proposes that "textual criticism is a complex discipline, involving a small amount of science and a large measure of art."[105] This is a key statement that clearly reflects the shift in his approach to the NT text.

Curiously, Epp seems to soften his stance on the goal of the discipline, as he states, "The preceding discussion should not be understood as a rejection of the traditional approach to New Testament textual criticism or its announced goal of removing errors to reveal the original (or better) the earliest attainable text," but later he reverts to his changing position and declares,

> We cannot move much farther back than the third or the end of the second century. For these reasons and others, the notion of original text has shown itself to be both elusive and illusive, and we are compelled to face the fact that the original text has exploded into a highly complex multivalent entity. It is the Holy Grail of textual criticism—conceivable, but likely unattainable.[106]

Epp admits his aim, along with some others, is to "breathe some life back into the process and to enlarge the vision of textual critics and of those who should profit from their labors."[107] He concludes,

> The New Testament text is a *living text*, and the meaningful variants can reveal the life, the liveliness, and the dynamism that existed in the churches, producing narratives parallel to those present in the selected text at the top of the pages in our critical editions. How, then, do we dare relegate these variants to *Sheol*? For untold numbers of Christians, these discarded snippets were part of their 'original' and sacred canonical Scripture and, what is more important, they were part of and evolved from their real life-experiences in the churches.[108]

A more recent article relating to the subject at hand is Epp's contribution to *The New Cambridge History of the Bible,* published in 2015. Although much of the discussion concerns the history of NTTC, he continues to define the goal of the discipline in *precisely* the same terms as expressed in his

---

105. Epp, "Why Does New Testament Textual Criticism Matter?," 425.
106. Epp, "Why Does New Testament Textual Criticism Matter?," 425–427.
107. Epp, "Why Does New Testament Textual Criticism Matter?," 428.
108. Epp, "Why Does New Testament Textual Criticism Matter?," 428 (emphasis original).

"It's All about Variants" essay, emphasizing NTTC as being both "science and art," with the initial goal being "the earliest attainable text" and then evaluating all other variants as "narratives of early Christian thought and life.[109] This egalitarian view of NT textual variants constitutes the new direction of the discipline and clearly repositions the text-critical goalpost in its approach.

CONCLUSION

Epp has been very instrumental in spearheading the new movement in shifting the goalpost in NTTC. His articles, especially "The Multivalence of the Term 'Original Text' in New Testament Textual Criticism," are repeatedly quoted in discussing the changing definition of the original text.

---

109. Refer to footnote 88 to compare. See Epp, "Critical Editions," 47–48.

6

J. Keith Elliott

J. Keith Elliott is a newcomer in changing the goalpost in NTTC, but he is no novice to the field. He studied textual criticism under the famed text-critic George Dunbar Kilpatrick at the University of Oxford.[1] After retiring a few years ago as Professor of New Testament Textual Criticism at the University of Leeds, he has continued a busy writing and speaking schedule. Elliott has written many books, numerous articles, and over 400 book reviews, many in the field of NTTC. Among his many accomplishments is his position of secretary of the International Greek New Testament Project and his editorship over the publishing of their Lucan material. Needless to say, Elliott is a major voice in the field of NTTC, whose inclusion in this study is because of the shift in his stance on the original text of the NT.

Although Elliott is not the most recent scholar to capitulate to the new movement in NTTC, he is the most vocal in his writings as of late. In a contributing chapter in the 2017 festschrift in honor of James Voelz, Elliott admits to the shift in his understanding of the goal of NTTC as follows:

> I too acknowledge a change in my own writing. When I first pronounced on these matters, I was confident that, with the 5,000 or so Greek New Testament manuscripts at our disposal, we were well equipped to locate at virtually every point the

---

1. Elliott also studied under Margaret Thrall at the University of Wales.

original, *authorial* text. Now such an aim is chimeric and the definition of our function and purpose needs nuancing.²

A couple of paragraphs earlier, he refers to the term "original" as a "weasel word," which "text-critics today hesitate to bandy around."³ He even chides Robinson and Pierpont for continuing to use the term in their 2005 edition, *The New Testament in the* Original *Greek*, which he likens to the arrogance of Kurt Aland a generation ago in calling his Nestle 26th edition the *Neue Standardtext*.⁴

The above example is not just a recent isolated digression, but one of many similar sentiments Elliott has expressed in recent years. As noted above, his view on the attainability of the original text has been shifting over the past twenty years. The following section will analyze the initial view of Elliott and the growing change in his understanding of the goal of NTTC.

ELLIOTT'S INITIAL VIEW ON THE ORIGINAL TEXT

Elliott has never identified with the evangelical tradition, as can be noticed in his 1982 work *Questioning Christian Origins*.⁵ Nonetheless, his views regarding the original text of the NT were always in line with the traditional quest of the discipline. In 1974, Elliott wrote an article titled "Can We Recover the Original New Testament?" which was filled with optimism regarding the retrievability of the original text of the NT. As if anticipating the recent distractions from the primary goals of NTTC, Elliott states in the introductory paragraph,

> Too often it is thought that the primary interest of the textual critic is in the distinctive reading of this or that manuscript or with the variations in word order in, say, the Latin or Syriac version. This would be a wrong assumption. Admittedly much research on New Testament manuscripts is concerned with these matters, but it would be incorrect to deduce that these are the main objects of such study. The principle purpose of textual

---

2. Elliott, "Relevance of Authorial Language," 81 (emphasis original).

3. Elliott, "Relevance of Authorial Language," 80.

4. Elliott, "Relevance of Authorial Language," 81. Note that Robinson/Pierpont utilized "Original Greek" primarily to imitate the title of Westcott and Hort's edition; their intent was to present a generally reliable text in the original *language* of inspiration and revelation—a text considered to be best reflected among a consensus of Byzantine manuscripts. This was discussed in a personal correspondence between the present author and Maurice A. Robinson.

5. Elliott, *Questioning Christian Origins*.

criticism is to establish so far as possible the original text of the books of the New Testament.[6]

He even considers the task of NTTC to be of paramount importance, stating,

> The need to establish the text so precisely is greater than for other ancient books in so far as the New Testament in particular forms not only the basis for Christian doctrine and practice but also represents the literary archives of a religion which is based on an historical revelation. Believers need to be convinced that the copy of the scriptures they possess is reliable and reproduces the words of the original authors. However, it must not be thought that the textual critic's work is of use only for those who use the Bible as scripture. The need to establish an ancient text for its own sake and for the sake of those who read it for historical, philological or other reasons is a perfectly respectable academic exercise.[7]

Not only is Elliott convinced regarding the traditional primary goal of NTTC, but he understands the value of it for the faith of the believers. He affirms this as the chief end of scholarship, reflecting a very clear definition of the traditional goal of NTTC.

Elliott appears well aware of the complications and challenges involved in pursuing the traditional goal of NTTC. He acknowledges the plethora of NT manuscripts, which at that time amounted to "85 papyri, 268 uncials, over 2,700 cursive manuscripts and nearly 2,200 lectionary texts," per Aland's handlist.[8] He also acknowledges the reality of corruptions by noting "it is probably true to say that no two of this number agree exactly."[9] Curiously, Elliott employed the designation "living text," almost two decades prior to David Parker, to describe the state of the text through the centuries prior to the printing press.[10] He is also quite aware there were more than just accidental changes made to the text. Many of the deliberate alterations served as witnesses to "changes in doctrine over the centuries from the variants in the manuscripts."[11] Furthermore, Elliott considers some of these changes to be significant. He dubs as "oversimplification"[12] the view of those who

6. Elliott, "Can We Recover the Original New Testament?," 338.
7. Elliott, "Can We Recover the Original New Testament?," 338–39.
8. Elliott, "Can We Recover the Original New Testament?," 339.
9. Elliott, "Can We Recover the Original New Testament?," 339.
10. Elliott, "Can We Recover the Original New Testament?," 339.
11. Elliott, "Can We Recover the Original New Testament?," 339.
12. Elliott, "Can We Recover the Original New Testament?," 340.

claim these variants had no impact on the fundamental doctrines of the Christian faith. He lists just a few of the many examples that prove that variants are significant to doctrine: Matthew 24:36; Mark 1:1; Luke 2:14; 10:1–7; 22:19b–20; John 7:53—8:11; Acts 7:56; 15:20, 29; Romans 5:1; 1 Corinthians 2:1; 15:51; 1 John 5:7.

Elliott also expresses discontent over the several printed editions of the Greek NT. He claims each "attempts to be a reconstruction of the original words of the New Testament" and yet they all "give a text which never existed as a manuscript of the New Testament."[13] It is obvious Elliott is making a case for rigorous or thoroughgoing eclecticism. He proposes that not only is the original text attainable, but his methodology is the only one capable of attaining it, claiming, "A text based on [thoroughgoing] eclectic principles stands a good chance of representing the original text of the New Testament authors"[14]—even though this, as with any method, necessarily results in a text which never existed in any known manuscript (since this is the most anyone can claim when talking about a putative original autograph text where the autograph is not extant and where mss regularly differ among themselves). Even so, Elliott would *not* go beyond existing manuscript testimony as he clearly states,

> Unlike some other ancient writings, conjectural emendations have no place in a reconstruction of the New Testament. . . . It is the task of textual critics to analyse the *manuscripts* and to decide at which points in the *manuscripts* the true reading is preserved. It is a painstaking and difficult task but it is one that is worthwhile if we are to establish the textual integrity of the New Testament.[15]

On the whole, this article presents one of the most convincing scholarly claims for the recoverability of the original text of the NT, assuming the theoretical validity of the thoroughgoing eclectic method.

A year later, Elliott published an article further defending the merits of thoroughgoing eclecticism in retrieving the original text of the NT. As expected, under the basic premises of thoroughgoing eclecticism, he dismisses the need to seek after conjectural emendations and advocates for projects that would add to the "apparatus criticus" of the NT text. After all, the "original reading has been preserved somewhere among the extant

---

13. Elliott, "Can We Recover the Original New Testament?," 341.

14. Elliott, "Can We Recover the Original New Testament?," 349.

15. Elliott, "Can We Recover the Original New Testament?," 352–53 (emphasis added).

manuscripts."[16] After giving several examples advocating his position, Elliott reiterates: "The science or art of textual criticism is concerned with the evaluation of actual variants, whatever method one adopts. Confronted with two or more alternatives one has to reach a decision as to which is likely to be original."[17] Through the years following, Elliott expressed similar confidence in the retrievability of the original text of the NT. An example of this can be seen in the concluding remark in his article, "The Relevance of Textual Criticism to the Synoptic Problem," where he wrote, "No one edition of the Greek New Testament nor any one synopsis is likely to be one hundred percent correct in printing the original text."[18] Even though the remark betrays his lack of confidence in any particular Greek NT's ability to reach the original text completely, it still reflects his assumption of an original text behind the myriad of NT manuscripts. Elliott's introductory article on thoroughgoing eclecticism in the 1995 compendium, *The Text of the New Testament in Contemporary Research: Essays on the Status Quaestionis*, also demonstrates the same confidence regarding the presence of an original text. Below are a few examples as stated by Elliott on this point:

- "In many places the majority of MSS do preserve the original text."
- "Unless one can be sure how many stages exist between any MS and the original, and unless one knows what changes were made at each copying, then age alone is no help in recovering the original words."
- "The validity of variants is debated: we need to be genuine *critics* applying our critical faculty in determining the original reading."
- "At Mark 1:41 it is more likely that the text describing Jesus as 'angry' is original."
- "A rule of thumb that one should apply is that a variant that makes parallel texts dissimilar is more likely to be original than one that makes parallels agree."[19]

Thus far, Elliott seems in line with the traditional quest of NTTC.

---

16. Elliott, "In Defence of Thoroughgoing Eclecticism," 96.
17. Elliott, "In Defence of Thoroughgoing Eclecticism," 109.
18. Elliott, "Relevance of Textual Criticism," 359.
19. Elliott, "Thoroughgoing Eclecticism," 321, 322, 325 (emphasis original), 325–26, 326.

ELLIOTT'S SHIFT ON THE ORIGINAL TEXT

Beginning in 2000, traces of Elliott's changing view regarding the original text of NT became apparent. On April 6–7, 2000, during the previously mentioned symposium on NT studies,[20] Elliott presented a defense of thoroughgoing eclecticism. He appears to have retained his confidence in the possibility of retrieving the original text of the NT, as can be seen in the comments below:

- "Usually these eclectic principles, consistently applied, serve as useful aids in the discussion of many types of variants and enable me to reach a decision about which reading is original and which secondary."
- "We also attempt not only to reach a decision about which reading is more likely to represent the original words of the original author but the motive for the change(s) found in the alternative reading(s)."
- "If, for instance, a witness regularly expands divine titles, possibly using established liturgical formulas, then we will be reluctant to accept its testimony as a reliable witness to the original text in this matter in a variation unit."[21]

After affirming the traditional view of the primary goal of NTTC, Elliott remarks he is no longer confident in the viability or necessity of trying to retrieve the original text of the NT. He begins by acknowledging the impact of Bart Ehrman's *The Orthodox Corruption of Scripture*:

> Thoroughgoing eclecticism is very much alert to the development of Christian doctrine and the awareness that this sometimes caused changes in the manuscript tradition. Bart Ehrman has put us very much in his debt with his *Orthodox Corruption of Scripture* by showing how various pressure groups in early Christianity left their fingerprints on manuscripts because their deliberate changes to the text, especially those relating to important issues of Christology and theology, caused changes to the text being transmitted in one direction or another in support of a particular party line. His reasoning can be harnessed when assessing textual variants; often his work is compatible with the aims and practices of thoroughgoing eclecticism.[22]

---

20. Regarding the symposium, refer to footnote 69 in chapter 5.
21. Elliott, "Case for Thoroughgoing Eclecticism," 107, 121–22.
22. Elliott, "Case for Thoroughgoing Eclecticism," 123–24.

Although the statement above might appear as an honest appraisal of a text-critical work in the field and its compatibility with the proponent's methodology, the conclusion that follows reveals a different intent:

> Thoroughgoing textual criticism should be concerned not only with establishing as far as possible the original words of the original authors; it should try to explain the likeliest direction of change and why the secondary texts arose. It may well be that modern textual criticism is less confident about the need to, or its ability to, establish the original text and that its best contribution to biblical studies is to show how variation arose, ideally in what directions, and to explain the significance of all variants.[23]

The statement above is the first blatant evidence of the departure in Elliott's confidence in the retrievability of the original text of the NT.

In the same year, July 2000, at the Lille Colloquium in France, Elliott reiterated his departure, remarking unequivocally what the new goal of NTTC should be:

> At one time I would certainly have argued that one needs to take into account all evidence—not only early evidence—because the task of the textual critic was the recovery of the original New Testament text. If asked whether our fund of 5,000 manuscripts together with the versional and patristic evidence enabled us to reestablish the original text I always used to answer in the affirmative—and I have written extensively along those lines. Now I am less confident that we can achieve that, or indeed if it is the job of textual criticism to do that. I have been persuaded to change my stance somewhat thanks to the writings of Bart Ehrman and David Parker.[24]

He quotes Helmut Koester's investigation of the "original [secret] Mark," (following Morton Smith), as an example of the fluidity and complexity of the term "original text." He also claims to be following in the footsteps of Kenneth Clark, who in 1966 referred to the original text as a "retreating mirage."[25] Overall, Elliott's essay takes on an agnostic and pessimistic tone toward the discipline of NTTC and the quest for the original text.

Ironically, three years later, Elliott still appeared optimistic regarding the possibility of retrieving the original text, and he continued to define thoroughgoing eclecticism as "the procedure for dealing with textual

---

23. Elliott, "Case for Thoroughgoing Eclecticism," 124.
24. Elliott, "Nature of the Evidence," 14–15.
25. Elliott, "Nature of the Evidence," 15. Cf. Clark, "Theological Relevance of Textual Variation," 15.

variation that prefers to debate each and every variant wherever these arise and to reach a decision not only on the reading most likely to represent the original words of the original author but also on the motives why the variant(s) arose."[26] Characteristically, he again dismisses the need for conjectural emendation: "That the original text has survived in our 5,000 extant Greek manuscripts and in the numerous versional manuscripts is a cornerstone of the method."[27] Nonetheless, he again expresses his kinship with the proponents of the new approach in NTTC and even restates the goal of thoroughgoing eclecticism as something that not

> merely seeks the original text, a will o' the wisp according to some like Amphoux, but, perhaps more importantly, it also tries to find likely motives for the perceived changes throughout the tradition, a view compatible with Ehrman's or Parker's recent views on the validity of *all* variants as part of the living text.[28]

This is far different from his original view in his 1974 article "Can We Recover the Original New Testament?"

Several articles between 2012 and the present reaffirm Elliott's shift regarding the goals of NTTC. In 2012, he wrote one examining the different variants in the book of Revelation to conclude,

> Apart from errors that merely expose scribal carelessness, most variation units are indicative of the thoughtful attention of copyists determined not simply to preserve doggedly a text that increasingly was becoming—or indeed had already become—accepted as authoritative, canonical, and scriptural, but also to make sure that that *living* text was being promoted as understandable in and for its own generation.[29]

In the same year, he wrote an article entitled "Recent Trends in the Textual Criticism of the New Testament: A New Millennium, A New Beginning?" in which he declares,

> Until recently, most text-critics and editors would have declared that their stock in trade was the re-establishing of the original text by which they would mean the authorial text. That is now seen as a chimera, and an increasing number of those writing on textual criticism and therefore its practitioners now state that

---

26. Elliott, "Thoroughgoing Eclecticism," 42.
27. Elliott, "Thoroughgoing Eclecticism," 42n10.
28. Elliott, "Thoroughgoing Eclecticism," 49 (emphasis original).
29. Elliott, "Revelations from the Apparatus Criticus," 23 (emphasis original).

their aim is to be a plotting of the history of the text from its earliest recoverable form.[30]

Again, he remarks,

> The new textual criticism is therefore reluctant to work toward the elusive authorial text. Instead, what we see is the more creative and rewarding pursuit of the nature of and reasons for the changeability of the wording. When and why was the text altered and which ginger groups undertook such 'orthodox corruption' are the relevant questions now.[31]

He credits Epp for spotlighting this approach through his "Multivalence" article.

The following year, in the second edition of *The Text of the New Testament in Contemporary Research: Essays on the Status Quaestionis*, Elliott repeats verbatim his statements regarding the original text from the first edition, including the following previously uncited comments:

- "A thoroughgoing critic would not accept as reasonable the claim that the original text is located in the largest number of manuscripts."
- "On a positive note, the thoroughgoing method of textual criticism assumes that the original reading has been preserved somewhere among the extant manuscripts."[32]

Along with several new sections bringing his research up to date, Elliott inserts different paragraphs highlighting the works of Ehrman and Parker. His support for the new trend in NTTC appears conflicted at best. On one hand, he supports the quest for the original text and, on the other, he appears to deny its existence. It is paradoxical to continue to claim the retrievability of the original text and concurrently emphasize the lack thereof. It would seem wiser to abandon one or the other. It may very well be that without the original text, all the theories and claims regarding modifications and alterations throughout church history seem illogical at best. If there were no baseline original text, then there is no measurement for the alleged changes.

Three years later in an article entitled "Using an Author's Consistency of Usage and Conjectures as Criteria to Resolve Textual Variation in the

---

30. Elliott, "Recent Trends," 127. Cf. also the discussion of Elliott's context on page 7 *supra*.

31. Elliott, "Recent Trends," 127.

32. Elliott, "Thoroughgoing Eclecticism in New Testament Textual Criticism," 745–46.

Greek New Testament," Elliott challenges text-critics to stop looking back to the "gold standard" original text and instead seek to understand the place of the previously discarded secondary readings.[33] He concludes: "the current shift away from trying to establish exclusively the author's published text comes alongside an allied recognition that *all* alternatives merit attention as stepping stones in the dense and varied history of the New Testament."[34] Although this reflects the traditional thoroughgoing eclectic position, it does not have the traditional goal in mind.

CONCLUSION

In his 2017 dedicatory article entitled "The Relevance of Authorial Language, Style and Usage in the Evaluation of Textual Variants in the Greek New Testament," he repeats the same sentiments in the previous article.[35] Another festschrift in 2017 for Dave Black reaffirms Elliott's understanding of the text and his new disregard for the original text:

> Fortunately, I have never been constrained by having to adhere to any particular party line, such as an acceptance of "inerrancy," which *pace* fundamentalist scholars, is an illogical and bizarre principle that flies in the face of the history of textual witnesses and refuses to recognize that all manuscripts, however maverick they be branded by modern scholarship, were nonetheless at one time the divine and sacred scriptures of the individuals, churches, and communities that happened to read *and use* each and every copy.[36]

Such statements clearly indicate the shift in Elliott's understanding of the goal of NTTC. He has not produced books and articles with examples like the other proponents. Nonetheless, it is clear from his many statements he has moved away from his former views regarding thoroughgoing eclecticism and its ability to establish an original form of text in favor of a new goalpost, and has categorized himself as an advocate for the recent trend in NTTC.

---

33. Elliott, "Using an Author's Consistency," 122–35.
34. Elliott, "Using an Author's Consistency," 125 (emphasis original).
35. Elliott, "Relevance of Authorial Language," 67–84.
36. Elliott, "Majority Text or Not," 81 (emphasis original).

7

The Coherence-Based Genealogical Method

The Coherence-Based Genealogical Method (CBGM) is the most recent contribution in shifting the goalpost in NTTC.[1] It has been hailed as a "major breakthrough in New Testament text-critical method,"[2] and stands against Epp's bleak assessment thirty years ago that NTTC had reached an impasse.[3] In spite of the new discoveries of papyri and other Greek manuscripts, the text of the Greek NT had remained virtually unchanged since the text of Westcott and Hort almost 100 years ago.[4] In contrast, the advocates of the CBGM have promised their methodology would be a breakthrough from the textual status quo and lead to a new text more securely based on history and standardized text-critical principles. Its originator, Gerd Mink, introduced his view of the genealogical structure of the manuscript tradition as far back as 1982, albeit in an embryonic form.[5] Through the years, especially in the last twenty years, his methodology has received much attention through his articles and some by his colleagues at the Institut für

---

1. A portion of this chapter was presented by Shah as "Bats in the Belfry."
2. Wasserman, "Criteria for Evaluating Readings," 605.
3. See Epp, "Twentieth Century Interlude," 386–414. Also, Epp, "Continuing Interlude," 131–51.
4. It should be pointed out that traditionalists like Kurt Aland and Gordon Fee suggested that this only meant that Westcott and Hort were on the right track.
5. Mink, "Zur Stemmatisierung," 100–114.

Neutestamentliche Textforschung (INTF) in Münster. In the process, the CBGM has been explained with complicated data charts and stemmatic diagrams, sometimes with tedious arguments and painstaking details. The CBGM is now applied to the Editio Critica Maior (ECM) in Acts and the Catholic Epistles, and to the Catholic Epistles in the Nestle-Aland 28. It is repeatedly claimed the CBGM will serve as the basis for all of the critical text editions yet to come under the INTF auspices.

On the one hand, any effort to bring life into an otherwise dead field of NTTC should be welcomed. On the other hand, it should be cautioned that what might appear to be a breakthrough may lead to a misguided and destructive methodology. In this section, some questions will be raised regarding the viability of the CBGM and the initial text it promotes. The lack of a concrete methodology and the abandonment of the traditional quest of NTTC qualifies the CBGM as a proponent of the new movement in NTTC.

THE HYPOTHESIS UNDERGIRDING THE CBGM

The adherents of the CBGM claim it counters the arbitrary nature of reasoned eclecticism in which readings are chosen by shifting the weight between external and internal evidences. It has also been admitted (with some helplessness) that modern text-critical praxis is devoid of any solid history of transmission. It is claimed the CBGM will offer a more tightly controlled and precise system of evaluating readings, thereby attaining a closer approximation to an initial text (*Ausgangstext*) of the NT. Prior to examining the claims of this new methodology, it will be beneficial to gain a basic understanding of its assumptions and praxis. This brief chapter will not attempt to explain the CBGM methodology. That is beyond its scope and has been attempted by its advocates, critics, and reviewers alike.[6] It will suffice here to raise only those salient points relevant for the present discussion.

For starters, the CBGM, etymologically, is a refinement of what Kurt and Barbara Aland labeled as the "local principle" or the "local-genealogical method," which was an attempt at "applying to each passage individually the approach used by classical philology for a whole tradition."[7] In their *Text of the New Testament*, Rule #8 explained that the "reconstruction of a stemma of readings for each variant (the genealogical principle) is an extremely important device, because the reading which can most easily explain the

---

6. Gerd Mink, Klaus Wachtel, Holger Strutwolf, Annette Hüffmeier, and Tommy Wasserman. For the latest introduction to the CBGM, see Wasserman and Gurry, *New Approach to Textual Criticism*. Also see Alexanderson, *Problems in the New Testament*.

7. Aland and Aland, *Text of the New Testament*, 34.

derivation of the other forms is itself most likely the original."[8] However, there are several important distinctions between the Alands' method and the CBGM. Unlike just the local stemma of the former, the latter attempts to go beyond and create a global stemma for each individual variation unit. Furthermore, at its core, the CBGM claims to be a variant-focused approach to the text rather than the previous "witness-focused" approaches. For the CBGM purposes, a "witness" is not a particular manuscript but the text it contains. The principle behind this distinction is that a manuscript might be late and minor in weight but the text might be early and highly valuable.

The following are some basic assumptions of the CBGM regarding the transmission of the NT text:

1. A scribe wants to copy the *Vorlage* with fidelity.
2. If a scribe introduces diverging variants, they come from another source (i.e., they are not "invented").[9]
3. The scribe uses few rather than many sources.
4. The sources feature closely related texts rather than less-related ones.[10]

Based on these assumptions, the collation of manuscripts is used to create the local stemma of variants at each variation unit. The local stemmata are then grouped to the global stemmata of witnesses through what is termed "coherence of witnesses." Internal coherence along with textual flow and stemmatic coherence are used to craft an initial text (*Ausgangstext*), which guides the construction and refinement of the local stemmata of variants.[11] The new stemmata are then used to create a "better" initial text, which is "constantly revised in light of the textual decisions, in an iterative process moving progressively from easier to more complex cases of textual variation."[12] Furthermore, variants that hypothetically are presumed to oc-

---

8. Aland and Aland, *Text of the New Testament*, 281.

9. Number 2 is questionable, since at least in many less consequential variants (particularly when not widespread) the individual scribes may be the creators of such.

10. Mink, "Coherence-Based Genealogical Method," 96–107.

11. This paragraph raises many questions: (1) Collation of which mss (all, some, or those determined not to be most characteristically Byzantine)? (2) What is the difference between "local stemma of variants" and the "global stemma of witnesses?" (3) What is the "coherence of witnesses?" (4) What is the difference between "internal coherence" and "stemmatic coherence?" (5) What is the "textual flow" and how is it determined? Even though the various explanations remain unclear, the most succinct definitions of each of the questions can be found in the glossary at the end of Wasserman and Gurry, *New Approach to Textual Criticism*, 133–39.

12. Wasserman, "Coherence-Based Genealogical Method," 208.

cur through mere coincidence are relegated to the side and focus is placed on those contaminations presumed to truly count.

As to the many intermediary states of the text that have been lost forever in the witnesses that are no longer extant, the CBGM attempts to construct a genealogical hypothesis, in which a hypothetical ancestor is built upon less complex structures and progresses into highly complex ones. Even though computer technology plays a major role in creating the stemmata, proponents clarify the CBGM is not a purely algorithmic approach. Wachtel explains it "also processes philological statements on the genealogy of variants and derives statements on the relationships between extant manuscript texts from them."[13] Obviously, all this is an immensely complicated undertaking since there are no original witnesses and it is claimed that the text is marred by a high degree of contamination due to "the multitude of copying processes and the large number of lost text states."[14]

The CBGM's proponents insist theirs is a meta-method that proponents holding various presuppositions regarding text and textual history can utilize. They repeatedly claim the exegete should be the final arbiter, examining an unbiased critical apparatus, and thereby, to "put the editor's decisions to the test,"[15] which seems to already have been the general practice long before the CBGM (assuming exegetes actually had the time or expertise to debate with the editor's text). It is promised that "so far its primary use is to document the work of the *ECM* editors because it presupposed their textual decisions. The next phase will be interactive, enabling users to make their own decisions and feed them back into the system."[16] To those who may be hesitant to accept a computer program's ability to determine a text that is characterized by a complex transmissional history, Wachtel clarifies the CBGM is not "a means of automating the reconstructing of the initial text, nor the 'royal way to it.'"[17] Overall, it appears the resultant loss of a concrete methodology and the resort to creating a text that is at the mercy of the exegete is typical of the current approaches intent on relocating the text-critical goalpost further from its traditional placement.

---

13. Wachtel, "Coherence-Based Genealogical Method," 128.

14. Mink, "Coherence-Based Genealogical Method: What is it about?," para. 3.

15. See Wachtel, "Coherence Method and History," 1. This article was originally a paper presented by Wachtel under the theme "Genealogical Method" at the New Testament Textual Criticism Session of the SBL Annual Meeting, San Diego, 2014.

16. Wachtel, "Coherence-Based Genealogical Method," 138.

17. Wachtel, "Towards a Redefinition of External Criteria," 127.

MAJOR OBJECTIONS REGARDING THE CBGM

Scholars such as Dirk Jongkind have raised significant questions regarding CBGM's assumptions that are far beyond the scope of this survey.[18] What follows lists only the distinct points of CBGM as they pertain to the present discussion. It is argued here that each of them contributes individually and also collectively toward the identification of CBGM as being within the new movement approach of NTTC.

The traditional text-types must be abandoned

Mink claims the "traditional text-type approach . . . should be avoided in favor of the structure that will emerge if we focus on the relationships between all individual witnesses and thus determine their places in the transmission history."[19] As well-meaning as this may be, this bold intention of the proponents of the CBGM is repeatedly ignored in praxis, wherein various textual clusters are repeatedly invoked to categorize readings as prior and secondary along with outside editorial judgments based on internal evidence. If the CBGM's true aim is to focus exclusively on external evidence, then any and all prejudgment of a witness should be discarded, which is an impossible task. Mink states, "Although preferences for certain witnesses may influence the final results, the complexity of procedures and the differences in approach . . . preclude consistent bias in favor of certain results."[20] The operative phrase here is "consistent bias," which betrays the CBGM's penchant for its favorite group of manuscripts. It seems to be constantly walking the tightrope between all witnesses are equal and no groupings are needed, and all witnesses are not equal and have to be grouped until they don't have to be. Furthermore, the "pregenealogical coherence" seems to be a disguised form of text-type grouping described as a "purely quantitative, therefore nonsubjective summation of agreements between the manuscript texts."[21] Overall, even though the data in the earliest stages of the methodology are claimed to represent the basic textual coherence of simple variants, the grouping of texts is unavoidable and is used without clear acknowledgment.

---

18. In his dissertation, Gurry has documented these important issues Jongkind raised regarding CBGM's methodology and the responses that followed from Mink. See Gurry, *Critical Examination*, 27–29, 149–57.

19. Mink, "Contamination, Coherence, and Coincidence," 148.

20. Mink, "Contamination, Coherence, and Coincidence," 150.

21. Hüffmeier, "CBGM Applied to Variants," 1. This article was originally a paper presented by Hüffmeier under the theme "Genealogical Method" at the New Testament Textual Criticism session of the SBL Annual Meeting, San Diego, 2014.

Eldon Epp brings up a critical objection regarding the contra-text-type assumptions of the CBGM: "So far [at the time Epp wrote] . . . the CBGM has been applied fully only to the Catholic Epistles, where, as most agree, text types or textual clusters play little role."[22] In fact, Epp strongly points out it is in the rest of the corpus (Gospels, Acts, and the Pauline Epistles) that the presence of text-types is more clearly encountered.[23] Given this objection, the proponents of the CBGM should be modest in their claims against text-types until some definitive results obtained from the ECM edition of Acts can be correlated with future results for the remaining portions of the NT. In other words, any claims regarding the viability or nonviability of the concept of text-type should be made only after the method has been adequately applied to the Gospels, Acts, and Pauline Epistles, which truly appear to involve the unavoidable presence of the text-types as seen in their relevant clustering patterns.[24]

High caution must be exercised against "trusted texts" like B

Similar to the last point, this claim is also more frequently retracted, and B is declared trustworthy only after further examination.[25] After lengthy explanations and tedious examples to demonstrate the CBGM's egalitarian outlook toward all manuscripts, Mink still betrays his preference for B. He concedes to "coming to decision at passages with unclear initial text by following 03 consistently, because it generally comes closest to the initial text."[26] So also Wasserman: "It is perhaps not surprising to find that Codex Vaticanus (03) has the initial text as the closest related potential ancestor

22. Epp, "Textual Clusters," 558.

23. Epp, "Textual Clusters," 558. ECM Acts now has applied the CBGM to that book, wherein text-types and clusters are extensive.

24. Whether termed "text-types" or "specified cluster patterns," a tendency toward a general grouping of manuscripts does exist. Unlike the older concept of text-types, however, the modern notion tends to avoid the presumption claimed by Westcott and Hort that any particular text-type is necessarily the product of formal recensional activity. (This was discussed in a personal correspondence with Maurice A. Robinson.)

25. In the description of the methodology, Mink remarks, "The best known, highly esteemed witnesses have to be treated with special caution. . . . Therefore the ECM editors treated B/03, a witness that tipped the scales in many previous text-critical decisions, with skepticism when they constructed the local stemmata." Immediately, in the footnote, he adds, "Nevertheless, it was confirmed that 03 is an outstanding witness agreeing more than any other with the reconstructed initial text. (See Mink, "Contamination, Coherence, and Coincidence," 161).

26. Mink, "Contamination, Coherence, and Coincidence," 203.

throughout the corpus."[27] Hüffmeier also examined the variant in Acts 18:17, where the majority of the manuscripts favor the "b" reading παντες οι ελληνες while a handful (P74 ℵ A B 629 1501 2374 and some Latin and Bohairic) have the "a" reading with only παντες. After much discussion and many diagrams, she asks,

> Might variant b be the initial text? After all, it is the longer and less flexible reading compared to variant a. From our experience with TP [Transcriptional Probability] we are more inclined to answer in the negative. . . . Since we have arguments on both sides, we had to weigh them carefully and not to forget about the GC [Genealogical Coherence] during the process. It would seem quite plausible to find the initial text A [*Ausgangstext*] represented by the witnesses P74 and 01–03 in variant a.[28]

J. Keith Elliott's charge of the "cult of the best manuscript" continues, albeit under a new heading.[29] The adherents of the CBGM claim text-critics of various persuasions may utilize their program by simply interchanging their favorite manuscripts or text-critical assumptions. While that may appear to be a neutral approach, it is far more complicated over many otherwise coherent ones. The method is inherently biased and solidly based upon the idea that a few divergent manuscripts are to be preferred over many coherent ones. As a result, it appears "coherence" is the goal unless such is encountered among the bulk of the Byzantine manuscripts.[30] Wasserman summarizes the sentiment, noting that a "preliminary step is also used to eliminate from further consideration the majority of Byzantine mss that witness to the late Byzantine text."[31] It therefore is hard to understand how the CBGM can remain unbiased.

Conjectural emendation should be accepted

At times, the text that is not found in any Greek manuscript is listed in the primary line of the ECM apparatus.[32] One of these, 2 Peter 3:10, has been

---

27. Wasserman, "Criteria for Evaluating Readings," 599.

28. Hüffmeier, "CBGM Applied to Variants," 11. Here "a" and "b" represent the witnesses to a variant.

29. Elliott, "Rational Criticism," 340.

30. Mink admits, "Perfect genealogical coherence is a feature of many large attestations particularly if the witnesses are predominantly Byzantine" (Mink, "Contamination, Coherence, and Coincidence," 179).

31. Wasserman, "Criteria for Evaluating Readings," 597.

32. There is also a new conjecture (or two) in the ECM Acts volume.

debated by text-critics and commentators for some time. Here the majority of the manuscripts read κατακαησεται ("will be burned up") while other significant manuscripts (ℵ B K P 323 424^Mg 1175 1241 1448 1739^mg 1852 1881 sy^phmss sy^hms) read ευρεθησεται ("will be found"). Metzger, in his *Textual Commentary*, gives the latter a "D" rating but maintains it was the "oldest reading and the one which best explains the origin of the others that have been preserved." He further acknowledges the "difficulty of extracting any acceptable sense from the passage."[33] The ECM editors in this case chose to override the CBGM data and to use ουχ ευρεθησεται (found only in the Sahidic version and some witnesses of the Philoxenian) as the baseline text, claiming it "may offer a conjecture that is both attractive and reasonable."[34]

The NT text can be shown to have gone through a "process" of development

According to this assumption, the text developed over time, culminating in the presumably "adulterated" Byzantine text.[35] Herein lies the most critical theoretical fault of the proponents of the CBGM, who suggest if the bulk of the missing manuscripts could be found, they would demonstrate the almost imperceptible shift in the text through the centuries. Maurice A. Robinson has suggested,

> If a small restricted sample is taken randomly from among the many extant post-sixth century manuscripts, this then would parallel the limited existing evidence available to CBGM from the first six centuries. In such a case, it should be demonstrable that even a small group of manuscripts belonging to a later period evince *no* distinct changes such as proposed by the CBGM.[36]

If so, Wachtel's aforementioned claim becomes a misrepresentation of the actual history of textual transmission, and betrays a lack of consistency in the assumptions crucial to the CBGM methodology. On the one hand, it is good to recognize texts are much older than the manuscripts that carry them and hence deserve an equal say in determining potential ancestors; on the other hand, it is uncritically presumed that later manuscripts are more likely to become corrupt over time, when the Byzantine consensus in

---

33. Metzger, *Textual Commentary on the Greek New Testament*, 636–37.
34. Aland et al., *Novum Testamentum Graecum*, 24, 252.
35. Wachtel, "Byzantine Text of the Gospels."
36. Ongoing personal conversations with Maurice A. Robinson, Spring 2016 and Winter 2019.

contrast displays a strong general consistency. While claiming to focus on the text rather than the witnesses, the CBGM still appears to give preference to the earlier witnesses, keeping the favored manuscripts at the top of the flow while locating the bulk of the manuscripts in a secondary or tertiary position. Another question that should be asked is: If ℵ and B generally represent the lines that best preserve the *Ausgangstext*, why would the scribes through the centuries not attempt to correct their text to reflect the earlier initial starting point (*Ausgangspunkt*) of the textual flow?

The CBGM process appears to be a cycle in futility

The CBGM's iterative process—meaning readings are funneled repeatedly through the computer program until the optimal reading appears—has grave weaknesses. As Wasserman succinctly notes, two basic options could often conflict: "Prefer a reading to the extent that (a) it is supported by witnesses that have the initial text as their closest potential ancestor and (b) the resulting local stemma is coherent with the predominant textual flow in the book or corpus."[37] It is not too far-fetched to predict most of the time the two options will not be in accord but will flip-flop. If the determination of the text can be either/or, it is hard to determine how iteration will bring the process any closer to the original text.

The CBGM is a meta-method

A major weakness of the CBGM is that it is the brainchild of one person, Gerd Mink. Although it has a strong following at the Münster Institute and among many NT scholars (mostly European, but also several American textual researchers), it has yet to be understood and embraced by most text-critics. Furthermore, the computer program developed by Mink has not been released publicly for independent testing.[38] There is a very limited software program available (Genealogical Queries) that generates "Coherence in Attestations" and "Coherence at Variant Passages."[39] Wasserman rightly observes, however, "In the public version the underlying genealogical database is fixed at this point, which is a serious limitation."[40] The outsider

---

37. Wasserman, "Criteria for Evaluating Readings," 605.

38. One such case is Gurry's supposed test with Byzantine taken as primary (Gurry, "Harklean Syriac," 183–200).

39. http://intf.uni-muenster.de/cbgm/GenQ.html

40. Wasserman, "Coherence-Based Genealogical Method," 208n6.

apparently is expected to take for granted any and all conclusions of the CBGM. On the one hand, it is claimed "the main advantage of the CBGM is it allows scholars with different emphases on criteria to correlate their textual decision in a single variation unit with the decisions throughout a whole book or corpus"; on the other hand, it is conceded "scholars may have different opinions about the assessment of the character of the textual witnesses in the initial stages."[41] Wachtel acknowledges the complexity and nondeterminability of the computer program as follows:

> Unfortunately it has hitherto not been possible to finish the global stemma for the Catholic Letters. Mink has constructed the top of it, but could not accomplish the whole task due to a lack of computing capacity. This capacity is available now, and as Acts will be the next volume of the ECM to appear, the first global stemma will be related to this edition.[42]

Yet even with the publication of ECM Acts, no such global stemma is presented, thus leaving Wachtel's promise unfulfilled.

The use of computer technology in the CBGM ensures objectivity

On this point an old article by Bonifatius Fischer on the use of computers in NTTC is pertinent:

> Two stages must be distinguished. In the first the relations between the manuscripts and the texts are defined on the basis of all their readings, irrespective of whether these readings are true or false: this stage is a purely mathematical process which can be done by a computer—indeed in so complicated a case as the New Testament it should be done by a computer. Then follows the second stage, the proper task of the textual critic, the judgment of the truth or falsity of the readings, the recension of the original text and perhaps also of its more subsequent forms, and the reconstruction of the history of its transmission. This is a task that only a [hu]man can perform: it is beyond the capacities of a computer. But it rests on the firm basis that the computer supplies.[43]

---

41. Wasserman, "Criteria for Evaluating Readings," 605–6.
42. Wachtel, "Coherence Method and History," 5.
43. Fischer, "Use of Computers," 297–308.

Maurice A. Robinson remarks: "Note that neither stage 1 nor 2 applies to the CBGM; rather stage 1 relates to cladistic grouping methods (nothing to do with pseudo-stemmatics or textual "flow"), while stage 2 involves normal human evaluation of variant readings as generally practiced within NTTC."[44] Computers are helpful, but they are not the miracle cure for subjectivity.

There are more methodological and practical issues regarding the CBGM

Peter Gurry has commented on various methodological and practical concerns related to the CBGM as follows:[45]

Methodological

- "The CBGM recognizes that witnesses may agree coincidentally. But the CBGM uses agreements to determine when this happens. At what point does this become viciously circular?"
- "How does the CBGM's distinction between 'manuscript' and 'text' affect its ability to represent historical development? Can this gap be bridged once it has been made?"

Practical

- "Even if the CBGM can tell us *when* a reading emerged multiple times, it can never tell us *why* it arose. The CBGM offers no tunnel into the minds of scribes."
- "Genealogical coherence cannot give direct evidence about scribal habits. A potential ancestor in the CBGM is not necessarily the same as the scribe's exemplar."

In a summary article of his dissertation in the *Tyndale Bulletin*, several statements echo similar sentiments:[46]

44. This was discussed in a personal conversation with Maurice A. Robinson.
45. Gurry, "How Your Greek NT is Changing," 2 (emphasis original).
46. For the summary of Peter Gurry's dissertation on the CBGM see Gurry, "Critical Examination," 317–19. Also see Wasserman and Gurry, *New Approach to Textual*

- "The official explanations are often dense and cumbersome and . . . misunderstanding has ensued . . . [resulting in] subsequent confusion [regarding the nature of the *Ausgangstext*] even among the editors of the ECM themselves."
- "The method is practically unnecessary for those who follow the Byzantine priority position even as it challenges key assumptions of thoroughgoing eclecticism. . . . It is a tool designed by and best used by reasoned eclectics."
- "The CBGM's current practice is inconsistent in some . . . cases and excludes valuable data in others."
- "The method can provide no shortcut to determine the cause (let alone a single cause) of variation."

Although some of these concerns have been answered by the proponents of CBGM, the methodology has not been accepted *en masse*.

The Ausgangstext is a critical outcome of the CBGM

The final outcome of the CBGM is the *Ausgangstext* (initial text), which also serves as the starting point for further refinement in an iterative process. Mink defines the *Ausgangstext* as "a hypothetical, reconstructed text, as it presumably existed, according to the hypothesis, before the beginning of its copying."[47] On the surface this appears to be the only available and viable option to reach the original text.[48] On closer examination, it severely undermines the concept entirely. Although in theory an original text is presumed, the shifting status of the initial text severely diminishes any hopes of ever retrieving anything earlier than the *Ausgangstext* (initial text). It should be kept in mind that the so-called "initial text" is not found in any manuscript but has to be constructed piecemeal from many manuscripts, which in itself remains a form of eclecticism. Such a procedure is based more on goalpost-moving presuppositions than standard human text-critical endeavor.

Criticism, 111–21.

47. Mink, "Problems of a Highly Contaminated Tradition," 25.

48. Wasserman and Gurry acknowledge, "Unfortunately, the new goal and its new term have led to as much confusion and debate as the term 'original text'! This is regrettable, not least because Gerd Mink, who coined the term *Ausgangstext*, has always been clear enough that the term has a single *meaning* with several possible *referents*" (Wasserman and Gurry, *New Approach to Textual Criticism*, 12).

CONCLUSION

The most problematic aspect of the CBGM is the difficulty in comprehending its description by its proponents, especially Mink. The long, wordy, complicated, and elusive explanations of the countless provisos and qualifications leave the reader in a text-critical headspin, with more questions than answers. Only if readers first submit intellectually to the concept can they move on to the conclusion, leaving it to the experts to deal with the intricate details and agreeing to take their word for it. One wonders whether this is due to the complexity of the method or only to its muddled methodology.

In a recent discussion on a NTTC Facebook page, Timothy Mitchell describes the CBGM methodology in not-so-glowing terms:

> It strips the textual history of the NT of any connection with reality. Instead of mss and transmission history, it becomes sterilized and mechanized into raw data. The reconstructed initial text is great because it utilizes more data and witnesses. But the initial text is a nebulous creation completely untethered from any actual transmission of mss. The Initial Text cannot be dated, has no ties to a geographical location, no church tradition that uses it. What is it then?[49]

It appears the confusion regarding the methodology of the CBGM is still ongoing and will require much more proof before it can be trusted.[50]

On the ETC blogsite, Maurice A. Robinson pertinently expressed a warning on this matter, quoting Richard Laurence's 200-year old comments on Griesbach's method that can apply, *mutatis mutandis*, to the CBGM:[51]

> It is natural therefore to expect, that every novel mode of ascertaining the validity of a reading will be at first received with caution, and long watched with jealousy. And notwithstanding the ability which has been displayed in support of Griesbach's theory, notwithstanding the high tone which it has assumed in the literary world, I must confess, that it is far from producing in my own mind complete conviction.

---

49. https://www.facebook.com/groups/11404207692//?ref=direct. Timothy Mitchell is a PhD student at the University of Birmingham (England), studying under Hugh Houghton.

50. Recently, more scholars have called into question the methodological biases in the CBGM that have resulted in questionable conclusions. See Carlson, "Bias at the Heart," 319-340. Also, Knight, "Reading between the Lines," 899-921.

51. Cited as a comment at http://evangelicaltextualcriticism.blogspot.com/2014/11/your-greek-new-testament-and-revisions.html.

> I shall . . . only be understood as urging the propriety of circumspection upon the points of the practical conception and application of Griesbach's particular hypothesis . . .: but as it is extremely liable to be misconceived as well as misapplied; is so intricate in its construction; is so difficult to be detailed with precision, or even to be made out in its subordinate arrangements; and is so readily convertible to party purposes; surely we should again and again contemplate it, and that in every possible point of view, before we consent to admit the conclusions which have been deduced from it into general currency.[52]

Evidently, the CBGM, in its claims, stands in the similar trend of moving away from the traditional goal of NTTC. Even though the proponents may hold to the importance of the original text, their methodology opens the door to "any text" and "many texts"—a standard assumption of the proponents of the new movement in NTTC.[53] CBGM contributes to changing the goalpost in NTTC.

---

52. Laurence, *Remarks*, 6–7.

53. The proponents of the CBGM offer their methodology as an aid in countering Ehrman's claim of "orthodox corruption." It is claimed that the stemmata produced by the CBGM confirm that "repeated and independent emergences of readings . . . speak against deliberate textual changes as effects of early Christological controversies" (Wasserman, "Coherence-Based Genealogical Method," 218). While it may be true that these changes can be attributed to scribal habits, it cannot prevent Ehrman from insisting that different scribes from various periods might make the same "orthodox corruption." In other words, repeated emergences of readings from noncoherent genealogies may still betray the same ideology.

8

Final Analysis and Critique

A point-by-point rebuttal of every example employed by each proponent in marshalling their view of the NT text is beyond the scope of this study.[1] Instead, Stephen Neill's wise dictum in his analysis of David Friedrich Strauss proves a helpful guide in critiquing the new approach in NTTC,

> In what sense is it ever possible to *answer* a great work of the intellect? It is possible to go through it point by point, indicating inaccuracies or errors in detail. Such demonstration is usually highly tedious; and for the most part it is ineffective, because it leaves the main structure unshaken. A principle may still be valid, even though the working out in detail of its applications may leave much to be desired.[2]

In other words, just exposing the factual inaccuracies in the myriad of examples used by the various proponents of the new approach will not ultimately confront the real issues underlying their methodology. Again, Neill's approach to Strauss serves as a valuable paradigm for the present critique:

---

1. As noted earlier, a limited scope of example-by-example analysis of Ehrman's use of manuscript evidence was conducted by Wasserman, "Misquoting Manuscripts?," 325–50. Wasserman identifies two flaws in Ehrman's methodology: first, overlooking (intentionally?) the tendencies of the individual witnesses; and second, neglecting the context of the individual passages and treating them mechanically.

2. Neill and Wright, *Interpretation of the New Testament*, 18 (emphasis original).

Either it must be shown that the method adopted is inappropriate to the material to be considered, or, granted that the method is not illegitimate, it must be shown that the application of the method has been vitiated from the start by concealed presuppositions and prejudices, by the neglect of relevant evidence, or by the failure to see what kind of conclusions really follow from the evidence adduced, and what kind of evidence must be produced if certain conclusions are to be maintained as tenable.[3]

Overall, the new approach is built upon four premises that have to be examined in detail, as displayed in the following diagram:

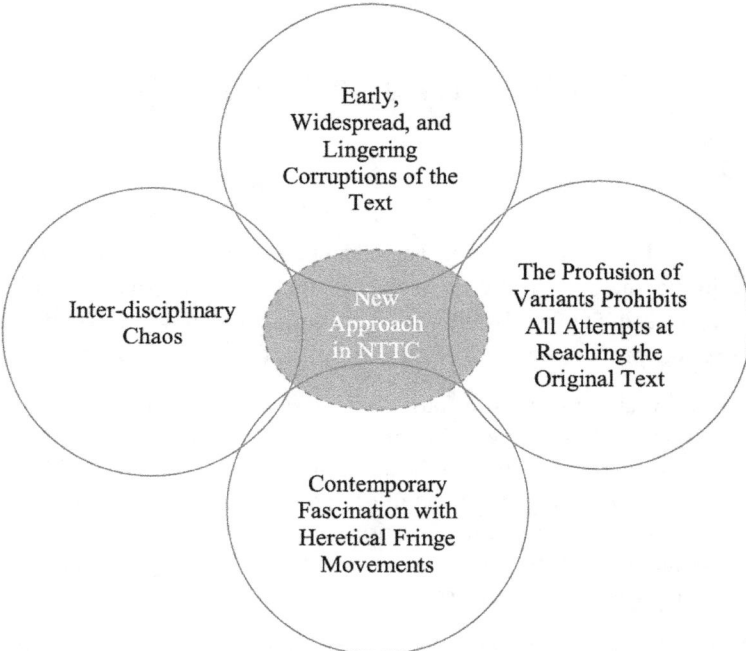

As the above figure demonstrates, the new approach does not depend solely on any one of the premises. Instead, it appears to take bits and pieces from each to create its own legitimacy. While some may consider this an interdisciplinary approach, it is anything but that. Rather, it picks and chooses whichever theory or conclusion best suits the immediate matter. It also fails, intentionally or unintentionally, to consider the limitations and unproven conclusions within each category. In addition, there is also some overlap

---

3. Neill and Wright, *Interpretation of the New Testament*, 18.

between the various issues and disciplines, which further complicates the discussion. It should also be clarified that the various proponents of the new approach are not unified in how they utilize each issue and discipline. Each of them places more weight on some issues and disciplines more than others. Overall, there are clear commonalities between them that warrant the following analysis.

PREMISE 1: CONTEMPORARY FASCINATION WITH HERETICAL FRINGE MOVEMENTS

The first major instance appeared in the mid-1980s with the Jesus Seminar movement and their manifesto, *The Five Gospels: The Search for the Authentic Words of Jesus*.[4] In a manner similar to that of Ehrman, the seminar claimed traditional forms of early Christianity were no better than the heretical fringe movements of that period. In fact, NT apocryphal and pseudepigraphal writings were not only to be considered on par with the canonical works but were also preferable to them at times. They deemed the gnostic Gospel of Thomas as more authentic in places than even the canonical Gospels, which themselves were considered 82 percent inauthentic.[5] The members of the seminar portrayed themselves as "liberators," setting the masses free from centuries of blind faith "to update and then make the legacy of two hundred years of research and debate a matter of public record."[6] Philip

---

4. The Jesus Seminar included a group of seventy-four scholars with a few recognizable names, like Robert Funk, Marcus Borg, and John Dominic Crossan. Blomberg notes that the majority of the remaining had "published at best two or three journal articles, while several are recent PhD's whose dissertations were on some theme of the Gospels.... Almost all are American; European scholarship is barely represented" (Blomberg, "Where Do We Start Studying Jesus?," 19–20). For more information, see Funk and Hoover, *Five Gospels*.

5. The seminar voted on the various sayings of Jesus found in the Gospels, utilizing a bead-counting method. They voted with only black (nonauthentic) and white (authentic) beads, and then determined the shading range from red to pink to gray to black on the basis of the proportion of the black or white beads cast by all the seminar members: a red shading meant Jesus definitely said it; a pink shading, he probably said it; a gray shading, he probably did not say it; and a black shading, he definitely did not say it. The seminar fellows found three red shading quotations in the Gospel of Thomas but just one red shading quotation in the Gospel of Mark and none in the Gospel of John. Scholars outside the seminar have argued against this equal status approach towards the Gospel of Thomas. Although the fourth-century Coptic work might have parallels with a second-century gnostic Greek fragment found a century ago, John Meier strongly argues it is more than likely based on the four canonical Gospels. See Meier, *Roots of the Problem and the Person*, 1:137.

6. Funk and Hoover, *Five Gospels*, 1.

Jenkins, in his book *Hidden Gospels: How the Search for Jesus Lost its Way*, gives the recipe for the movement in the following words,

> If we can borrow the language of detective stories, the new gospel finds provided the *means* for new directions in research, while the expansion of the academic world supplied the *opportunity*: even so, a *motive* was still required, and this came from the new intellectual currents and theories which focused attention on topics once relegated to the academic fringe.[7]

For a while, the seminar basked in the spotlight of media coverage by popular news sources, like the *Los Angeles Times* and *U.S. News and World Report*,[8] especially during the Christmas and Easter seasons, but eventually it faded away by the end of the last century.

The second instance appeared at the beginning of the new millennium in the form of a mystery thriller by popular novelist Dan Brown entitled *The Da Vinci Code*, followed by a movie of the same name.[9] The novel was far from scholarly, but Brown claimed its storyline was a culmination of the most up-to-date scholarship. Frequent references were made to gnostic writings like the *Gospel of Philip* and the *Gospel of Mary of Magdala* to create a page-turner. Between high-speed chases, murder plots, and sexual rites, characters debated the veracity of the Bible and the development of Christianity. At the mid-point of the book the naïve character in the storyline, Sophie Neveu, received a lecture on the scholarly "cover-up" of Christianity by the protagonist,

> The Bible did not arrive by fax from heaven. . . . The Bible is a product of *man*. . . . Not of God . . . it has evolved through countless translations, additions, and revisions. History has never had a definitive version of the book. . . . More than *eighty* gospels were considered for the New Testament. . . . The Bible,

---

7. Jenkins, *Hidden Gospels*, 16 (emphasis original).

8. See Funk, "How Should the Jesus Seminar's Conclusions Be Viewed?," F18–19; Thomas, "Did the Jesus Seminar Draw from Faulty Assumptions?," F18–19; Sheler et al.,, "In Search of Jesus," 47–53.

9. Brown, *Da Vinci Code*. This work questions the biblical and traditional account of the person and work of Christ. It raises questions as to whether Jesus actually died on the cross, was married, has a modern bloodline that leads back to him, and if hidden evidence exists to support these claims. Much of the matter was based on the 1982 international bestseller by Baigent, et al., *Holy Blood, Holy Grail*. Baigent and Leigh wrote another controversial nonfictional work in 1991, *The Dead Sea Scrolls Deception*, which accused the Roman Catholic Church of suppressing detrimental information from the Dead Sea Scrolls regarding early Christianity. See Baigent and Leigh, *Dead Sea Scrolls Deception*.

> as we know it today, was collated by the pagan Roman emperor Constantine the Great.... By fusing pagan symbols, dates, and rituals into the growing Christian tradition, he created a kind of hybrid religion that was acceptable to both parties.... Jesus' establishment as "the Son of God" was officially proposed and voted on by the Council of Nicaea ... the early Church literally *stole* Jesus from His original followers, hijacking His human message, shrouding it in an impenetrable cloak of divinity, and using it to expand their own power.... Constantine commissioned and financed a new Bible, which omitted those gospels that spoke of Christ's *human* traits and embellished those gospels that made him godlike ... the earlier gospels were outlawed, gathered up, and burned.... Fortunately for historians ... some of the gospels ... managed to survive.[10]

Darrell Bock investigated the claims of the novel and concluded, "Popular and cultural beliefs often emerge out of what the culture comes to embrace as top-drawer scholarship, and the claims of *The Da Vinci Code* are a prime example of such a phenomenon."[11] There is no doubt that such revisionist theories have found a market among less-informed, yet curious armchair scholars. Luke Timothy Johnson remarks in his book *The Real Jesus*,

> Recent years have been very good for the Jesus business in America. I don't mean the Jesus business that goes on in churches, but the profitable trade in Jesus by a variety of publications that by creating a commotion in both the academy and the church also create a media-fed demand for more of the same. Sales in scandal are high, stocks in shock are rising, and futures on the historical Jesus are sound. Commerce in the Christ has rarely been better.[12]

Over three decades ago, Patrick Henry listed some insightful reasons for this continuing trend:

> First, there is the excitement generated by any major new discovery of unanticipated primary source material.... Second,

---

10. Brown, *Da Vinci Code*, 250–54. Needless to say, some well-timed media coverage of the alleged *Gospel of Judas* no doubt gave a nudge towards the blockbuster success of the novel and the movie. The novel was rebutted by several competent scholars in books, articles, and forums. See Bock, *Breaking the Da Vinci Code*; Garlow and Jones, *Cracking Da Vinci's Code*; Kennedy and Newcombe, *Da Vinci Myth*; and many others. See also Ehrman, *Lost Gospel of Judas Iscariot*.

11. Bock, *Breaking the Da Vinci Code*, 156.

12. Johnson, *Real Jesus*, 1.

> just as the quest for the historical Jesus has frequently been motivated by a desire to get behind the church's picture of Jesus in order to have a base from which to criticize the church, so the effort to demonstrate the temporal priority and religious superiority of heresy may be part of an attempt to legitimate various contemporary forms of radical Christianity. Third, we in the academic world have developed in the past decade or two a rather romantic notion that those who are rebellious are honest and self-aware . . . the current fascination is more with heretics than with heresies. . . . Fourth—and perhaps most fundamental—our paradigm for the world is *politics*. We tend to see everything in terms of power struggles, manipulations, negotiations, lobbying, trade-offs, compromises, revolutions.[13]

In this fertile soil of fascination with heretical fringe movements, the new trend in NTTC has also flourished, reflecting this line of thought in its approach to text-critical matters. It is not necessary to trace lines of descent or dependence to prove this. Neither is it necessary to find references to the proponents of the new approach or their texts to justify the connection. The presence of the tendencies defined above are enough to establish that the contemporary fascination with heresies has and continues to influence the new movement in NTTC. According to this view, the text at hand is not necessarily original but merely that which won out in the sociopolitical struggle of early Christianity. In such an era, it is worth following the advice of Wisse:

> Our dependence on these texts is absolute. It is the only "hard" evidence available to the historian and interpreter. . . . If the critic questions the reliability of a text . . . the result is usually not scholarly gain but loss. . . . The risk of undermining the scholarly usefulness of the limited amount of evidence that is available should put a burden on the critic to protect this evidence against arbitrary treatment and unwarranted doubts.[14]

Ultimately, novel and baseless claims of sociopolitical struggles in early Christianity, unfounded charges of orthodox conspiracy to manipulate the canon and the text, and a sensational history of textual transmission have no place in responsible NTTC. The proponents of the new trend in NTTC exemplify a penchant for such claims, some more so than others.

---

13. Henry, "Why is Contemporary Scholarship?," 63–67 (emphasis original). The work was first published in *Studia Patristica* 17:1, 123–26.

14. Wisse, "Textual Limits," 167–68.

PREMISE 2: THE PROFUSION OF VARIANTS PROHIBITS ALL ATTEMPTS AT REACHING THE ORIGINAL TEXT[15]

Bart Ehrman has often repeated the claim that with only 138,000 words in the NT, there are as many as 400,000 or more variants in the NT manuscript tradition.[16] His claim is meant to shock the untrained readers and leave them hopeless regarding all attempts at retrieving the original text. Underlying his claim is the assumption that the growing number of manuscripts has led to a growing total count of variants, as he reasons,

> Whereas Mill knew of or examined some one hundred Greek manuscripts to uncover his thirty thousand variations, today we know of far, far more. At last count, more than fifty-seven hundred Greek manuscripts have been discovered and catalogued. That's fifty-seven *times* as many as Mill knew about in 1707.[17]

To the contrary, the root cause of the growing total count of variants is not the growing number of extant manuscripts but the changing definition of the variant unit, as will be shown below.

Even prior to the coming of the new approach in NTTC, the number of variants has steadily risen: John Mill posited 30,000 variants,[18] Scrivener 120,000 variants,[19] Eberhard Nestle and Leon Vaganay 150,000 to 250,000

---

15. Most of this section was presented as a paper titled "From Mill to Muenster" at the Annual Meeting of the Evangelical Theological Society, Baltimore, MD, on 20 November 2013.

16. Ehrman, *Misquoting Jesus*, 89. Similarly, Wallace has suggested in his often-quoted article, "The Number of Textual Variants: An Evangelical Miscalculation," that "with the work done on Luke's Gospel by the International Greek New Testament Project, Tommy Wasserman's work on Jude, and Muenster's work on James and I Peter, the estimates today are closer to 400,000" (Wallace, "Number of Textual Variants," para. 13).

17. Ehrman, *Misquoting Jesus*, 88–89. There is no doubt John Mill made a valuable contribution to the field of NTTC by listing the variants at the bottom of each page. After thirty years of tireless effort, he produced in 1707 an unprecedented edition of the Greek NT. See Bristol, "New Testament Textual Criticism," 101; Nineham, "In Memory of a Forgotten Scholar," 185–89. It is misleading, however—albeit sensational—for Ehrman to continue referring to Mill's "30,000" to estimate the exponential growth of such based on the discovery of new manuscripts. If Mill's data were recorded according to today's standards and progress in the field, it would prove to be much less spectacular.

18. See Fox, *John Mill and Richard Bentley*, 105. Fox notes Gerard von Maestricht was the first to list the number of variants in Mill in his work titled *Dissertation on the Collections and Collectors of Variant Readings*. Later, Richard Bentley mentioned this repeatedly in his *Remarks upon a Late Discourse of Free-Thinking*. Portions of it are found in Tregelles, *Account of the Printed Text*, 49–57.

19. See Scrivener, *Plain Introduction*, 1:3. He notes, "If the number of these variants

variants,[20] and IGNTP[21] 300,000 variants. The claims have now risen to 400,000 to 800,000, and to even more variants. Peter Gurry, in his recent article, "The Number of Variants in the Greek New Testament: A Proposed Estimate," has given the most comprehensive and up-to-date survey of all the proposals regarding the total number of variants in the NT manuscript tradition, noting,

> We often have no idea who produced the estimate. The use of the passive voice to introduce these numbers is rampant. Phrases like "some say . . . " or "one speaks of . . . " or "it has been estimated that . . . " or "there have been counted . . ." pave a long trail of unverified estimates. By citing the number this way, those who cite them are able to make use of the number while at the same time avoiding any real responsibility for it. The problem is made worse when the number is presented as one of "the best estimates," "competent estimates" (*kundiger Schätzung*) [sic], or the like. The impression on the reader is that someone somewhere has taken the trouble to work out a sound method of estimating; but no such source appears forthcoming.[22]

Even though Gurry acknowledges there are more variants than previously claimed, these hypothetical totals have proven extremely beneficial under the new trend that thrives on the sensational.

By raising the status of a singular reading to a significant reading, the characteristics peculiar to that individual manuscript and scribe are now considered of equal importance for gaining an understanding of the much broader history of transmission. According to Epp, a "reading" can be deemed either "significant" or "insignificant," hinging on the boundaries of the broader tasks of NTTC, which Epp lists as "Determination of a MS's relationship with all other MSS, the location of a MS within the textual history and transmission of the NT, and the ultimate goal of establishing the original text."[23] Hence, for Epp, a variant is a reading that still stands as a valid candidate to be considered as part of the original text and is also useful for locating the "genetic and genealogical tracking."[24]

---

was rightly computed at thirty thousand in Mill's time, a century and a half ago, they must at present amount to at least fourfold that quantity."

20. Nestle, *Einführung in das Griechische*, 23; Vaganay and Amphoux, *Introduction to New Testament Textual Criticism*, 2.

21. The International Greek New Testament Project.

22. Gurry, "Number of Variants," 97–121. For an updated treatment of the subject, see Gurry's new essay, "Myths about Variants," 191–210.

23. Epp, "Toward the Clarification," 57.

24. Epp, "Toward the Clarification," 57.

Elsewhere, Epp becomes even more explicit in recasting the goal of NTTC. In his now-well-known article, "The Multivalence of the Term 'Original Text' in New Testament Textual Criticism," he postulates four categories that redefine the idea of an original text.[25] First is the "predecessor text-form," which he considers to be the "precanonical" text. This text represents the hypothetical sources available to the author at the time of writing the text—a position which more properly belongs to the realm of higher rather than lower (textual) criticism. The second is the "autographic" text form—the actual text as actually penned by the author or his amanuensis. The third is the "canonical text-form," i.e., the "textual form of a book (or a collection of books) at the time it acquired consensual authority or when its canonicity was (perhaps more formally) sought or established." The fourth is the "interpretive text-form," which represents the later, nonauthorial reformulations of the original text. With such a broad definition of what constitutes the "original text," it is quite obvious previously discarded readings are now back in the mix.

In a sequel article titled "It's All about Variants: A Variant-Conscious Approach to New Testament Textual Criticism," Epp unequivocally declares,

> The text becomes a virtual museum, with its variation-units comprising exhibits of narratives and interpretations located, whenever possible, contextually in time and place. This phenomenon of variation reveals the dynamism of the Christian community and the wealth of interpretive possibilities and creative impulses that Christians sensed were inherent in the text. Naturally, most of the estimated one third of a million variant readings among the New Testament manuscripts are most likely unintentional changes—scribal errors—yet the meaningful and presumably intentional alterations are legion, witnessing to the hermeneutical ferment in the life of the church.[26]

Epp takes issue with the NA, UBSGNT and the *ECM* texts for discarding readings to the "netherworld" that are deemed as inviable contenders for the original text.[27] Instead, for Epp, every reading is equally "significant"[28]— not for the establishment of the original text but to aid in the reconstruction of the history of the text.

The above discussion demonstrates the boundaries of what constitutes a variant have extended as the quest for the original text has

---

25. Epp, "Multivalence of the Term 'Original Text,'" 276–77.
26. Epp, "It's All about Variants," 291–92.
27. Epp, "It's All about Variants," 297.
28. Epp, "It's All about Variants," 298.

diminished. In fact, with growing pessimism regarding any hope of retrieving the original text, the focus has now shifted to recreating many texts in the history of transmission. Along with this shift, the count of variants has also grown exceedingly, with patently secondary readings being elevated to primary status. Recently, Peter Gurry estimated 500,000 variants, but cautioned,

> [I]t is still an *estimate* . . . based on a sample size of about three percent of the entire Greek New Testament and includes minuscules, majuscules, and some lectionaries. Except for Revelation, it is based on data from portions of every book and therefore does not assume that all books were copied with the same frequency or the same accuracy. It does not include variants from patristic citations, versions, amulets, or inscriptions.[29]

Earlier, Kenneth Clark was far more pessimistic regarding any total count of variants. Although he acknowledges "the simple fact of massive textual variations (small and large) is beyond denial or refutation,"[30] he cautions that "counting words is a meaningless measure of textual variation, and all such estimates fail to convey the theological significance of variable readings."[31] Although Clark's intent is to decry any attempt to minimize the impact variations can make on doctrine, the principle is just as valuable for the present discussion. Numbers carry the fallacy of hasty generalization and only serve to create sensation.

In conclusion, the numbers game can be counterproductive to a proper understanding and representation of the number of variants. Whether they are used to defend the Bible or to attack it, the fact is, apart from the limited number of viable original text variants,[32] we never had a number, and we probably never will have an accepted and definitive one regarding all *possible* variants. All attempts at using numbers for shock value or to discourage any and all attempts at retrieving the original text of NT are misleading and without basis.

---

29. See Gurry, "Number of Variants," 97–121 (emphasis original).
30. Clark, "Theological Relevance of Textual Variation," 3.
31. Clark, "Theological Relevance of Textual Variation," 4.
32. Greenlee claimed significant variants made up the "few thousand" remaining variants that do make a difference, but qualified that they are "only of a small portion of the New Testament text" (Greenlee, *Scribes, Scrolls, and Scripture*, 37–39).

PREMISE 3: EARLY, WIDESPREAD, AND LINGERING CORRUPTIONS PROHIBIT ALL ATTEMPTS AT REACHING THE ORIGINAL TEXT

NT text-critics recognize the text was corrupted early and the corruption was widespread. They also agree the corruption lingered on for the first several centuries of Christianity. Although this is true, it does not preclude responsible efforts at retrieving the original text of the NT. Yet, some of the proponents have a dismal view of ever reaching this text. Even if attempts are made, they argue there is no guarantee the text will be the original text. The proponents insist such futile efforts must be abandoned and redirected toward understanding the history of the variants in their various hypothetical settings. Some even claim there was never any authoritative original text. Instead, readers should create the text that best fits their individual needs.[33]

Major text-critics from the early days of the discipline have long acknowledged the portentous challenge in retrieving the original text. Tischendorf remarked, "I have no doubt that in the very earliest ages after our Holy Scriptures were written, and before the authority of the Church protected them, willful alterations, and especially additions, were made in them."[34] So also, Westcott and Hort contended the earliest text was rife with variants, as Hort remarked:

> The conception of new Scriptures standing on the same footing as the Scriptures of the Old Testament was slow and unequal in its growth, more especially while the traditions of the apostolic and immediately succeeding generations still lived; and the reverence paid to the apostolic writings, even to the most highly and most widely venerated among them, was not of a kind that exacted a scrupulous jealousy as to their text as distinguished from their substance. As was to be expected, the language of the historical books was treated with more freedom than the rest: but even the Epistles, and still more the Apocalypse, bear abundant traces of a similar type of transcription. After a while changed feelings and changed circumstances put an end to the early textual laxity, and thenceforward its occurrence is altogether exceptional; so that the later corruptions are most wholly those incident to transcription in the proper sense, errors

---

33. Cf. Parker, "Through a Screen Darkly," 402. "I do not mean that the texts we are creating are necessarily superior to earlier creations. It is more significant that they are the texts that we *need* to create." Emphasis added.

34. Tischendorf, *New Testament*, xv.

arising from careless performance of a scribe's work, not from an imperfect conception of it.³⁵

Scrivener agrees, saying, "It is no less paradoxical in sound that the worst corruptions to which the New Testament has ever been subjected, originated within a hundred years after it was composed."³⁶ Zuntz also cautions, "Modern criticism stops before the barrier of the second century; the age, so it seems, of unbounded liberties with the text."³⁷ Colwell too concurs in his nontechnical work on NTTC, *What is the Best New Testament?*: "The first two Christian centuries witnessed the creation of the large majority of all variations known to scholars today."³⁸ He summarizes this turbulent period as follows,

> The originals perished; they perished early. There is nothing mysterious or puzzling about this. . . . The early manuscripts were written to be read. They were read until their pages fell out or were torn. . . . [T]he rapid multiplication of [Christian converts] created a demand for copies of these books. . . . And in the first one hundred and fifty years of Christian history copies of copies multiplied.³⁹

Gordon Fee even extends this period to the fourth century, claiming, "The vast majority of the errors in the NT mss occurred during the period that is also the most difficult to reconstruct—the first four Christian centuries."⁴⁰ Harry Gamble expresses similar sentiments in his *Books and Readers in the Early Church: A History of Early Christian Texts*, as he claims,

> It was not until the fourth century that Christian books began to be produced to a professional and literary bibliographic standard. This was in part because of the increasing popularity of the codex for non-Christian literary texts, which reduced the disparity of format, but more significantly it was the result of the establishment of Christianity as the religion of the empire.⁴¹

---

35. Westcott and Hort, *Introduction and Appendix*, 7. Also, Hort's name alone is used because the authors themselves attest to the fact that Hort was the primary writer "of this volume and the other accompaniments of the text" (18).

36. Scrivener, *Plain Introduction*, 2:264.

37. Zuntz, *Text of the Epistles*, 11.

38. Colwell, *What is the Best New Testament?*, 52.

39. Colwell, *What is the Best New Testament?*, 51–52.

40. Fee, "Textual Criticism of the New Testament," 1:425. Again, "Most of the copying errors that made their way into the stream of history were created during the first 300 years of Christianity" (Fee, "Text Criticism," 1110).

41. Gamble, *Books and Readers*, 79.

Thus, prior to the codex there was a greater possibility for the text to be changed.

It is obvious from the brief discussion above it is a unified assumption among text-critics that the earliest centuries were the period of the creation and dissemination of most of the variants found in the NT textual tradition today. Nonetheless, most of the text-critics mentioned above were also optimistic in their ability to reach the original text utilizing responsible textual criticism. To the contrary, the proponents of the new approach are far more pessimistic regarding the ability of any methodology to retrieve the original text. They exaggerate the corruption to such an extent that any attempt at claiming original text or practicing the discipline to reach it is dismissed as impossible or unnecessary. Here are some counterarguments against the premise discussed above.

Early corruption was not unchecked

Many NT text-critics often claim the second century was marked by unchecked and now even orthodox-church-sponsored deliberate corruption of the NT text. The evidence from the earliest sources of Christianity is contrary to such claims. The early fathers acknowledged through their writings that there was some corruption in the early centuries by the heretics, but also affirmed the text was not up for grabs. Below are two major quotes from early fathers attesting the corruption of the NT text. First, Origen, in his work *Against Celsus*, observed,

> Now I know of no others who have altered the Gospel, save the followers of Marcion, and those of Valentinus, and, I think, also those of Lucian. But such an allegation is no charge against the Christian system, but against those who dared so to trifle with the Gospels. And as it is no ground of accusation against philosophy, that there exist Sophists, or Epicureans, or Peripatetics, or any others, whoever they may be, who hold false opinions; so neither is it against genuine Christianity that there are some who corrupt the Gospel histories, and who introduce heresies opposed to the meaning of the doctrine of Jesus.[42]

Also, Eusebius expressed a similar opinion, as can be seen in his lengthy quote of Gaius in his *Ecclesiastical History*:

---

42. Origen, *Against Celsus*, 2.27. English translation taken from Roberts et al., *Ante-Nicene Fathers*, 4:443.

> For this reason is it they have boldly laid their hands upon the divine Scriptures, alleging that they have corrected them. And that I do not state this against them falsely, any one who pleases may ascertain. For if any one should choose to collect and compare all their copies together, he would find many discrepancies among them. The copies of Asclepiades, at any rate, will be found at variance with those of Theodotus. And many such copies are to be had, because their disciples were very zealous in inserting the corrections, as they call them, i.e., the corruptions made by each of them. And again, the copies of Hermophilus do not agree with these; and as for those of Apollonius, they are not consistent even with themselves. For one may compare those which were formerly prepared by them with those which have been afterwards corrupted with a special object, and many discrepancies will be found. And as to the great audacity implied in this offence, it is not likely that even they themselves can be ignorant of that. For either they do not believe that the divine Scriptures were dictated by the Holy Spirit, and are thus infidels; or they think themselves wiser than the Holy Spirit, and what are they then but demoniacs? Nor can they deny that the crime is theirs, when the copies have been written with their own hand; nor did they receive such copies of the Scriptures from those by whom they were first instructed in the faith and they cannot produce copies from which these were transcribed.[43]

According to Eusebius, Dionysius of Corinth (ca. 170), in his now-nonextant letters, discussed the notorious tendency of the heretics to corrupt not only his letters but also the Scriptures.[44] Sometimes the corruptors were actually attempting to reach back to the original text. One case in point were the Theodotians, who attempted a critical recension of the text in order to refute Galen, an early critic of Christianity. Metzger remarks concerning them, "Ironically enough, the earliest efforts to ascertain the original text of the New Testament seem to have been made by those who were excommunicated as heretics by the authoritarian Bishop of Rome, Pope Victor (AD 187–98)."[45]

Regarding the extent of such corruptions to the NT text, there have been different opinions. From an earlier perspective, John Burgon is more

---

43. Eusebius, *Ecclesiastical History*, 5.28. English Translation taken from Roberts et al., *Ante-Nicene Fathers*, 5:602.

44. Eusebius, *Ecclesiastical History*, 4.23. See Crusé, *Eusebius' Ecclesiastical History*, 135–36.

45. Metzger, *Text of the New Testament*, 150. These Theodotians apparently were followers of the same Theodotus cited by Eusebius.

cautious in his judgment as to how widespread were such corruptions. He writes,

> All that is intended by such statements is that these old heretics retained, altered, transposed, just so much as they pleased of the fourfold Gospel: and further, that they imported whatever additional material they saw fit—not that they rejected the inspired text entirely, and substituted something of their own invention in its place.[46]

On the other hand, from a similar perspective, Amy Donaldson is far more open to widespread corruptions in the early period and its lingering effect past the second century. She claims, "These examples illustrate that anyone with a stylus and enough education was able to make their own 'corrections' to the text."[47] She adds,

> The 2nd century in particular is often acknowledged as a time of relative freedom for the NT text, the period during which the majority of textual variants were introduced. Thus, any accusations by Irenaeus, Origen, Eusebius, or Jerome pertaining to the earliest generation of copyists fit well with modern theories about that early period. But the criticisms of Origen, and especially Jerome, carry that distrust into the third, fourth, and even fifth centuries.[48]

While it is true the "accusations" of the early fathers validate the early contamination of the text, they also serve to prove they had a high regard for preserving the original text of the NT. Irenaeus, living in the latter half of the second century, instructed any who would copy his own work against heretics to be extra careful and even apply some textual criticism:

> I adjure you who shall copy out this book, by our Lord Jesus Christ and by his glorious advent when he comes to judge the living and the dead, that you compare what you transcribe, and correct it carefully against this manuscript from which you copy; and also that you transcribe this adjuration and insert it in the copy.[49]

If Irenaeus was so cautious regarding the transmission of his own work, one can only imagine how highly he would have regarded the

---

46. Burgon, *Causes of the Corruption*, 198.
47. Donaldson, "Explicit References," 289.
48. Donaldson, "Explicit References," 301.
49. Irenaeus, in Metzger and Ehrman, *Text of the New Testament*, 33.

transmission of the biblical text. So also, Origen observed in his homily on Matthew, "Nowadays, as is evident, there is a great diversity between the various manuscripts, either through the negligence of certain copyists, or the perverse audacity shown by some in correcting the text, or through the fault of those who, playing the part of correctors, lengthen or shorten it as they please."[50] Even though such statements are rare, they are not such due to a diminished view of the original text but due to a dearth of early sources. While it is true some textual corruption happened in the early period of church history, it was not as unchecked nor widespread as is often claimed.

As to the length of the period of contamination, the issue is far from settled. Contrary to what is often assumed, it seems it was not a long period of time. Barbara Aland argues, in response to Marcion's tampering with the text, there was a greater text-consciousness at the end of the second century.[51] George Dunbar Kilpatrick points to Origen's own unsuccessful attempt to fix the text after the second century, as an example of textual stability:

> Origen's treatment of Matt. 19:19 is significant in two other ways. First he was probably the most influential commentator of the Ancient Church and yet his conjecture at this point seems to have influenced only one manuscript of a local version of the New Testament. The Greek tradition is apparently quite unaffected by it. From the third century onward even an Origen could not effectively alter the text.
>
> This brings us to the second significant point—his date. From the early third century onward the freedom to alter the text which had obtained earlier can no longer be practised. Tatian is the last author to make deliberate changes in the text of whom we have explicit information. Between Tatian and Origen Christian opinion had so changed that it was no longer possible to make changes in the text whether they were harmless or not.[52]

In fact, Larry Hurtado, in his article "The New Testament in the Second Century," brings out a relevant factor that may have impacted the situation: "I suggest that what changes in the post-150 CE period is a greater tendency to see texts as the *works of authors*, and so to cite them as such, rather than simply appropriating the contents of texts."[53]

---

50. Origen, *In Matthew*, xv.14. For text see Swete, *Introduction to the Old Testament in Greek*, 60. Compare Metzger, "Explicit References," 78–79.

51. Aland, "Die Rezeption," 5–21.

52. Kilpatrick, "Atticism," 129–30.

53. Hurtado, "New Testament in the Second Century," 27 (emphasis original).

This brief survey demonstrates the exaggerated claims of unchecked and widespread corruption of the NT text in the early centuries is contrary to the historical evidence. It is only sensational and must be abandoned. The evidence from the early fathers demonstrates an awareness of corruption followed by a high regard to preserve the original text. Most major text-critics have affirmed this view.

Earliest extant papyri are far more unified than commonly assumed

Some text-critics often claim the NT papyri give evidence of a period of textual fluidity and chaos. Ehrman remarks in his *The Orthodox Corruption of Scripture*,

> The majority of textual variants that are preserved in the surviving documents, even the documents produced in a later age, originated during the first three Christian centuries. The conviction is not based on idle speculation. In contrast to the relative stability of the New Testament text in later times, our oldest witnesses display a remarkable degree of variation. The evidence suggests that during the earliest period of its transmission the New Testament text was in a state of flux, that it came to be more or less standardized in some regions by the fourth century, and subject to fairly rigid control (by comparison) only in the Byzantine period. As a result, the period of relative creativity was early, that of strict reproduction late. Variants found in later witnesses are thus less likely to have been generated then than to have been reproduced from earlier exemplars.[54]

Such claims were also made by others prior to the new movement in NTTC. Decades earlier, George Dunbar Kilpatrick gave the following observation regarding the text of the papyri,

> Let us take our two manuscripts of about this date [AD 200] which contain parts of John, the Chester Beatty Papyrus [P45] and the Bodmer Papyrus [P66]. They are together extant for about seventy verses. Over these seventy verses they differ some seventy-three times apart from mistakes.
>
> Further, in the Bodmer Papyrus the original scribe has frequently corrected what he first wrote. At some places he is correcting his own mistakes but at others he substitutes one form of phrasing for another. At about seventy-five of these substitutions

---

54. Ehrman, *Orthodox Corruption of Scripture* (1993), 28.

both alternatives are known from other manuscripts independently. The scribe is in fact replacing one variant reading by another at some seventy places so that we may conclude that already in his day there was variation at these points.[55]

Kenneth Clark made a similar claim in his remarks on P75: "The papyrus vividly portrays a fluid state of the text at about AD 200. Such a scribal freedom suggests that the gospel text was little more stable than the oral tradition."[56] Colwell also weighed in on the matter by sifting the Chester Beatty and Bodmer Papyri through the grid of text-types. Contrary to what was often assumed (that early text-types were a creation of certain fathers, such as Lucian, Hesychius, and Origen), he argued text-types were a result of a process during the first few centuries of upheaval in the manuscript history. In his words, "The first action required by the new evidence is to split the fourth-century date for the origin of the text-types in half and to push the halves apart."[57] By this he means the processes leading to the formation of the text-types began quite early in the manuscript tradition but were not in their final form until the mid-fourth century. Many of the readings of the text-types can be noted in the early papyri but not in the completed form as noted later. Colwell utilizes Zuntz's research of P46, wherein both the Alpha and the Beta-type readings can be found with the Beta taking over the Alpha.[58] Overall, "all witnesses are mixed in ancestry (or individually corrupted, and thus parents of mixture)."[59] Elsewhere, Colwell illustrates the matter by a parabolic analogy,

> The original New Testament may be likened to a collection of dresses. These dresses were worn out, cut up, and put into a scrap bag. This process was completed in the second century. Then frugal and industrious Christians came along, reached into the bag for material, and made patchwork quilts out of it. When they lacked a needed piece, they found it elsewhere; when a piece was misshapen, they trimmed it to fit. Some of these quilt-makers liked long narrow quilts; some liked square ones; some had an antipathy to green color and would not use any material which contained it; others doted on red scraps. But most of the material came out of the scrap bag. In the fourth

---

55. Kilpatrick, "Transmission of the New Testament," 128–29.
56. Clark, "Theological Relevance of Textual Variation," 15.
57. Colwell, "Method in Locating," 47.
58. The Alpha were the earlier (Alexandrian and Western) and the Beta the later Byzantine.
59. Colwell, "Method in Locating," 52.

and later centuries some of the earlier quilts were ripped up and put back in the bag, from which again new quilts were made—pieced out where necessary with new material. Many of these patterns became popular and were copied widely but, until the industrial revolution, never with complete accuracy.[60]

Similar arguments, or some variation thereof, are often repeated by the text-critics being discussed who claim the earliest period of the transmission of the NT text was endemic of textual fluidity. While reasoned eclectics have remained optimistic in their ability to sift through the early material, variant by variant, and reach a generally acceptable form of the original text of the NT, many present-day text-critics have given up in the face of presupposed insurmountable odds.

Recent research has shown that the earliest papyri were not as divided or chaotic as is often assumed. Maurice A. Robinson demonstrated this in his paper at the Evangelical Theological Society in 2005, titled "The Integrity of the Early New Testament Text: A Collation-Based Comparison Utilizing the Papyri of the Second and Third Centuries."[61] He begins by noting the reliability of the NT text was affirmed by Westcott and Hort in the "prepapyrus era" to "at least seven-eighths of the NT text (87.5 percent)."[62] Robinson then puts their statement to the test in light of the many papyri discoveries in the past 100 years and more. His methodology is based on the commonly accepted fact regarding the varied nature of the papyri text, described by Barbara Aland and Klaus Wachtel as follows: "The papyri and majuscules are for the most part individual witnesses: despite sharing general tendencies in the forms of their texts, they differ so widely from one another that it is impossible to establish any direct genealogical ties among them."[63] Robinson stated his methodology for the experiment as follows,

> Some 30 randomly selected early mss of the second and third centuries are collated against the Byzantine Textform (Robinson-Pierpont edition). Such a collation is particularly appropriate, since it is well known that none of those early documents—indeed no extant Greek NT manuscript prior to the mid-fourth century—yet reflects a thoroughly Byzantine type of text. Thus, the amount of textual diversity and divergence should be maximized in such a test.[64]

60. Colwell, *What is the Best New Testament?*, 71.
61. Robinson, "Integrity of the Early New Testament Text."
62. Robinson, "Integrity of the Early New Testament Text," 3.
63. Aland and Wachtel, "Greek Minuscule Manuscripts," 46.
64. Robinson, "Integrity of the Early New Testament Text," 4.

Robinson begins by comparing the Byzantine textform against the Westcott-Hort text. While the W-H Greek text is a thoroughgoing Alexandrian text from the fourth-century manuscripts and their later close relatives, the Byzantine text utilized for this analysis is based on manuscripts from the fourth to the eleventh century. The study of the sample text (the rich man and Lazarus narrative, Luke 16:19–31) reveals the text of both printed editions is 93 percent identical. Robinson continues the comparison between the text-types on randomly selected larger units (Matt 13, Acts 13, Rom 13, Heb 13, Rev 13). The results again showed the text remained identical on a range of 91.6 percent (low) to 96.8 percent (high).[65] Next, along with some major papyri, Robinson compares some randomly selected minor papyri against the Byzantine text form.[66] Again, the result showed identical readings in approximately 92.2 percent of their text. Overall, Robinson's study demonstrates the early extant papyri were not as varied as is often assumed.

Recently, Alan Mugridge came to the same conclusion by examining the scribal practice of early scribes of NT papyri. In a similar vein as Haines-Eitzen's thesis, he challenges the popular assumption that "the early Christians had their texts reproduced 'in-house,' making little or no use of 'secular' or 'professional' scribes."[67] To the contrary, his research shows the early scribes exercised great care in reproducing the text as close as possible to the original. Zachary Cole deems it a myth that the "*unpretentious scripts* of early New Testament papyri indicate an *unprofessional standard of copying*. That is, unattractive and pretentious writing must mean 'untrained' scribes and poor standards of transcription."[68] Instead, he offers three points in favor of faithful preservation by the early scribes:

> First, due to the wealth of our evidence, we have a paradoxical safety in numbers. Second, we have strong evidence that the text has been carefully transmitted in at least one stream of manuscripts. Third, when we look at the nature of our textual variants, they do not appear to be the kind of variants that would arise if scribes were in the habit of writing whatever they wanted.[69]

---

65. Robinson, "Integrity of the Early New Testament Text," 7–9.

66. The papyri selected are as follows: Century II—P46, P52, P66, P75, P90, P98; Century II/III— P77+103; Century III—P5, P13, P15, P20, P27, P37, P39, P45, P47, P49, P50, P53, P72, P86, P101, P106, P108, P100, P110, P111, P114, P115.

67. Mugridge, *Copying Early Christian Texts*, 1.

68. Cole, "Myths about Copyists," 135 (emphasis original).

69. Cole, "Myths about Copyists," 144.

Peter Malik argues on the basis of scribal corrections in the early papyrus P66, the late minuscule GA 61, and even the noncanonical Egerton Gospel that the "scribes' main goal was not to innovate, and when they did it was often accidental."[70] Ehrman affirms this as well: "By far the vast majority [of variants] are purely 'accidental,' readily explained as resulting from scribal ineptitude, carelessness, or fatigue."[71] Nonetheless, in practice, Ehrman portrays the intentional changes as far more prevalent and irreparable.

Ultimately, the assertion by the proponents of the new approach that the early text was so fluid or chaotic that any attempt to reach the original text is hopeless does not stand in the face of text-critical scrutiny and scribal habits of early scribes. More and more research is proving the early period was far more stable and reflective of the original text. Furthermore, scribes were much more competent and concerned about the accuracy of the text they copied than is often assumed. Corruptions did arise, but they did not render the original text beyond repair or recovery.

Patristic citations are not the best gauge for the state of the early text

In the new movement in NTTC, patristic citations are often held up as key evidence the text was not only corrupted early and was widespread, but that it continued to be contaminated for the first few hundred years of Christianity. This allegation of corruption in the third and fourth century is then taken as evidence to prove there was corruption even in the second century. Primary in employing this reasoning is Bart Ehrman. In his *The Orthodox Corruption of Scripture*, he uses scriptural quotations from the early Greek fathers to make his case the orthodox fathers often manipulated the text in order to safeguard their pet doctrines. Inherent in his argument was the presumed retrievability of the original text, albeit through much sifting. However, his goal is not to retrieve the original text through patristic citations, but to stretch the alleged examples of corruption back to the second century and place the same indictment of corruption against the hypothetical proto-orthodox scribes. It is guilt by speculation based on scanty evidence and unproven arguments. The focus is not on whether later orthodox fathers had any link to earlier proto-orthodox scribes. That is impossible to prove or disprove due to a lack of historical evidence. Instead, the focus is on the legitimate use of patristic evidence in text-critical research. Most of Ehrman's arguments blatantly disregard the proper use of patristic citations.

70. Malik, "Myths about Copying," 152, 154–69.
71. Ehrman, *Orthodox Corruption of Scripture* (1993), 27.

Ehrman's previous writings on patristic sources reveal he is well aware of the many caveats and qualifications necessary in accurately evaluating the citations. He acknowledges the writings of the church fathers are "incomplete and survive by chance, and the quotations of Scripture in them are spotty, often paraphrastic, and likewise subject to the vagaries of textual transmission."[72] Nonetheless, he considers them to be the missing link to establishing the original text, since the papyri are fragmentary and nothing more than the "accidents of history and climate."[73] It is hard to follow Ehrman's convoluted argument on the significance and retrievability of the original text. It appears he only wants to utilize the patristic citations to peer into the "window" of early Christianity,[74] while simultaneously adhering to and denying the original text concept, as noted in the following remark:

> The only real access we have to the Christian milieu of the period is through our literary sources—i.e., the writings of the Church Fathers (and those they opposed). Once again, then, the key to understanding this aspect of the textual tradition lies in our Patristic sources—not so much through seeing how the Fathers themselves quote the text (although this can sometimes prove useful as well) as through seeing the kinds of issues that they discuss and dispute.[75]

In an earlier work, Ehrman had chastised Marie-Émile Boismard[76] for giving too much credence to patristic testimony regarding the original text, saying, "The Patristic sources provide primary evidence for the history of the transmission of the NT text but only secondary evidence for the original text itself."[77] Yet, in *The Orthodox Corruption of Scripture*, Ehrman seems to have fallen into the same error by holding to the viability of the original text, albeit corrupted and irretrievable, as found in the patristic citations. The following discussion will briefly survey the evaluation of past and present text-critics on the value of patristic citations to NTTC.

Although it is popularly claimed there are enough patristic citations to recreate the NT text, such is far from the truth.[78] Text-critics of the past were skeptical of the value of patristic citations in ascertaining the history

---

72. Ehrman, "Use and Significance," 249.
73. Ehrman, "Use and Significance," 248.
74. Ehrman, "Text as Window," 803–30.
75. Ehrman, "Use and Significance," 261.
76. Boismard, "Critique Textuelle," 388–408; Boismard, "Lectio Brevior, Potior," 161–68.
77. Ehrman, *Didymus the Blind*, 5n2.
78. Blaski "Myths about Patristics," 228–52.

of the NT text in the early period. Over a century ago, Westcott and Hort cautioned against placing excessive weight on patristic evidence: "Whenever a transcriber of a patristic treatise was copying a quotation differing from the text to which he was accustomed, he had virtually two originals before him, one present to his eyes, the other to his mind; and, if the difference struck him, he was not unlikely to treat the written exemplar as having blundered."[79] In 1890, John Montfort Bebb cautioned against the "critical value of the printed editions" of the fathers because many of the printed editions were put together at a time when the issue of "best manuscripts, or groups of manuscripts" was not as important as it is regarded today.[80] Even as late as 1957, M. Jack Suggs brought up the same issue regarding a lack of critical patristic editions.[81] Although some progress has been made since then in reconstructing critical texts of some of the Greek fathers' use of the NT,[82] there is still much work to be done and there are still many methodological issues that remain to be clarified regarding the accuracy of their citations.

Although critical editions of the fathers are very helpful, they do not resolve all the issues inherent in patristic citations. As Suggs noted, "A critical edition gives us confidence, but it is not infallible."[83] The jury is still out over how to assess the citations. Sometimes the longer passages are more accurately quoted than the shorter ones.[84] Others have proposed "the problem of *memoriter* [from memory] citation is perhaps the most critical of all."[85] Suggs had even suggested passages quoted for polemical purposes tended to be more accurate than those for homiletical purpose (for example, Chrysostom).[86] As to the Gospels, he noted the "quotations from memory tend to be harmonized and it is often almost impossible to determine to which Gospel the citation is supposed to refer."[87] With regard to "argument from silence," Bebb had cautioned earlier against making weighty decisions

---

79. Westcott and Hort, *Introduction and Appendix*, 202–3.

80. Bebb, "Evidence of the Early Versions," 196.

81. Suggs, "Use of Patristic Evidence," 140.

82. Ehrman, *Didymus the Blind*; Brooks, *New Testament Text of Gregory of Nyssa*; Ehrman et al., Text of the *Fourth Gospel*; Hannah, *Text of I Corinthians*; Racine, *Text of Matthew in the Writings of Basil*; Osburn, *Text of the Apostolos*; Mullen, *New Testament Text of Cyril of Jerusalem*; Donker, *Text of the Apostolos in Athanasius of Alexandria*; Cosaert, *Text of the Gospels in Clement of Alexandria*.

83. Suggs, "Use of Patristic Evidence," 141.

84. Bebb, "Evidence of the Early Versions," 216; Suggs, "Use of Patristic Evidence," 142.

85. Suggs, "Use of Patristic Evidence," 141.

86. Suggs, "Use of Patristic Evidence," 143.

87. Suggs, "Use of Patristic Evidence," 141.

just because a certain father does not mention a passage or a word that is deemed important today.[88] Overall, Bebb's remark reflects the overall sentiment of past text-critics regarding the value of patrisitic citations in doing responsible textual criticism: "The evidence of patristic quotations merits the severest scrutiny before it is thrown into the balance on one side or the other."[89]

The caution against patristic citations is also shared by many contemporary text-critics. Metzger concludes patristic, along with versional, quotations only serve to provide "indirect evidence" for a confirmatory purpose rather than for establishing text.[90] He warns earlier that often a "Father quotes the same passage more than once but never twice in the same wording."[91] Gordon Fee lists three major problems in utilizing patristic evidence from the Greek fathers. The first concerns their citation habits; the second deals with the transmission of the text, where he cautions that even though the critical editions are helpful, "they must themselves be used critically by those seeking to recover those texts."[92] The third is the need to understand the intricacies of patristic studies. He elsewhere classifies three evidences of the patristic text of the NT: citations, adaptations, and allusions.[93] Carroll Osburn, in his article "Methodology in Identifying Patristic Citations in NT Textual Criticism," incorporates Fee's guidelines to propose more acceptable criteria for assessing the patristic citations. Under the subheading "Accurate Citation with Partial Omission," he chides Ehrman for claiming an "orthodox omission" of θεος at 1 Corinthians 10:5 by Irenaeus. Since the supposed omission is at the end of the quote, "It cannot be used as textual evidence."[94] He concludes,

> Even when discriminate use is made of a critically edited patristic text, simple verbal precision in a patristic quotation is sometimes insufficient basis [sic] for including it in determining the reading of a Father's biblical exemplar, or for including it in the apparatus of the Greek NT. Each citation should be read in its patristic context in order to determine more precisely how the

---

88. Bebb, "Evidence of the Early Versions," 218.
89. Bebb, "Evidence of the Early Versions," 219.
90. Metzger, "Patristic Evidence," 395.
91. Metzger, "Patristic Evidence," 380.
92. Fee, "Use of the Greek Fathers," 194.
93. Fee, "Text of John," 169–70.
94. Osburn, "Methodology in Identifying, Patristic Citations" 326.

text is actually used and in what way it probably reflects a text known to the Father.[95]

Barbara Aland rightly differentiates between the accuracy of the fathers in quoting the text and the accuracy of the scribes in copying the text. The former were far more lenient but the latter were far stricter.[96] Robinson also offers similar important guidelines in evaluating patristic citations:

> First, the supposed "text of a Father" is based upon a gratuitous assumption: namely, that a Father in any single locale or at any particular time used one and only one manuscript. In fact, a Father may have switched manuscripts daily in some cases . . . most manuscripts available to him in that region would reflect the local text of the area; but what if now and then another manuscript from a different region came his way? It becomes no surprise to find that some Fathers possess a text that is "mixed" in a significant degree. . . . Second, Fathers often paraphrase, quote faultily from memory, or deliberately alter a quotation to make a point. . . . The goal of the Fathers was theological rather than primarily text-critical.[97]

After discussing all the qualifications to keep in mind when evaluating patristic evidence, Amy Donaldson remarks, "Once the caveats described in this chapter are taken into account, the actual concrete data is much more limited than the list of references to variants,"[98] and again, "to use these citations for reinforcement of the MS evidence or to argue for text types, one must proceed with great care."[99]

The brief discussion above demonstrates the leading scholars in NTTC, past and present, remain divided over the true value and the proper use of the fathers in NTTC. Although the scriptural citations by the fathers offer much valuable information in understanding the history of the transmission of the NT text, caution still needs to be exercised when using them to decide such critical matters as the attainability of the original text of the NT. Those who are attempting to shift the goalpost in NTTC should abandon their use of patristic citations to make sweeping claims regarding the irretrievability of the original text or for conjuring hypothetical and fanciful settings for the emergence of variants.

95. Osburn, "Methodology in Identifying, Patristic Citations" 342–43.
96. Aland, "Die Rezeption," 30.
97. Robinson and Pierpont, *New Testament in the Original Greek* (1991), xxxiii.
98. Donaldson, "Explicit References," 44.
99. Donaldson, "Explicit References," 44.

PREMISE 4: INTERDISCIPLINARY STUDIES RESOLVE TEXT-CRITICAL PROBLEMS

The proponents of the new quest in NTTC repeatedly utilize other disciplines to shed light on text-critical issues. They claim such interaction opens new vistas to previously gridlocked matters. To the contrary, weak and even outmoded conclusions of other disciplines are being utilized with erroneous results. This is not in any way a suggestion that interdisciplinary studies are off-limits. There have been tremendous benefits and strides made through the intermingling and cross-learning of disciplines. In fact, it is vital text-critical scholars engage and interact with scholars of other disciplines. It leads to more responsible studies where the collaborations can help resolve conundrums in individual fields. Albert C. Outler makes an excellent comment with regard to the need for such interaction between disciplines such as NT studies and patristics,

> "New Testament" scholars seem not to be as interested as one might think they should be in the historical aftermath of the production of the New Testament. . . . Patrologists, for their part, return the compliment by regarding the New Testament and the first century as theologically underdeveloped. Even when taken as prototype, the New Testament requires the fourth–sixth century development as climax. Small wonder, then, that these two academic cadres co-exist in the modern university but not often as constant colleagues.[100]

Outler's comment can be extended historically to refer to isolationist tendencies among NTTC scholars regarding other fields of biblical studies and individual disciplines within NT studies. Many times, commonly accepted and long-established principles and conclusions in other fields of studies are categorically ignored or dismissed. It is imperative NTTC scholars interact with other fields (historical theology, patristics, intertestamental studies, etc.) and disciplines (redaction criticism, social-scientific criticism, canonical criticism, etc.). However, this has to be done responsibly.

The current movement in NTTC betrays many examples of interdisciplinary irresponsibility, usually displayed in two major ways: First, principles that may apply to other major disciplines and even criticisms within NT studies are crudely emulated in text-critical analysis; second, inconclusive and even discredited theories of other disciplines and criticisms are utilized in NTTC without any qualifications. The new quest is

---

100. Outler, "Methods and Aims," 13.

replete with such examples, resulting in a foundationless structure, as depicted in the following diagram:

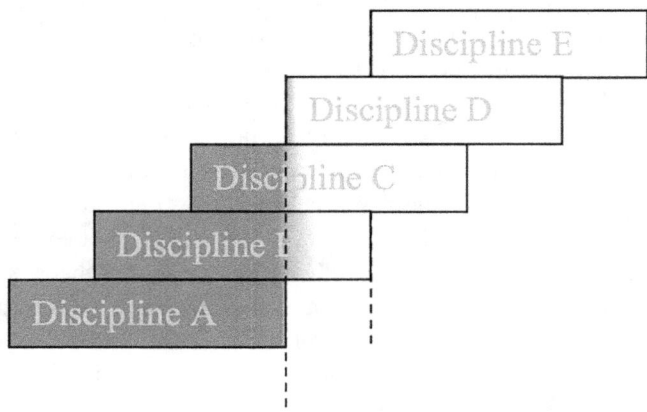

Each of the five boxes in the above figure represents a major discipline (patristics, biblical theology, systematic theology, etc.) or type of criticism (form, source, redaction, reader-response, etc.) in the field of NT. The darker portion of the box represents the well-tested and established conclusions in the field. The lighter portion represents the inconclusive and even the disproven theories in the field. The stacking of the boxes represents the interaction between the various disciplines and/or criticisms and the usage of data and conclusions from them.

As demonstrated in the figure, the foundation begins with Discipline/Criticism A. This is built upon by Discipline/Criticism B, which, for the most part, rests securely upon Discipline/Criticism A. This is followed by Discipline/Criticism C, which also sits more or less securely upon Discipline/Criticism B. Yet, the next box, Discipline/Criticism D, does not rest upon the foundation of Discipline/Criticism A. As the dotted line demonstrates, it barely touches the side of Discipline/Criticism A. Worst of all is Disciplines/Criticism E which, the dotted line shows, does not touch the foundation of either Discipline/Criticism A or Discipline/Criticism B. Many of the conclusions of the new quest in NTTC reflect a similar lack of foundational basis. Furthermore, the faulty and weak presuppositions of one discipline are knowingly or unknowingly carried over and uncritically accepted by the next. Even though the disciplines appear to intersect, not every conclusion is equally valid. The following section will briefly examine the inherent weakness of the criticisms that are often intermingled with NTTC and the unsteady conclusions that follow.

The proponents of the new approach rely heavily on some of the unresolved conclusions of source, form, and redaction criticisms in NT studies to prove their thesis. Each of these disciplines has provided valuable helps in the understanding of the NT text but not without some major qualifications and warnings. As Grant Osborne notes regarding form, tradition, redaction, and narrative (literary) criticism, "Each discipline presupposes the validity of and builds upon its predecessor, yet each also has originated partly because of inherent weaknesses in the preceding approaches."[101] Regarding redaction criticism specifically, Osborne observes "the discipline is prone to highly speculative theories because the conclusions depend entirely upon how one chooses and organizes the data. If the search is not complete and if the changes are not studied carefully, virtually opposite theories can be promulgated."[102] Redaction criticism and the presumed Markan priority are both major tools in the handling of the text. This is not to say these are not valid hypotheses, but just that, at the end of the day, these are still hypotheses. Apparently, the Markan priority hypothesis is taken for granted in the evaluation of variants without leaving room for other hypotheses that may reflect the data differently or even more accurately. Arthur Bellinzoni rightly cautions, "Since Markan priority is an assumption of so much of the research of the last century, many of the conclusions of that research would have to be redrawn and much of the literature rewritten if the consensus of scholarship were suddenly to shift."[103] Some eighty-five years ago, James Ropes, who advocated that Luke used Mark as a source and not a hypothetical Q source to construct his gospel, also warned against the uncritical acceptance of Synoptic criticism:

> That Mark, in substantially its present form, was drawn on by Matthew and Luke for the greater part of their narrative of events and incidents, can be regarded as an achieved result of Synoptic criticism, and can be used without scruple as the basis of modern study. But it is surprising, and a little mortifying to scholarship, to have to admit that this fundamental conclusion is the only assured result of the vast amount of incessant labour which has been expended on the so-called Synoptic Problem in the whole of the past hundred years and more.[104]

---

101. Osborne, "Redaction Criticism," 199.

102. Osborne, "redaction criticism," 204. Another important weakness to note is "the exceptions to the generalization or the agreements of Matthew and Luke against Mark in sections of triple tradition" (Thomas, "redaction criticism," 235).

103. Bellinzoni, *Two-Source Hypothesis*, 9.

104. Ropes, *Synoptic Gospels*, 92.

The most harmful aspect of this dependence and interaction with other critical disciplines is the sharing of the inherent historical skepticism regarding the text. Many of the conclusions of source, form, and redaction criticisms challenge the historicity of the biblical narratives. Richard Longenecker warns regarding the use of form criticism that "*Formgeschichte* has performed a service in reminding us of the kerygmatic nature of the New Testament materials, though we may question its extremely negative attitude toward questions of historical reliability."[105] Robert Stein's remark is also typical of some of the practitioners of the criticisms: "It would appear that materials in a Gospel that reflect an Evangelist's unique theological emphasis are probably less authentic or historical, especially if they appear only in his unique material (M in Matthew and L in Luke) or in his redactional work (summaries, explanatory clauses, seams, etc.)."[106] In the new quest in NTTC, such historical skepticisms are not limited to the Synoptic Gospels, (which are conducive to comparisons and speculations regarding redaction), but are also extended to the Gospel of John. Ehrman's remark regarding the authenticity of John 1:1–18 and chapter 21 is just one such example:

> What does that do for the textual critic who wants to reconstruct the "original" text? Which original is being constructed? All our Greek manuscripts contain the passages in question. So does the textual critic reconstruct as the original text the form of the Gospel that originally contained them? But shouldn't we consider the "original" form to be the *earlier* version, which lacked them? And if one wants to reconstruct that earlier form, is it fair to stop there, with reconstructing, say, the first edition of John's Gospel? Why not go even further and try to reconstruct the *sources* that lie behind the Gospel, such as the signs sources and the discourse sources, or even the oral traditions that lie behind them.[107]

Such questions go beyond the domain of proper NTTC, as Wisse commented earlier, noting "The result is usually not scholarly gain but loss."[108] It appears the primary target of all such undertakings is the historicity of Jesus. In addressing the issue of the criteria for the methodology, Koester makes an incisive observation:

---

105. Longenecker, *Christology of Early Jewish Christianity*, 9.
106. Stein, *Studying the Synoptic Gospels*, 157.
107. Ehrman, *Misquoting Jesus*, 61–62 (emphasis original).
108. Wisse, "Textual Limits to Redactional Theory," 167–68.

> [T]he task of the historian and of the theologian are [sic] identical and cannot be divided into the free inquiry of the one and the dogmatic security of the other. The search for the decisive criterion for the distinction between true and false belief coincides with the historical quest for the essential characteristics of Early Christianity as such. . . . [T]he quest for the individuality and singularity of Christianity is inevitably bound up with the problem of the historical Jesus.[109]

Ultimately, all such speculations regarding sources and skepticisms regarding the historical Jesus, innate in other critical disciplines, are now utilized wholesale as standard guidelines and operating procedures in the new quest in NTTC.[110] To complicate matters, many of the principles and conclusions that might hypothetically characterize a redactor are carried over and applied indiscriminately to the copyist. Thus, the scribe is now awarded the status of a redactor with the prerogative to freely alter the NT text to fit his theological agenda.

As often pointed out by critics, most of Ehrman's critical arguments are based on speculation rather than textual evidence. The sources of these speculations are usually the conclusions or principles derived from other critical disciplines. Where data is lacking, Ehrman often appeals to historical-critical studies with their speculative and skeptical tendencies. One such example is found in his chapter on supposed anti-adoptionist alterations in the NT text by the proto-orthodox scribes. Ehrman posits,

> Most of the later adoptionists that we can actually identify—the Ebionites, Theodotus, Artemon—located the time of Jesus' adoption not at his resurrection, but at his baptism. One would naturally expect that unless they invented this notion themselves, traces of it should be found in earlier traditions. Such traces do in fact exist, and most of them, as we shall see, were changed in one way or another by various scribes during the history of their transmission.[111]

109. Koester, "ΓΝΩΜΑΙ ΔΙΑΦΟΡΟΙ," 281.

110. Compare in this regard the recent comment from Tommy Wasserman on the ETC blog under the discussion on "'First-Century Mark' SBL Panel": "[F]or me a high view of Scripture is a matter of personal belief. I have no intention of trying to prove that this or that textual variant is the original word of God. I would like to work as a text-critic as if God didn't exist, so to speak. On the other hand, I have a personal faith which certainly affects also my scholarship, and I try to be honest about that. I am certain that other people's belief or disbelief affects what they do too. I prefer not to be put in a box of privileged white male text-critics who just pretend to do real scholarship" (http://evangelicaltextualcriticism.blogspot.com/2019/11/first-century-mark-sbl-panel.html #comments).

111. Ehrman, *Orthodox Corruption of Scripture* (1993), 49.

Ehrman thus assumes later heresies have their source in earlier heresies, unidentified in church history but now identifiable through traces of scribal alterations. To make his case in the preceding paragraph, Ehrman discusses the disputed "bipartite christological creed" in Romans 1:3-4. He is not concerned with the role of the scribes but that of the redactor behind those verses. There is no discussion of variants but a form-critical analysis of those verses from the works of Johannes Weiss, Eduard Schweizer, Eta Linnemann, Heinrich Schlier, J. D. G. Dunn, and Klaus Wengst.[112] Ehrman concludes from his brief survey there must have been a belief predating the NT text that Christ was adopted as son after the resurrection.

Ehrman also appeals to Paul's speeches in Acts that supposedly point to Christ's attainment of sonship at the point of his resurrection. Again, he utilizes form-critical analysis of the Pauline speech in Acts 13 to conclude there must have been an earlier belief in Christ's resurrection-based adoption.[113] Anticipating the objection, based on form criticism, that the speeches are not necessarily historical but composed by Luke, Ehrman simply remarks in a footnote "the judgment concerning earlier materials in the speeches of Acts holds true even though the speeches themselves are by and large Luke's own composition."[114] This statement is problematic because it implies Luke knowingly accepted and utilized sources that espoused an adoptionist Christology, which is contrary to any responsible examination of the Luke-Acts material. Furthermore, there is no textual evidence for any attempt by the scribes to harmonize the variants between Luke and Acts. Ehrman's reply to this is in two parts: first, Lucan writings exemplify many such "tensions" and "inconsistencies" that are difficult to explain but nevertheless are relevant to the discussion of the variants; and second, it is further evidence of scribal tampering rather than otherwise.[115] Such cavalier dismissal is unsatisfactory and unscientific.

Ehrman then turns his attention toward the true adoptionists—Ebionites, Theodotus, and Artemon—who considered Jesus's adoption to occur at his baptism. It would seem this would debunk Ehrman's case since they held to Jesus's baptism and not resurrection as the actual point of adoption—but such is not to be. He claims the baptism adoptionists must demonstrate similar earlier traces, such as those claimed by form critics regarding the resurrection

---

112. Ehrman, *Orthodox Corruption of Scripture* (1993), 99. It should be noted that Eta Linneman later repudiated all her earlier discussions and conclusions in favor of a traditional, conservative, evangelical position.

113. Ehrman, *Orthodox Corruption of Scripture* (1993), 49.

114. Ehrman, *Orthodox Corruption of Scripture* (1993), 100.

115. Ehrman, *Orthodox Corruption of Scripture* (1993), 64-67.

adoptionists. Ehrman thus takes the weak and inconclusive arguments of form criticism and applies them to NTTC. He approaches passages that have not been discussed regarding any purported preliterary source and marshals a case for scribal alteration that *might* have been motivated by a theological agenda. According to Ehrman, whereas the preliterary source argument assumes a source predating the edited NT text, the scribal alteration theory thus increases the presumed greater legitimacy and originality that favors the unaltered text. Since the preliterary source theory stands on shaky ground, Ehrman's application of its conclusions to his proto-orthodox scribal alteration theory also fails to stand. The inconsistencies in intermingling the different criticisms can be seen in the table below:

Resurrection Adoptionists	Baptism Adoptionists
Discipline being applied: Form-criticism	*Discipline being applied*: Textual criticism
Applied by: Author/Redactor(s)	*Applied by*: Scribe(s)
Group in question: Adoptionists who believed Jesus was adopted after the resurrection.	*Group in question*: Adoptionists who believed Jesus was adopted at baptism.
Legitimizing principle: Preliterary sources carry greater weight than the NT text as they predate the latter.	*Legitimizing principle*: Since there were preliterary sources that antedate the NT text and hence legitimize the presence of other strands of equal weight in early Christianity, there could also be scribal alterations that evidence the presence of other strands of equal weight in early Christianity.
Progression of study: From early Christianity toward the era of christological controversy.	*Progression of Study*: From the era of christological controversy to early Christianity. (In essence, it is a reversal of the lefthand column.)

Many of Ehrman's text-critical arguments are based on similar weak, insufficient, and contradictory conclusions of other critical disciplines and fail to stand under scrutiny. Similar tendencies are also demonstrated by Parker and Epp in their treatment of the NT text. The proponents of the new approach in NTTC should base their evidence on much more solid research—but they don't, nor do they seem to feel any need to do so. This demonstrates the four major premises often employed by the proponents of the new trend in NTTC are based on a shaky foundation and must be abandoned.

Finally, the proponents of the new trend in NTTC claim under their thesis the NT text is rendered an ordinary writing devoid of any claim of being inerrant. The following section will attempt to explain and rebut common misconceptions regarding the relationship of NTTC and inerrancy.

THE CHALLENGE TO THE INERRANCY OF THE NT TEXT

The proponents of the new approach in NTTC balk at any suggestion of inerrancy of the NT text. Ehrman characteristically asks,

> [H]ow does it help us to say that the Bible is the inerrant word of God if in fact we don't have the words that God inerrantly inspired, but only the words copied by the scribes—sometimes correctly but sometimes (many times!) incorrectly? What good is it to say that the autographs (i.e., the originals) were inspired? We don't *have* the originals! We have only error-ridden copies, and the vast majority of these are centuries removed from the originals and different from them, evidently, in thousands of ways.[116]

Even though such explicit statements against inerrancy are not expressed by the other proponents of the new movement, they share similar views. This derision for the doctrine of inerrancy is nothing novel. It began as the byproduct of the higher-critical conclusions through European universities in the nineteenth century. In the early decades of the twentieth century, it was the battleground of the fundamentalist-modernist struggle over the uniqueness and historicity of the Bible. The post-World War II neoevangelical movement of the late 1940s also questioned the limits of inerrancy. Finally, from the 1960s onward began what J. I. Packer called the "Thirty Years' War" over the nature of revelation.[117] Many rebuttals were given by scholars through the years, but none as comprehensive as that in 1978 by the International Council on Biblical Inerrancy in Chicago. Concerned over the erosion of biblical authority and accuracy, a group of scholars drafted nineteen articles on inerrancy along with a preamble and an official commentary. It was signed by nearly 300 scholars from many evangelical persuasions in the United States, with great implications in the years following.[118] Here it will suffice to note this statement has been instrumental in shaping the understanding of biblical inerrancy.

116. Ehrman, *Misquoting Jesus*, 7 (emphasis original).

117. Packer, "Thirty Years' War," 25–44.

118. It is credited as being instrumental in turning around several evangelical entities. One major example is the conservative resurgence in the Southern Baptist Convention.

Regrettably, no statement of faith or confession has a permanent impact.[119] As Norman Geisler writes in his recent defense of inerrancy, "A new generation has arisen that knows not Lindsell, Henry, Archer, Schaeffer, Gerstner, Nicole, or Boice—all of whom have passed on to their reward— and once again inerrancy is being challenged."[120] Several publications, even from within evangelical circles, have challenged the traditional definition of inerrancy. These include Peter Enns' *Inspiration and Incarnation: Evangelicals and the Problem of the Old Testament*,[121] Andrew Thomson Blake McGowan's *The Divine Authenticity of Scripture: Retrieving an Evangelical Heritage*,[122] and Kenton L. Sparks's *God's Word in Human Words: An Evangelical Appropriation of Critical Biblical Scholarship*.[123]

There is yet another contender in the ring against biblical inerrancy. It is not armed with theological or epistemological arguments but with transmissional history and variant choice. Textual criticism—long considered to be a friend of inerrancy and the inerrantists' best friend—is now a foe. This section will discuss the changes in the understanding of the relationship between NTTC and inerrancy, and the rebuttals that have followed.

Traditional relationship between Inerrancy and NTTC

Until recently, inerrancy justified the need for textual criticism and not vice versa. In an editorial in *Christianity Today* in 2002, J. I. Packer was asked, "How can I reconcile my belief in the inerrancy of Scripture with comments in Bible translations that state that a particular verse is not 'in better manuscripts'?" He answered,

> Inerrantists should welcome the work of textual scholars, who are forever trying to eliminate the inauthentic and give us exactly what the biblical writers wrote, neither more nor less. Text criticism serves inerrancy; they are friends. Inerrancy treasures the meaning of each writer's words, while text criticism checks

---

119. The reason for this shift, notes John D. Woodbridge, is "during the past forty years an influential historiography has emerged arguing that biblical inerrancy is a doctrinal innovation—the provenance of which is American fundamentalism, itself portrayed as a doctrinally innovative movement and thus suspect" (Woodbridge, "Evangelical Self-Identity," 107–8).

120. Geisler and Roach, *Defending Inerrancy*, 23. Notably, Geisler himself, as a leading defender of inerrancy, has now (2019) also "passed on to his reward." Similar issues have been taken up in MacArthur, *Inerrant Word*.

121. Enns, *Inspiration and Incarnation*.

122. McGowan, *Divine Authenticity of Scripture*.

123. Sparks, *God's Word in Human Words*.

that we have each writer's words pure and intact. Both these wisdoms are needed if we are to benefit fully from the written Word of God.[124]

This understanding was also clearly articulated in Article X of the 1978 *Chicago Statement on Biblical Inerrancy*,

> We affirm that inspiration, strictly speaking, applies only to the autographic text of Scripture, which in the providence of God can be ascertained from available manuscripts with great accuracy. We further affirm that copies and translations of Scripture are the Word of God to the extent that they faithfully represent the original.
>
> We deny that any essential element of the Christian faith is affected by the absence of the autographs. We further deny that this absence renders the assertion of Biblical inerrancy invalid or irrelevant.[125]

Several papers presented at that 1978 conference reiterated the importance of textual criticism, but subjected it to the primacy of inerrancy. Paul D. Feinberg defends inerrancy in relation to the concept of the original text by stating, "When all the facts are known, the Scriptures in their original autographs and properly interpreted will be shown to be wholly true in everything that they affirm, whether that has to do with doctrine or morality or with the social, physical, or life sciences."[126] Lack of the original autographs is not deemed a significant issue since the original text is presumed to exist somewhere among the multitude of manuscripts.[127] In other words, the text appearing among the nonautographical manuscripts continues to hold the same authority as the now-absent autographical manuscripts.[128]

---

124. Packer, "Text Criticism and Inerrancy," 102.

125. For the above definition see "Appendix" in Geisler, *Inerrancy*, 496.

126. Feinberg, "Meaning of Inerrancy," 294.

127. Harris, *Inspiration and Canonicity of the Bible*, 88–89. He writes, "Reflection will show that the doctrine of verbal inspiration is worthwhile even though the originals have perished.... Suppose we wish to measure the length of a certain pencil. With a tape measure we measure it at 6 1/2 inches.... Careful measurement with a steel scale under laboratory conditions reveals it to be 6.577 inches.... Not satisfied still, we send the pencil to Washington, where master gauges indicate a length of 6.5774 inches. The master gauges themselves are checked against the standard United States yard marked on a platinum bar preserved in Washington... [S]uppose... a clever criminal had run off with the platinum bar and melted it down.... What difference would this make to us? Very little.... These approximate measures derive their value from their being dependent on more accurate gauges. But even the approximate has tremendous value if it has had a true standard behind it."

128. Bahnsen, "Inerrancy of the Autographa," 159. Bahnsen gives some pertinent

It was also understood the extant manuscripts are not exempt from errors and God did not obligate himself to protect the copies. As Moisés Silva rhetorically asks,

> If an enemy of Christianity took it in hand to copy a biblical book, must God prevent him from distorting the material? More to the point: did our Lord ever promise that any fool who wished to copy some portion of Scripture would automatically be kept from error? Dare a modern printer for that matter, forego proofreading when producing copies of the Bible?[129]

Furthermore, text-critics of yesteryear readily and repeatedly affirmed the usefulness of NTTC involved only a very minute portion of the text, since that text stood virtually strong in nearly all variant units. Frederick Kenyon's oft-repeated statement is a good representation: "The Christian can take the whole Bible in his hand and say without fear or hesitation that he holds in it the true Word of God, handed down without essential loss from generation to generation, throughout the centuries."[130] So also, A. T. Robertson declares, "The real conflict in the textual criticism of the New Testament is concerning this thousandth part of the entire text"[131]—repeating the heavily overstated claim of Westcott and Hort, but essentially on the right track. It was also understood that, overall, the Bible would largely remain the same even if all the possible variants were substituted.[132] In essence, the faith of a believer was in no way threatened by applying text-critical principles to the NT text.

Major evangelical systematic theologies through the years also have maintained the same understanding while advocating the responsible use of textual criticism. Millard Erickson writes, "The doctrine of inerrancy applies in the strict sense only to the originals, but in a derivative sense to copies and translations, that is, to the extent that they reflect the original."[133] Wayne Grudem also notes the presuppositional theological basis for

---

biblical examples in which later copies were cited as being of equal authority with the autograph: "And keep the charge of the Lord . . ., as it is written in the Law of Moses" (1 Kgs 2:3); "These also are proverbs of Solomon which the men of Hezekiah king of Judah copied" (Prov 25:1); Jesus reading the copy of Isaiah (Luke 4); "Jesus answered them, 'Is it not written in your law?' (John 10:34)"; Timothy having known (copies of) the Holy Scriptures from his youth, etc. (2 Tim 3:15); "Bring the cloak that I left with Carpus at Troas when you come and the books, especially the parchments" (2 Tim 4:13).

129. Silva, "New Testament Use of the Old Testament," 147.
130. Kenyon, *Our Bible and the Ancient Manuscripts*, 23.
131. Robertson, *Introduction to the Textual Criticism*, 22.
132. Stuart, "Inerrancy and Textual Criticism," 98.
133. Erickson, *Christian Theology*, 265.

inerrancy, stating, "If we have mistakes in the copies (as we do), then these are only the *mistakes of men*. But if we have mistakes in the *original manuscripts*, then we are forced to say not only that men made mistakes, but that *God himself* made a mistake and spoke falsely. This we cannot do."[134] Paul Ellingworth remarks in view of this concept, "A group of Christians who believed that every word of the Bible was inerrant and/or infallible would give the highest priority to establishing what the exact wording of the Bible was."[135] In summary, under the traditional understanding, inerrancy calls for NTTC, but NTTC does not determine inerrancy. NTTC is necessary but is not in itself a threat to inerrancy.[136]

From friends to foes

Under the new approach, however, NTTC dismantles inerrancy. The major proponents discussed in previous chapters all share the same nonevangelical view regarding the integrity of the NT text. They basically agree with Ehrman's noted maxim, "The winners not only write the history, they also reproduce the texts."[137] Hence, the text-critic is no longer concerned with reaching the original text in its entirety. Seeming discrepancies in the textual traditions are not to be resolved so much as to be used as a "window" into the world of the early church and the issues they faced.[138] Thus, NTTC is no longer about an original text but about *many* original and fluid texts that developed over time to meet the needs of their individual communities. As Ehrman has claimed, "There are more differences among our manuscripts than there are words in the New Testament."[139] Consequently, for the proponents of the new trend in NTTC, inerrancy has become indefensible. As John Brogan deems it,

---

134. Grudem, *Systematic Theology*, 97 (emphasis original).

135. Ellingworth, "Theological Reflections," 122.

136. In a recent article, Timothy Mitchell affirms the "proposed definition of 'autographs,' as found in various inerrancy doctrinal statements, stands." By comparing Greco-Roman publications of the time, he clarifies the definition of "autographs" as "the completed authorial works which were released by the author for circulation and copying, not earlier draft versions or layers of composition" ("What are the NT Autographs?," 307). For a discussion of the interrelation between inerrancy and NTTC, also see Kruger, "Do We Have a Trustworthy Text?," 304–18.

137. Ehrman, *Orthodox Corruption of Scripture* (1993), 27.

138. Ehrman, "Text as Window."

139. Ehrman, *Misquoting Jesus*, 10.

> At best, the theological construct of an inerrant autograph is only a semantic chimera that defends an indefensible position. At worst, it is an intellectually dishonest escape from critical thinking.[140]

This statement captures well the current despair regarding the interrelation between NTTC and inerrancy among many evangelicals, especially noninerrantist evangelicals.

Two weak rebuttals

Rebuttals by evangelical scholars committed to inerrancy can be categorized under two basic forms: first, an appeal to divine preservation; and second, an appeal to responsible textual criticism. Both camps assume inerrancy will be safeguarded, provided their respective premises are upheld. In actuality, both miss the true foundation of inerrancy and place undue emphasis on textual criticism as the determining factor over inerrancy. The following is a brief discussion of the weakness of these two forms of rebuttals in maintaining the traditional relationship between inerrancy and textual criticism.

The first form suggests divine preservation guarantees inerrancy. This rebuttal is built on the following presuppositional claims:

a. The original autographs were inerrant.

b. The original autographs are no longer extant.

c. God in his providence has preserved the original text among the extant copies.

d. Textual criticism can establish the preserved text and safeguard inerrancy.

The first claim is theological and the second is factual, but the third and fourth claims are problematic, as Ehrman asserted in his master's thesis,

> Any claim that God preserved the text of the New Testament intact, giving His church actual, not theoretical, possession of it, must mean one of three things—either 1) God preserved it in all the extant manuscripts so that none of them contain any textual corruptions, or 2) He preserved it in a group of manuscripts, none of which contain any corruptions, or 3) He preserved it in a solitary manuscript which alone contains no corruptions.[141]

---

140. Brogan, "Can I Have Your Autograph?," 109. For a survey of the different views on the matter, see Bovell, "Inerrancy," 91–106.

141. Ehrman, "New Testament Textual Criticism," 44.

Ehrman is accurate in drawing the above conclusions. The idea of precise textual preservation does not have any scriptural or historical backing and creates more problems than solutions.[142]

As a prime example, consider Wilbur Pickering's view that God "preserved the Text though a normal process of transmission, done by careful people, such that we can identify the original wording on the basis of the consensus of the independent, reliable, witnesses (determined empirically)."[143] Pickering's claim is not much different than the three postulates mentioned by Ehrman, since it equally lacks any scriptural or historical data beyond the mere existence of manuscripts from which a reasonable textual consensus could be constructed. In his article "Inspiration, Preservation, and New Testament Textual Criticism," Wallace rightly chides those who argue that "inspiration and preservation are intrinsically linked to one another. . . . That is to say, the doctrine of verbal-plenary inspiration necessitates the doctrine of providential preservation."[144] Just because God providentially preserved the original writers from any errors does not necessitate God also providentially preserved the copied text of the NT. The mere existence of variants in all the extant manuscripts proves that. In the end, any absolute claims of divine providence or preservation over the transmissional process create more theological obstacles than solutions.

The second form suggests responsible textual criticism in and of itself will lead to inerrancy. This rebuttal is built on the following claims:[145]

142. For a more balanced perspective on the matter of preservation in conjunction with responsible textual criticism, see Robinson, "Absent from the Handbooks?"

143. Pickering, *Identity of the New Testament Text*, 121. This comment is no longer present in his updated 4th edition of 2014, although he does say (4th ed., 101n1): "I really do believe that God has preserved the original wording to our day, and that we can know what it is on the basis of a defensible procedure"; cf. also 101n7, which gives his added theological emphasis to "preservation": "God and Satan exist, and both [!] have been involved in the transmission of the NT text." Further, the authorship summary on Amazon.com declares, "This includes the position that the *precise* original wording has been preserved to our day and that we can know what it is. . . . For some time Dr. Pickering has felt that . . . surely God would have preserved the original wording. . . . [H]e has concluded that God used a certain line of transmission to preserve that wording. . . . That archetypal form has been empirically, objectively identified by a wide comparison of family representatives, and it is indeed error free" https://www.amazon.com/Greek-New-Testament-According-Family/dp/0989827372; emphasis added). Also from his essay "In Defense of the Objective Authority of the Sacred Text," he says: "Given my presuppositions, I consider that I have good reason for declaring the divine preservation of the precise original wording of the New Testament Text, to this day" (4, 6).

144. Wallace, "Inspiration, Preservation, and New Testament Textual Criticism," 22.

145. See Wallace, "Gospel According to Bart," 327–49; Wallace, "Challenges in New Testament Textual Criticism," 79–100; Komoszewski et al., *Reinventing Jesus*; Köstenberger and Kruger, *Heresy of Orthodoxy*.

a. More manuscripts are available for the NT than any other ancient text.[146]
b. The majority of the variants are inconsequential.
c. The oldest manuscripts must be the best preserved and are preferred as being closest to the time of the autograph.
d. Textual criticism can generally reach the original text and safeguard inerrancy.

Although the four claims mentioned above have some merit, they too fail to stand against the new approach. Interestingly, the new approach agrees with the first two claims. Ehrman repeatedly affirms in his written works and debates the plethora of NT manuscripts and the inconsequentiality of most variants. He does take issue, however, with the third and fourth claims. His reason for that is fourfold: first, the original autographs are no longer extant; second, most of the variants entered very early in the history of transmission, thus corrupting the manuscript tradition; third, some of the oldest extant manuscripts are filled with blatant errors; and fourth, there is no guarantee the original autograph text itself did not contain errors.

The first two contentions by Ehrman can be easily answered. The loss of the autographs is not as significant as it may seem, because the issue regards not an autographic codex, but the autographic text, which remains extant among the multitude of NT manuscripts. Greg Bahnsen clarified years ago, "The message conveyed by the words of the autographa, and not the physical page on which we find printing, is the strict object of inspiration."[147] As to the matter of the early entrance of variants and total or even massive corruption of the manuscript tradition, this premise is farfetched. Although text-critics agree most sensible variants entered the NT manuscripts before the second century, there is much debate over whether the manuscript tradition is indeed hopelessly corrupt, as discussed earlier in this chapter. To the claim the papyri reflect an unstable stage of transmission, several studies have shown the papyri were not as chaotic as once assumed, as witnessed in the previously mentioned study by Maurice A. Robinson regarding an approximate 90 percent or greater stability level among the papyri.[148]

The third contention of Ehrman regarding corruption in some of the oldest extant manuscripts makes their reliability and authority based on

---

146. Jacob W. Peterson and James B. Prothro have each confronted the weakness of this premise, the former in "Math Myths," 48–69, the latter in "Myths about Classical Literature," 70–89.

147. Bahnsen, "Inerrancy of the Autographa," 161.

148. Robinson, "Integrity of the Early New Testament Text."

mere age hard to defend in places. One case in point that was noted earlier is the Alexandrian text addition to Matthew 27:49. At the conclusion of verse 49, the major Uncial manuscripts (ℵ B C L), along with a number of minuscule manuscripts, include the words "another one, having taken the spear, pierced his side, and water and blood came out."[149] According to these highly regarded manuscripts, the piercing occurred before Jesus's death. Obviously, this is a problem that appears in the oldest extant manuscripts.

As to the fourth contention regarding errors in the original text itself, no amount of textual criticism can affirm or deny that claim. Ehrman goes far beyond the scope of legitimate NTTC and utilizes historical-critical conclusions that remove any hope of textual integrity. As a result, both the first and the second rebuttals fail to stand in light of the new approach's argument.

The proper domain of NTTC

The place to begin is to remove textual criticism from the position of judge or arbiter over the doctrine of biblical inerrancy. It is imperative to understand the true source of inerrancy is not NTTC, but inspiration. According to Erickson, "[Inerrancy] is a corollary of the doctrine of full inspiration of the Bible. The view of the Bible held and taught by the writers of Scripture implies the full truthfulness of the Bible."[150] So also, Bahnsen asserts,

> It is not a doctrine derived from empirical investigation of certain written texts; it is a theological commitment rooted in the teaching of the Word of God itself. The nature of God (who is truth Himself) and the nature of the biblical books (as the very words of God) require that we view the original manuscripts, produced under the superintendence of the Holy Spirit of truth, as wholly true and without error.[151]

The key is the doctrine of inerrancy is rooted in Scripture and not in the discipline of textual criticism. Paul Feinberg lists five scriptural phenomena that undergird inerrancy:[152]

    a. The biblical teaching on inspiration

    b. The biblical teaching concerning the accreditation of God's message and messengers

---

149. Shah, "Alexandrian Presumption of Authenticity," 92–99.
150. Erickson, *Christian Theology*, 255.
151. Bahnsen, "Inerrancy of the Autographa," 189.
152. Feinberg, "Meaning of Inerrancy," 276–87.

  c. The Bible's teaching concerning its own authority

  d. The way in which Scripture is used by Scripture

  e. The biblical teaching concerning the character of God

  As the list demonstrates, text-critical matters do not depend on biblical inerrancy. To begin with, inerrancy as a theological construct is not on trial. Next, a loss of text does not negate inerrancy any more than the loss of an arm or a leg negates the personhood of any individual. It only places the burden on text-critics to research and retrieve the original text. It is a challenge to reevaluate text-critical methodologies and histories of transmission, which should always be up for debate. Variants can indeed serve as a window to the history of the church but must be utilized cautiously, and should be carefully sifted when attempting to establish the original NT text. As to the hypothetical question of the loss of some inspired portion of the NT text, it is safe to assume, in light of the multitude of manuscripts and the inconsequentiality of the majority of variants, any presumed extensive loss is highly unlikely. Conjectural emendation may be necessary in other historical documents but it fails to be convincing for the vast NT manuscript tradition. Based on the quantity of evidence and the technological advances in recent years, it seems well-nigh impossible any part of the inspired text would be lost forever from every known copy, particularly as more and more data to the contrary tends to accumulate.

CONCLUSION

Not every premise inherent in the new movement in NTTC has been addressed in this section. The main objective has been to demonstrate the weaknesses in the major claims of the new trends in NTTC. It is imperative such maverick theories be answered and put to the test. If left unchecked, the changing of the goalpost of NTTC will remove every possibility of retrieving the original text of the NT. Without an authoritative text, the door is left open to create *any* text promoting *any* system of beliefs that might suit the individual or group.

9

Conclusion

National Geographic recently ran a cover story titled, "Bible Hunters: Scholars, Schemers, and the Search for Ancient Texts." In a magazine long known for bringing exciting stories of exploration and new discoveries to curious minds, one would have expected an article highlighting the latest manuscript finds and prospects of research. Instead, the article reads like an investigative report with some sprinklings of relevant information. Robert Draper, the author, seeks to expose those evangelicals who will do whatever it takes to procure sacred texts. Draper is far from neutral on the matter of the original text, as can be noted in his following remark,

> Assuming for the moment that the God of the Bible actually exists and that he somehow spoke to the authors of the ancient biblical documents—do we have now what they wrote then? After all, none of their original writings, what scholars call the autographs, have been found. Their words survive only because they were hand copied countless times until the invention of the printing press in the fifteenth century. And even conservative scholars admit that no two copies are exactly alike.[1]

Although his statement relates to both the text of the OT and the NT, it accurately reflects the popular understanding in the contemporary culture

---

1. Draper, "Bible Hunters," 74. Note that the first *Greek* editions of the NT appeared in the *sixteenth* century, while Draper's mention of the fifteenth century would apply only to Gutenberg's printing of the Latin Vulgate.

regarding the original text of the NT. In a world in which objective truth is scorned and conspiracy theories are celebrated, there is no place for claiming a basically inerrant or infallible original among the currently available editions of the Greek NT.

Unfortunately, the same sentiment has been growing in the academic world for some time. This study has documented this trend among NTTC scholars who have deemed it far more profitable to focus upon the motivation of the scribes in creating particular variants and the significance of the text thus created for the community in which it was used, rather than to seek after an elusive and even an illusive original text. It is now stated as a matter of fact there is no going back to the traditional goal of NTTC. Obviously, this has devastating consequences for the conservative/evangelical academic study of the NT.

In a recent article titled, "Accidental Publication, Unfinished Texts and the Traditional Goals of New Testament Textual Criticism," author Matthew Larsen baldly declared, "Recovering the 'original text' has been challenged, and textual critics have defenestrated the idea of recovering the original text of the New Testament as an obtainable goal of New Testament textual criticism."[2] This matter-of-fact statement is the new normal under this way of thinking. Larsen is not remotely interested in the prospect or the possibility of retrieving the original text of the NT. He further argues, in a manner similar to the *National Geographic* article, the modern obsession with the original text is a by-product of the printing press since "publication was not a clean, linear process in the ancient world."[3] He surveys ancient Jewish, Greek, Roman, and early Christian writings to prove textual unfinishedness, accidental publications, postpublication revisions, and multiple authorized versions of the same work were far more commonplace than assumed. He applies those categories to the gospels to conclude

> it would be anachronistic to categorize Matthew as creating a separate piece of literature from Mark, especially since Matthew's alterations of Mark, from the point of view of ancient writing practices, are fairly minor. Read in this way, it makes more sense to categorize what we are now calling the Gospel of Matthew as a continuation of the same mushrooming textual tradition of the gospel. . . . What we are calling the Gospel of

2. Larsen, "Accidental Publication," 364.
3. Larsen, "Accidental Publication," 364. Timothy Mitchell counters Larsen's claim by demonstrating through a survey of Greco-Roman literary world that "[t]he text was fluid in some respects . . . but the authors (in this case Martial, Quintilian, Galen, and Octavius) clearly distinguished between these altered texts and their initially released versions" (Mitchell, "Myths about Autographs," 39).

Matthew would be a vertical revision of an unfinished textual tradition, and the various endings of the Gospel of Mark would be a horizontal revision.[4]

What Larsen therefore proposes in his particular approach to Markan priority is a presumption that certain aspects of higher criticism (form, source, and redaction) that already represent a hypothesized assumption on the part of (generally) more liberal critics should then force conclusions in regard to lower (textual) criticism. Previously those two disciplines were kept well-separated, clearly recognizing that establishment of the base or autographic text was prerequisite to any application of higher critical views. Larsen's present reversal of the critical order amounts to a blurring of the lines between form, source, redaction, and textual criticism. This procedure is disingenuous at best and dangerous at worst, since such is *totally* predicated on the current assumption there is *no* authorial, original, or final text, and thus the critics can do as they please in such matters.[5]

Such examples will only continue to abound, and they are a result of the changing goalpost in NTTC.[6] To reemphasize the principle stated at the beginning of this dissertation: without a generally settled original text, there can be no settled biblical theology, and this in turn will result in an unsettled Christian faith and practice.[7] To counter this trend, the traditional quest of the original text of the NT should be reclaimed and emphasized, requiring fresh approaches toward the issues at hand.[8]

---

4. Larsen, "Accidental Publication," 378.

5. This paragraph relates to a correspondence-based discussion with Maurice A. Robinson (February 2019) who noted specifically that "Larsen's position regarding the authorship, content, and transmission of the gospel documents presumes not only Markan priority, but a higher-critical rather than a text-critical view."

6. A recent example is the controversy that erupted on the Evangelical Textual Criticism blogsite in regard to several guest posts by Elizabeth Schrader, whose "text-critical" theory in John 11 involved the "replacement" of Mary with Martha at a time *preceding* the supposed *Ausgangstext*—a higher-critical theory based on nothing more substantial than a scattering of singular readings found among a few early and many late mss. Most surprising was the rush of many contemporary textual critics actually to *defend* her thesis as being within the legitimate bounds of NTTC, even while many other comments were systematically deleted for calling that hypothesis into question on proper theological and traditional evangelical grounds. See http://evangelicaltextualcriticism.blogspot.com/2019/08/is-martha-interpolation-into-johns.html and http://evangelicaltextualcriticism.blogspot.com/2019/09/is-martha-interpolation-into-johns_7.html, as well as Schrader, "Was Martha of Bethany Added?," 360–92.

7. See chapter 1, pages 2, 10–11.

8. In a recent article, Peter Williams proposed a clearer terminology of the key terms in NTTC, rolling the burden of proof on those who challenge the integrity of the NT text. Regarding the former, he suggested the terms "Bible," "original," and "text"

The battle for the traditional evangelical view of Scripture has to be fought anew in every generation, facing constantly changing forms of opposition. It is vital for those in Christian academia who hold to the importance of the original text of the NT to provide scholarly and effective responses, reaffirming the nature and authority of the Scriptures. A major step toward this is to reaffirm the traditional goal of the NTTC to seek the original text. Furthermore, NTTC should be taught and emphasized as a major part of a seminary's curriculum so future pastors and teachers may accurately handle text-critical issues for their personal understanding and the benefit of their congregations. It is also imperative to seek and share accurate information regarding NT text-critical matters, especially by those who are interested in apologetics. More research in text-critical matters should be encouraged and funded by those who believe in the importance of the Scriptures for daily life and practice. Ultimately, it is incumbent upon those who hold to a high view of Scripture to find clearer and more relevant ways to emphasize the importance of the original text of the NT and to reaffirm the traditional goal of NTTC.

---

should be abandoned since they place emphasis on the physical document rather than the content of a work. A document may not be extant, but its content may be. As to the latter, he declares "the presumption that we have the authorial wording until evidence arises to the contrary seems a more reasonable position than to refuse to believe that we have the authorial wording until an impossibly high level of proof be obtained that we do." This serves as just one example of the fresh approaches needed in answering the current challenges to the authority of NT writings. Williams thus draws a distinction between "text on a document" and the "text [= content] of a work" (Williams, "Ehrman's Equivocation," 398, 401–2).

Bibliography

Ackroyd, Peter R., and Christopher Francis Evans, eds. *From the Beginnings to Jerome.* Vol. 1 of *The Cambridge History of the Bible.* 3 vols. Cambridge: Cambridge University Press, 1970.
Akin, Daniel L., and Thomas W. Hudgins, eds. *Getting into the Text: New Testament Essays in Honor of David Alan Black.* Eugene, OR: Pickwick, 2017.
Aland, Barbara. "Der textkritische und textgeschichtliche Nutzen früher Papyri, demonstriert am Johannesevangelium." In *Recent Developments in Textual Criticism: New Testament, Other Early Christian and Jewish Literature,* edited by Wim Weren and Dietrich-Alex Koch, 19–38. Studies in Theology and Religion 8. Assen, The Netherlands: Royal Van Gorcum, 2003.
———. "Die Rezeption des neutestamentlichen Textes in den ersten Jahrhunderten." In *The New Testament in Early Christianity: La Réception des Écrits Néotestamentaires dans le Christianisme Primitif,* edited by Jean-Marie Sevrin, 5–21. Bibliotheca Ephemeridum Theologicarum Lovaniensium 86. Leuven: Leuven University Press, 1989.
———. "Kriterien zur Beurteilung kleinerer Papyrusfragmente des Neuen Testaments." In *New Testament Textual Criticism and Exegesis: Festschrift J. Delobel,* edited by Adelbert Denaux, 1–13. Bibliotheca Ephemeridum Theologicarum Lovaniensium 161. Leuven: Leuven University Press, 2002.
———. "New Testament Textual Research, its Methods and its Goals." In *Translating the New Testament: Text, Translation, Theology,* edited by Stanley E. Porter and Mark Boda, 13–26. McMaster New Testament Studies. Grand Rapids: Eerdmans, 2009.
———. "The Significance of the Chester Beatty Papyri in Early Church History." In *The Earliest Gospels: The Origins and Transmission of the Earliest Christian Gospels—The Contribution of the Chester Beatty Gospel Codex P45,* edited by Charles Horton, 108–21. Journal for the Study of the New Testament Supplement Series 258. London: T. & T. Clark, 2004.
Aland, Barbara, and Joël Delobel, eds. *New Testament Textual Criticism, Exegesis, and Early Church History: A Discussion of Methods.* Kampen, The Netherlands: Pharos, 1994.
Aland, Barbara, and Klaus Wachtel. "The Greek Minuscule Manuscripts of the New Testament." In *The Text of the New Testament in Contemporary Research: Essays on the Status Quaestionis,* edited by Bart D. Ehrman and Michael W. Holmes, 43–60. Studies and Documents 46. Grand Rapids: Eerdmans, 1995.

Aland, Barbara, et al., eds. *Novum Testamentum Graecum Editio Critica Maior Bd. II The Letters of Peter*. Stuttgart: Deutsche Bibelgesellschaft, 2000.

Aland, Kurt. "Der neue 'Standard Text' in seinem Verhältnis zu den frühen Papyri und Majuskeln." In *New Testament Textual Criticism: Its Significance for Exegesis: Essays in Honour of Bruce M. Metzger*, edited by Eldon J. Epp and Gordon D. Fee, 257–75. Oxford: Oxford University Press, 1981.

———. *The Problem of the New Testament Canon*. Contemporary Studies in Theology 2. London: Mowbray, 1962.

Aland, Kurt, and Barbara Aland. *The Text of the New Testament: An Introduction to the Critical Editions and to the Theory and Practice of Modern Textual Criticism*. Translated by Erroll F. Rhodes. 2nd rev. and enl. ed. Grand Rapids: Eerdmans, 1989.

Alexanderson, Bengt. *Problems in the New Testament: Old Manuscripts and Papyri, the New Genealogical Method (CBGM) and the Editio Critica Maior (ECM)*. Acta, Regiae Societatis Scientiarum et Litterarum Gothoburgensis, Humaniora 48. Gothenburg, Sweden: Kungl. Vetenskaps- och Vitterhets-Samhället, 2014.

Amphoux, Christian-Bernard, and J. Keith Elliott, eds. *The New Testament Text in Early Christianity: Proceedings of the Lille Colloquium, July 2000*. Histoire du texte biblique 6. Lausanne: Zèbre, 2003.

Anderson, Amy S., and Wendy Widder. *Textual Criticism of the Bible*. Edited by Douglas Mangum. Rev. ed. Lexham Methods Series 1. Bellingham, WA: Lexham, 2018.

Bahnsen, Greg L. "The Inerrancy of the Autographa." In *Inerrancy*, edited by Norman Geisler, 151–93. Grand Rapids: Zondervan, 1980.

Baigent, Michael, and Richard Leigh. *The Dead Sea Scrolls Deception*. New York: Touchstone, 1991.

Baigent, Michael, et al. *Holy Blood, Holy Grail*. New York: Doubleday, 1982.

Bartelt, Andrew H., et al., eds. *The Press of the Text: Biblical Studies in Honor of James W. Voelz*. Eugene, OR: Pickwick, 2017.

Bauer, Walter. *Orthodoxy and Heresy in Earliest Christianity*. Edited by Gerhard Krodel and Robert Kraft. Translated by Robert Kraft. Philadelphia: Fortress, 1971.

———. *Rechtgläubigkeit und Ketzerei im ältesten Christentum*. Tübingen: Mohr/Siebeck, 1934.

Baur, F. C. *Paul: The Apostle of Jesus Christ*. Vol. 1. 2 vols. London: Williams and Norgate, 1876.

Baur, Ferdinand Christian, and Allan Menzies. *The Church History of the First Three Centuries*. 3rd ed. 3 vols. London: Williams and Norgate, 1878.

Bebb, John Montfort. "The Evidence of the Early Versions and Patristic Quotations on the Text of the Books of the New Testament." In *Studia Biblica et Ecclesiastica II*, edited by Samuel Rolles Driver et al., 195–240. Oxford: Clarendon, 1890.

Becker, Eve-Marie, and Anders Runesson, eds. *Mark and Matthew I. Comparative Readings: Understanding the Earliest Gospels in Their First-Century Settings*. Wissenschaftliche Untersuchungen zum Neuen Testament 271. Tübingen: Mohr/Siebeck, 2011.

Bell, Lonnie D. *The Early Textual Transmission of John: Stability and Fluidity in its Second and Third Century Greek Manuscripts*. New Testament Tools, Studies, and Documents 54. Leiden: Brill, 2018.

Bellinzoni, Arthur J., ed. *The Two-Source Hypothesis: A Critical Appraisal*. Macon, GA: Mercer, 1985.

Billington, Mark, and Peter Streitenberger, eds. *Digging for the Truth: Collected Essays Regarding the Byzantine Text of the Greek New Testament: A Festschrift in Honor of Maurice A. Robinson*. Norden, Germany: FocusYourMission KG, 2014.

Binzler, Josef, et al., eds. *Neutestamentliche Aufsätze: Festschrift für Josef Schmid zum 70 Geburtstag*. Regensburg, Germany: Pustet, 1963.

Birdsall, J. Neville. "Current Trends and Present Tasks in New Testament Textual Criticism." *The Baptist Quarterly* 17.3 (1957) 109–14.

———. "The New Testament Text." In *The Cambridge History of the Bible, Vol. 1, From the Beginnings to Jerome*, edited by Peter R. Ackroyd and Christopher Francis, 308–77. 3 vols. Cambridge: Cambridge University Press, 1970.

———. "Review of *The Living Text of the Gospels*." *Journal of Theological Studies* 50.1 (1999) 275–88.

Birdsall, J. Neville, and Robert W. Thomson, eds. *Biblical and Patristic Studies in Memory of Robert Pierce Casey*. Freiburg: Herder, 1963.

Black, David Alan. *New Testament Textual Criticism: A Concise Guide*. Grand Rapids: Baker, 1994.

Black, David Alan, ed. *Rethinking New Testament Textual Criticism*. Grand Rapids: Baker Academic, 2002.

Black, David Alan, and David S. Dockery, eds. *New Testament Criticism and Interpretation*. Grand Rapids: Zondervan, 1991.

Blaski, Andrew. "Myths about Patristics: What the Church Fathers Thought about Textual Variation." In *Myths and Mistakes in New Testament Textual Criticism*, edited by Elijah Hixson and Peter J. Gurry, 228–52. Downers Grove, IL: IVP Academic, 2019.

Blomberg, Craig L. "Where Do We Start Studying Jesus?" In *Jesus Under Fire*, edited by Michael J. Wilkins and James Porter Moreland, 18–50. Grand Rapids: Zondervan, 1995.

Bock, Darrell L. *Breaking the Da Vinci Code: Answers to the Questions Everybody's Asking*. Nashville: Thomas Nelson, 2004.

———. *The Missing Gospels: Unearthing the Truth behind Alternative Christianities*. Nashville: Thomas Nelson, 2006.

Boismard, Marie-Émile. "Critique Textuelle et Citations Patristiques." *Revue Biblique* 57.3 (1950) 388–408.

———. "Lectio Brevior, Potior." *Revue Biblique* 58.2 (1951) 161–68.

Bovell, Carlos R. "Inerrancy: A Paradigm in Crisis." In *Interdisciplinary Perspectives on the Authority of Scripture: Historical, Biblical, and Theoretical Perspectives*, edited by Carlos R. Bovell, 91–106. Eugene, OR: Pickwick, 2011.

Bovell, Carlos R., ed. *Interdisciplinary Perspectives on the Authority of Scripture: Historical, Biblical, and Theoretical Perspectives*. Eugene, OR: Pickwick, 2011.

Bristol, Lyle O. "New Testament Textual Criticism in the Eighteenth Century." *Journal of Biblical Literature* 69.2 (1950) 101–12.

Brogan, John J. "Can I Have Your Autograph? Uses and Abuses of Textual Criticism in Formulating an Evangelical Doctrine of Scripture." In *Evangelicals & Scripture: Tradition, Authority and Hermeneutics*, edited by Dennis L. Okholm et al., 93–111. Wheaton Theology Conference Series. Downers Grove, IL: IVP Academic, 2004.

Brooks, James A. *The New Testament Text of Gregory of Nyssa*. New Testament in the Greek Fathers 2. Atlanta: Scholars, 1991.

Brown, Dan. *The Da Vinci Code*. New York: Anchor, 2003.

Brown, Peter. *The World of Late Antiquity: AD 150–750*. New York: Norton, 1989.
Burgon, John William. *The Causes of the Corruption of the Traditional Text of the Holy Gospels*. Edited by Edward Miller. 1896. Reprint. Collingswood, NJ: Dean Burgon Society, 1998.
Capes, David B., et al., eds. *Israel's God and Rebecca's Children—Christology and Community in Early Judaism and Christianity: Essays in Honor of Larry W. Hurtado and Alan F. Segal*. Waco, TX: Baylor University Press, 2007.
Carlson, Stephen C. "A Bias at the Heart of the Coherence-Based Genealogical Method (CBGM)." *Journal of Biblical Literature* 139.2 (2020) 319–340.
Carson, D. A., ed. *The Enduring Authority of the Christian Scriptures*. Grand Rapids: Eerdmans, 2016.
Carson, D. A., and John D. Woodbridge, eds. *Scripture and Truth*. Grand Rapids: Zondervan, 1983.
Chatraw, Josh D. "Disunity and Diversity: The Biblical Theology of Bart Ehrman." *Journal of the Evangelical Theological Society* 54.3 (2011) 449–65.
Childers, Jeff W., and David C. Parker, eds. *Transmission and Reception: New Testament Text-Critical and Exegetical Studies*. Texts and Studies 3:4. Piscataway, NJ: Gorgias, 2006.
Clark, Kenneth Willis. "The Theological Relevance of Textual Variation in Current Criticism of the Greek New Testament." *Journal of Biblical Literature* 85.1 (1966) 1–16.
Cole, Zachary J. "Myths about Copyists: The Scribes Who Copied Our Early Manuscripts." In *Myths and Mistakes in New Testament Textual Criticism*, edited by Elijah Hixson and Peter J. Gurry, 132–51. Downers Grove, IL: IVP Academic, 2019.
Colwell, Ernest Cadman. "Method in Locating a Newly Discovered Manuscript." In *Studies in Methodology in Textual Criticism of the New Testament*, edited by E. C. Colwell, 26–44. New Testament Tools and Studies 9. Leiden: Brill, 1969.
———. *Studies in Methodology in Textual Criticism of the New Testament*. New Testament Tools and Studies 9. Leiden: Brill, 1969.
———. *What is the Best New Testament?* Chicago: University of Chicago Press, 1952.
Comfort, Philip Wesley. *The Quest for the Original Text of the New Testament*. Grand Rapids: Baker, 1992.
Conn, Harvie M., ed. *Practical Theology and the Ministry of the Church, 1952–1984: Essays in Honor of Edmund P. Clowney*. Phillipsburg, NJ: Presbyterian and Reformed, 1990.
Conzelmann, Hans. *The Theology of St Luke*. Translated by Geoffrey Buswell. London: Faber and Faber, 1960.
Cosaert, Carl P. *The Text of the Gospels in Clement of Alexandria*. New Testament in the Greek Fathers 9. Atlanta: SBL, 2008.
Crusé, Christian Frederic. trans. *Eusebius' Ecclesiastical History*. Complete and Unabridged, New Updated Edition. Peabody, MA: Hendrickson, 1998.
Delobel, Joël. "Focus on the 'Western' Text in Recent Studies." *Ephemerides Theologicae Lovanienses* 73.4 (1997) 401–10.
Denaux, Adelbert, ed. *New Testament Textual Criticism and Exegesis: Festschrift J. Delobel*. Bibliotheca Ephemeridum Theologicarum Lovaniensium 161. Leuven: Leuven University Press, 2002.

Desjardins, Michel R. "Bauer and Beyond: On Recent Scholarly Discussions of *Haeresis* in the Early Christian Era." *Second Century* 8.2 (1991) 65–82.

Dever, William G. *What Did the Biblical Writers Know, and When Did They Know it?: What Archaeology Can Tell Us about the Reality of Ancient Israel*. Grand Rapids: Eerdmans, 2001.

Doble, Peter, and Jeffrey Kloha, eds. *Texts and Traditions: Essays in Honour of J. Keith Elliott*. New Testament Tools, Studies, and Documents 47. Leiden: Brill, 2014.

Donaldson, Amy. "Explicit References to New Testament Variant Readings among Greek and Latin Church Fathers, Vol. 1." PhD diss., University of Notre Dame, 2009.

Donker, Gerald J. *The Text of the Apostolos in Athanasius of Alexandria*. New Testament in the Greek Fathers 8. Atlanta: SBL, 2011.

Draper, Robert. "Bible Hunters: Scholars, Schemers, and the Search for Ancient Texts." *National Geographic Magazine* 234.6 (Dec 2018) 40–75.

Duff, Jeremy. "P46 and the Pastorals: A Misleading Consensus?" *New Testament Studies* 44.4 (1998) 578–90.

Dungan, David L., ed. *The Interrelations of the Gospels: A Symposium Led by M.-É. Boismard, William R. Farmer, F. Neirynck, Jerusalem 1984*. Leuven: Leuven University Press, 1990.

Ebeling, Gerhard. *The Problem of Historicity in the Church and its Proclamation*. Philadelphia: Fortress, 1967.

Ehrman, Bart D., ed. *After the New Testament: A Reader in Early Christianity*. Oxford: Oxford University Press, 1999.

———. *The Bible: A Historical and Literary Introduction*. 2nd ed. Oxford: Oxford University Press, 2018.

———. *Did Jesus Exist?: The Historical Argument for Jesus of Nazareth*. New York: HarperOne, 2012.

———. *Didymus the Blind and the Text of the Gospels*. New Testament in the Greek Fathers 1. Atlanta: Scholars, 1986.

———. *Forged: Writing in the Name of God—Why the Bible's Authors are Not Who We Think They are*. New York: HarperOne, 2011.

———. *Forgery and Counterforgery: The Use of Literary Deceit in Early Christian Polemics*. Oxford: Oxford University Press, 2013.

———. *God's Problem: How the Bible Fails to Answer Our Most Important Question—Why We Suffer*. New York: HarperOne, 2008.

———. *How Jesus Became God: The Exaltation of a Jewish Preacher from Galilee*. New York: HarperOne, 2014.

———. *Jesus, Apocalyptic Prophet of the New Millennium*. Oxford: Oxford University Press, 1999.

———. *Jesus before the Gospels: How the Earliest Christians Remembered, Changed, and Invented Their Stories of the Savior*. New York: HarperOne, 2016.

———. *Jesus, Interrupted: Revealing the Hidden Contradictions in the Bible (and Why We Don't Know about Them)*. New York: HarperOne, 2009.

———. *Lost Christianities: The Battles for Scripture and the Faiths We Never Knew*. Oxford: Oxford University Press, 2003.

———. *The Lost Gospel of Judas Iscariot: A New Look at Betrayer and Betrayed*. Oxford: Oxford University Press, 2006.

———. *Lost Scriptures: Books That Did Not Make it into the New Testament*. Oxford: Oxford University Press, 2003.

———. *Misquoting Jesus: The Story behind Who Changed the Bible and Why*. New York: HarperCollins, 2005.

———. *The New Testament: A Historical Introduction to the Early Christian Writings*. Oxford: Oxford University Press, 1997.

———. *The New Testament and Other Early Christian Writings: A Reader*. Oxford: Oxford University Press, 1998.

———. "New Testament Textual Criticism: Quest for Methodology." MDiv thesis, Princeton Theological Seminary, 1981.

———. *The Orthodox Corruption of Scripture: The Effect of Early Christological Controversies on the Text of the New Testament*. Oxford: Oxford University Press, 1993.

———. *The Orthodox Corruption of Scripture: The Effect of Early Christological Controversies on the Text of the New Testament*. Updated ed. Oxford: Oxford University Press, 2011.

———. *Peter, Paul, and Mary Magdalene: The Followers of Jesus in History and Legend*. Oxford: Oxford University Press, 2006.

———, ed. *Studies in the Textual Criticism of the New Testament*. New Testament Tools and Studies 33. Leiden: Brill, 2006.

———. "The Text as Window: New Testament Manuscripts and the Social History of Early Christianity." In *The Text of the New Testament in Contemporary Research: Essays on the Status Quaestionis*, edited by Bart D. Ehrman and Michael W. Holmes, 803–30. New Testament Tools, Studies, and Documents 42. Leiden: Brill, 2013.

———. *The Triumph of Christianity: How a Forbidden Religion Swept the World*. New York: Simon and Schuster, 2018.

———. *Truth and Fiction in the Da Vinci Code: A Historian Reveals What We Really Know about Jesus, Mary Magdalene, and Constantine*. Oxford: Oxford University Press, 2004.

———. "The Use and Significance of Patristic Evidence for NT Textual Criticism." In *New Testament Textual Criticism, Exegesis, and Early Church History: A Discussion of Methods*, edited by Barbara Aland and Joël Delobel, 118–35. Kampen, The Netherlands: Pharos, 1994.

———. "Video: Bart Ehrman vs. James White Debate." https://ehrmanblog.org/video-bart-ehrman-vs-james-white-debate/.

Ehrman, Bart D., and Michael W. Holmes, eds. *The Text of the New Testament in Contemporary Research: Essays on the Status Quaestionis*. New Testament Tools, Studies and Documents 46. Grand Rapids: Eerdmans, 1995.

———. *The Text of the New Testament in Contemporary Research: Essays on the Status Quaestionis*. New Testament Tools, Studies, and Documents 42. Leiden: Brill, 2013.

Ehrman, Bart D., and Andrew S. Jacobs, eds. *Christianity in Late Antiquity, 300–450 C.E: A Reader*. Oxford: Oxford University Press, 2004.

Ehrman, Bart D., and Zlatko Pleše, eds. *The Apocryphal Gospels: Texts and Translations*. Oxford: Oxford University Press, 2011.

———. *The Other Gospels: Accounts of Jesus from Outside the New Testament*. Oxford: Oxford University Press, 2014.

Ehrman, Bart D., et al. *The Text of the Fourth Gospel in the Writings of Origen.* New Testament in the Greek Fathers 3. Atlanta: Scholars, 1992.

Ellingworth, Paul. "Text, Translation, and Theology: The New Testament in the Original Greek?" *Filología Neotestamentaria* 13.25–26 (2000) 61–73.

———. "Theological Reflections on the Textual Criticism of the Bible." *The Bible Translator* 46.1 (1995) 119–25.

Elliott, J. Keith. "Can We Recover the Original New Testament?" *Theology* 77.649 (1974) 338–53.

———. "The Case for Thoroughgoing Eclecticism." In *Rethinking New Testament Textual Criticism*, edited by David Alan Black, 101–24. Grand Rapids: Baker Academic, 2002.

———. "Foreword to the English Translation." In *An Introduction to New Testament Textual Criticism*, 2nd ed., by Léon Vaganay and Christian-Bernard Amphoux, xiii–xv. Revised and updated by Christian-Bernard Amphoux. Translated by Jenny Heimerdinger. English ed. amplified and updated by Christian-Bernard Amphoux and Jenny Heimerdinger. Cambridge: Cambridge University Press, 1991.

———. "In Defence of Thoroughgoing Eclecticism in New Testament Textual Criticism." *Restoration Quarterly* 21.2 (1978) 95–115.

———. "Majority Text or Not: Which Criteria Should Be Adopted When Assessing Textual Variation in the Greek New Testament?" In *Getting into the Text: New Testament Essays in Honor of David Alan Black*, edited by Daniel L. Akin and Thomas W. Hudgin, 77–89. Eugene, OR: Pickwick, 2017.

———. "The Nature of the Evidence Available for Reconstructing the Text of the New Testament in the Second Century." In *The New Testament Text in Early Christianity: Proceedings of the Lille Colloquium, July 2000*, edited by Christian Bernard Amphoux and J. Keith Elliott, 9–18. Histoire du texte biblique 6. Lausanne: Zèbre, 2003.

———, ed. *New Testament Textual Criticism, the Application of Thoroughgoing Principles: Essays on Manuscripts and Textual Variation.* Supplements to Novum Testamentum 137. Leiden: Brill, 2010.

———, ed. *The Principles and Practice of New Testament Textual Criticism: Collected Essays of G. D. Kilpatrick.* Bibliotheca Ephemeridum Theologicarum Lovaniensium 96. Leuven: Peeters, 1990.

———. *Questioning Christian Origins.* London: SCM, 1982.

———. "Rational Criticism and the Text of the New Testament." *Theology* 75.625 (1972) 338–43.

———. "Recent Trends in the Textual Criticism of the New Testament: A New Millennium, a New Beginning?" *Bulletin de l'Académie Belge pour l'Étude des Langues Anciennes et Orientales* 1 (2012) 117–36.

———. "The Relevance of Authorial Language, Style, and Usage in the Evaluation of Textual Variants in the Greek New Testament." In *The Press of the Text: Biblical Studies in Honor of James W. Voelz*, edited by Andrew H. Bartelt et al., 67–84. Eugene, OR: Pickwick, 2017.

———. "The Relevance of Textual Criticism to the Synoptic Problem." In *The Interrelations of the Gospels: A Symposium Led by M.-É. Boismard, William R. Farmer, F. Neirynck, Jerusalem 1984*, edited by David L. Dungan, 348–59. Leuven: Leuven University Press, 1990.

———. "Revelations from the Apparatus Criticus of the Book of Revelation: How Textual Criticism Can Help Historians." *Union Seminary Quarterly Review* 63.3–4 (2012) 1–23.

———. "Review of *The Living Text of the Gospels*." *Novum Testamentum* 41.2 (1999) 176–81.

———. "Review of *The Orthodox Corruption of Scripture: The Effect of Early Christological Controversies on the Text of the New Testament*." *Novum Testamentum* 36.4 (1994) 405–6.

———. "Review of *The Quest for the Original Text of the New Testament*." *Novum Testamentum* 36.3 (1994) 284–87.

———. "Thoroughgoing Eclecticism." In *New Testament Textual Criticism, the Application of Thoroughgoing Principles: Essays on Manuscripts and Textual Variation*, edited by J. Keith Elliott, 41–49. Supplements to Novum Testamentum 137. Leiden: Brill, 2010.

———. "Thoroughgoing Eclecticism in New Testament Textual Criticism." In *The Text of the New Testament in Contemporary Research: Essays on the Status Quaestionis*, edited by Bart D. Ehrman and Michael W. Holmes, 321–35. Studies and Documents 46. Grand Rapids: Eerdmans, 1995.

———. "Thoroughgoing Eclecticism in New Testament Textual Criticism." In *The Text of the New Testament in Contemporary Research: Essays on the Status Quaestionis*, edited by Bart D. Ehrman and Michael W. Holmes, 745–70. New Testament Tools, Studies, and Documents 42. Leiden: Brill, 2013.

———. "Using an Author's Consistency of Usage and Conjectures as Criteria to Resolve Textual Variations in the Greek New Testament." *New Testament Studies* 62.1 (2016) 122–35.

Enns, Peter. *Inspiration and Incarnation: Evangelicals and the Problem of the Old Testament*. 2nd ed. Grand Rapids: Baker Academic, 2015.

Epp, Eldon J. "Anti-Judaic Tendencies in the D-text of Acts: Forty Years of Conversation." In *The Book of Acts as Church History: Text, Textual Traditions and Ancient Interpretations/Apostelgeschichte als Kirchengeschichte: Text, Texttraditionen und antike Auslegungen*. Beihefte zur Zeitschrift für die Neutestamentliche Wissenschaft und die Kunde der Älteren Kirche, edited by Michael Tilly and Tobias Nicklas, 111–46. New York: De Gruyter, 2003.

———. "Are Early New Testament Manuscripts Truly Abundant?" In *Israel's God and Rebecca's Children: Christology and Community in Early Judaism and Christianity: Essays in Honor of Larry W. Hurtado and Alan F. Segal*, edited by David B. Capes et al., 77–117. Waco, TX: Baylor University Press, 2007.

———. "The Codex and Literacy in Early Christianity and at Oxyrhynchus: Issues Raised by Harry Y. Gamble's *Books and Readers in the Early Church*." *Critical Review of Books in Religion* 11 (1998) 15–37.

———. "A Continuing Interlude in New Testament Textual Criticism." *Harvard Theological Review* 73.1–2 (1980) 131–51.

———. "Critical Editions and the Development of Text-Critical Methods, Part 2: From Lachmann (1831) to the Present." In *From 1750 to the Present*, edited by John Riches, 13–48. Vol. 4 of *The New Cambridge History of the Bible*. 4 vols. Cambridge: Cambridge University Press, 2015.

———. "Decision Points in Past, Present, and Future New Testament Textual Criticism." In *Perspectives on New Testament Textual Criticism: Collected Essays,*

1962–2004, edited by Eldon J. Epp, 227–83. Supplements to Novum Testamentum 116. Leiden: Brill, 2005.

———. "Decision Points in Past, Present, and Future New Testament Textual Criticism." In *Studies in the Theory and Method of New Testament Textual Criticism*, edited by Eldon J. Epp and Gordon D. Fee, 17–44. Studies and Documents 45. Grand Rapids: Eerdmans, 1993.

———. "The Eclectic Method in New Testament Textual Criticism: Solution or Symptom?" *Harvard Theological Review* 69.3–4 (1976) 211–57.

———. "The 'Ignorance Motif' in Acts and Anti-Judaic Tendencies in Codex Bezae." *Harvard Theological Review* 55.1 (1962) 51–62.

———. "In the Beginning was the New Testament Text, but Which Text? A Consideration of 'Ausgangstext' and 'Initial Text.'" In *Texts and Traditions: Essays in Honour of J. Keith Elliott*, edited by Peter Doble and Jeffrey Kloha, 35–70. New Testament Tools, Studies, and Documents 47. Leiden: Brill, 2014.

———. "Introduction: A Half-Century Adventure with New Testament Textual Criticism." In *Perspectives on New Testament Textual Criticism: Collected Essays, 1962–2004*, edited by Eldon J. Epp, xxvii–xl. Supplements to Novum Testamentum 116. Leiden: Brill, 2005.

———. "Issues in New Testament Textual Criticism: Moving from the Nineteenth Century to the Twenty-First Century." In *Rethinking New Testament Textual Criticism*, edited by David Alan Black, 17–76. Grand Rapids: Baker Academic, 2002.

———. "Issues in the Interrelation of New Testament Textual Criticism and Canon." In *The Canon Debate: On the Origins and Formation of the Bible*, edited by Lee Martin McDonald and James A. Sanders, 485–515. Peabody, MA: Hendrickson, 2002.

———. "It's All about Variants: A Variant-Conscious Approach to New Testament Textual Criticism." *Harvard Theological Review* 100.3 (2007) 275–308.

———. "The Multivalence of the Term 'Original Text' in New Testament Textual Criticism." *Harvard Theological Review* 92.3 (1999) 245–81.

———. "The New Testament Papyri at Oxyrhynchus in Their Social and Intellectual Context." In *Sayings of Jesus: Canonical and Non-Canonical: Essays in Honour of Tjitze Baarda*, edited by William Lawrence Petersen et al., 47–68. Supplements to Novum Testamentum 89. Leiden: Brill, 1997.

———. "New Testament Papyrus Manuscripts and Letter Carrying in Greco-Roman Times." In *The Future of Early Christianity: Essays in Honor of Helmut Koester*, edited by Birger A. Pearson, 35–56. Minneapolis: Fortress, 1991.

———. "New Testament Textual Criticism in America: Requiem for a Discipline." *Journal of Biblical Literature* 98.1 (1979) 94–98.

———. "The NT Papyrus Manuscripts in Historical Perspective." In *To Touch the Text: Biblical and Related Studies in Honor of Joseph A. Fitzmyer*, edited by Maurya P. Horgan and Paul J. Kobelski, 261–88. New York: Crossroad, 1989.

———. "The Oxyrhynchus New Testament Papyri: 'Not without Honor Except in Their Hometown'?" *Journal of Biblical Literature* 123.1 (2004) 5–55.

———. "The Papyrus Manuscripts of the New Testament." In *The Text of the New Testament in Contemporary Research: Essays on the Status Quaestionis*, edited by Bart D. Ehrman and Michael W. Holmes, 3–21. Studies and Documents 46. Grand Rapids: Eerdmans, 1995.

———, ed. *Perspectives on New Testament Textual Criticism: Collected Essays, 1962–2004*. Supplements to Novum Testamentum 116. Leiden: Brill, 2005.

———. "The Significance of the Papyri for Determining the Nature of the New Testament Text in the Second Century: A Dynamic View of Textual Transmission." In *Gospel Traditions in the Second Century: Origins, Recensions, Text, and Transmission*, edited by William Lawrence Petersen, 71–103. Christianity and Judaism in Antiquity 3. Notre Dame: University of Notre Dame Press, 1989.

———. "Textual Clusters: Their Past and Future in New Testament Textual Criticism." In *The Text of the New Testament in Contemporary Research: Essays on the Status Quaestionis*, edited by Bart D. Ehrman and Michael W. Holmes, 519–77. New Testament Tools, Studies, and Documents 42. Leiden: Brill, 2013.

———. "Textual Criticism in the Exegesis of the New Testament, with an Excursus on Canon." In *Handbook to Exegesis of the New Testament*, edited by Stanley E. Porter, 45–97. New Testament Tools and Studies 25. Leiden: Brill, 1997.

———. *The Theological Tendency of Codex Bezae Cantabrigiensis in Acts*. Society for New Testament Studies Monograph Series 3. Cambridge: Cambridge University Press, 1966.

———. "Toward the Clarification of the Term 'Textual Variant.'" In *Studies in the Theory and Method of New Testament Textual Criticism*, edited by Eldon J. Epp and Gordon D. Fee, 47–61. Studies and Documents 45. Grand Rapids: Eerdmans, 1993.

———. "Traditional 'Canons' of New Testament Textual Criticism: Their Value, Validity, and Viability—or Lack Thereof." In *The Textual History of the Greek New Testament: Changing Views in Contemporary Research*, edited by Klaus Wachtel and Michael W. Holmes, 79–128. Text-Critical Studies 8. Atlanta: SBL, 2011.

———. "The Twentieth Century Interlude in New Testament Textual Criticism." *Journal of Biblical Literature* 93.3 (1974) 386–414.

———. "Why Does New Testament Textual Criticism Matter? Refined Definitions and Fresh Directions." *Expository Times* 125.9 (2014) 417–31.

Epp, Eldon J., and Gordon D. Fee, eds. *New Testament Textual Criticism: Its Significance for Exegesis: Essays in Honour of Bruce M. Metzger*. Oxford: Oxford University Press, 1981.

———. *Studies in the Theory and Method of New Testament Textual Criticism*. Studies and Documents 45. Grand Rapids: Eerdmans, 1993.

Erickson, Millard J. *Christian Theology*. 2nd ed. Grand Rapids: Baker, 1998.

Fee, Gordon D. "Text Criticism." In *Encyclopedia of Early Christianity*, edited by Everett Ferguson et al., 1110–1112. 2nd ed. New York: Garland, 1997.

———. "The Text of John in the Jerusalem Bible: A Critique of the Use of Patristic Citations in New Testament Textual Criticism." *Journal of Biblical Literature* 90.2 (1971) 163–73.

———. "Textual Criticism." In *Dictionary of Jesus and the Gospels*, edited by Joel B. Green et al., 827–31. Downers Grove, IL: IVP, 1992.

———. "The Textual Criticism of the New Testament." In *The Expositor's Bible Commentary*, edited by Frank E. Gaebelein, 1:419–33. 12 vols. Grand Rapids: Zondervan, 1979.

———. "The Use of the Greek Fathers for New Testament Textual Criticism." In *The Text of the New Testament in Contemporary Research: Essays on the Status*

Quaestionis, edited by Bart D. Ehrman and Michael W. Holmes, 191–207. Studies and Documents 46. Grand Rapids: Eerdmans, 1995.

Feinberg, Paul D. "The Meaning of Inerrancy." In *Inerrancy*, edited by Norman Geisler, 267–304. Grand Rapids: Zondervan, 1980.

Ferguson, Everett. *Backgrounds of Early Christianity*. 3rd ed. Grand Rapids: Eerdmans, 2003.

Ferguson, Everett, et al., eds. *Encyclopedia of Early Christianity*. 2nd ed. New York: Garland, 1997.

Fischer, Bonifatius. "The Use of Computers in New Testament Studies, with Special Reference to Textual Criticism." *Journal of Theological Studies* 21.2 (1970) 297–308.

Flora, Jerry R. "A Critical Analysis of Walter Bauer's Theory of Early Christian Orthodoxy and Heresy." PhD diss., Southern Baptist Theological Seminary, 1972.

Fox, Adam. *John Mill and Richard Bentley: A Study of the Textual Criticism of the New Testament, 1675–1729*. Oxford: Blackwell, 1954.

Funk, Robert Walter, and Roy W. Hoover. *The Five Gospels: The Search for the Authentic Words of Jesus: New Translation and Commentary*. New York: Macmillan, 1993.

———. "How Should the Jesus Seminar's Conclusions Be Viewed?" *Los Angeles Times*, 6 April 1991, F18–19. https://www.latimes.com/archives/la-xpm-1991-04-06-ca-1580-story.html.

Gaebelein, Frank E., ed. *The Expositor's Bible Commentary*. 2 vols. Grand Rapids: Zondervan, 1979.

Gamble, Harry Y. *Books and Readers in the Early Church: A History of Early Christian Texts*. New Haven: Yale University Press, 1995.

———. *The New Testament Canon: Its Making and Meaning*. Guides to Biblical Scholarship: NT Series. Philadelphia: Fortress, 1985.

Garlow, James L., and Peter Jones. *Cracking Da Vinci's Code*. Colorado Springs: Victor, 2004.

Geisler, Norman L. *Inerrancy*. Grand Rapids: Zondervan, 1980.

Geisler, Norman L., and William C. Roach. *Defending Inerrancy: Affirming the Accuracy of Scripture for a New Generation*. Grand Rapids: Baker, 2011.

Goehring, James E., et al., eds. *Gospel Origins and Christian Beginnings: In Honor of James M. Robinson*. Forum Fascicles 2. Sonoma, CA: Polebridge, 1990.

Grant, Robert M. *Eusebius as Church Historian*. Oxford: Clarendon, 1980.

Green, Joel B., et al., eds. *Dictionary of Jesus and the Gospels*. Downers Grove, IL: IVP, 1992.

Greenlee, J. Harold. *Introduction to New Testament Textual Criticism*. Rev. ed. Peabody, MA: Hendrickson, 1995.

———. *Scribes, Scrolls, and Scripture: A Student's Guide to New Testament Textual Criticism*. Grand Rapids: Eerdmans, 1985.

Grudem, Wayne A. *Systematic Theology: An Introduction to Biblical Doctrine*. Grand Rapids: Zondervan, 1994.

Gurry, Peter J. *A Critical Examination of the Coherence-Based Genealogical Method in New Testament Textual Criticism*. New Testament Tools, Studies, and Documents 55. Leiden: Brill, 2017.

———. "A Critical Examination of the Coherence-Based Genealogical Method in the Catholic Epistles." *Tyndale Bulletin* 68.2 (2017) 317–19.

———. "The Harklean Syriac and the Development of the Byzantine Text: A Historical Test for the Coherence-Based Genealogical Method (CBGM)." *Novum Testamentum* 60.2 (2018) 183–200.

———. "How Your Greek New Testament is Changing: An Introduction to the Coherence-Based Genealogical Method (CBGM)." https://www.academia.edu/11926275/How_Your_Greek_New_Testament_Is_Changing_An_Introduction_to_the_Coherence_Based_Genealogical_Method_CBGM_.

———. "The Number of Variants in the Greek New Testament: A Proposed Estimate." *New Testament Studies* 62.1 (2016) 97–121.

———. "Myths about Variants: Why Some Variants are Insignificant and Why Some Can't Be Ignored." In *Myths and Mistakes in New Testament Textual Criticism*, edited by Elijah Hixson and Peter J. Gurry, 191–210. Downers Grove, IL: IVP Academic, 2019.

Haines-Eitzen, Kim. *Guardians of Letters: Literacy, Power, and the Transmitters of Early Christian Literature*. New York: Oxford University Press, 2000.

Hannah, Darrell D. *The Text of 1 Corinthians in the Writings of Origen*. New Testament in the Greek Fathers 4. Atlanta: Scholars, 1997.

Hanson, Richard Patrick Crosland. "Review of *The Theological Tendency of Codex Bezae Cantabrigensis in Acts*." *New Testament Studies* 14.2 (1968) 282–86.

Harris, R. Laird. *Inspiration and Canonicity of the Bible: An Historical and Exegetical Study*. Rev. ed. Contemporary Evangelical Perspectives. Grand Rapids: Zondervan, 1971.

Harvey, Anthony Ernest. "Review of *The Living Text of the Gospels*." *Theology* 101.800 (1998) 141–42.

Hauser, Alan J., and Duane F. Watson, eds. *A History of Biblical Interpretation, vol. 3: The Enlightenment through the Nineteenth Century*. 3 vols. Grand Rapids: Eerdmans, 2017.

Head, Peter M. "Review of *The Living Text of the Gospels*." *Evangelical Quarterly* 74.4 (2002) 359–61.

Henry, Patrick. "Why is Contemporary Scholarship so Enamored of Ancient Heretics?" *Epiphany* 12.4 (1992) 63–67.

———. "Why is Contemporary Scholarship so Enamored of Ancient Heretics?" In *Studia Patristica* 17:1, edited by Elizabeth A. Livingstone, 123–26. New York: Pergamon, 1982.

Hixson, Elijah, and Peter J. Gurry, eds. *Myths and Mistakes in New Testament Textual Criticism*. Downers Grove, IL: IVP Academic, 2019.

Hodges, Zane Clark. "The Greek Text of the King James Version." *Bibliotheca Sacra* 125.500 (1968) 334–45.

———. "Modern Textual Criticism and the Majority Text: A Response." *Journal of the Evangelical Theological Society* 21.2 (1978) 143–55.

———. "Rationalism and Contemporary New Testament Textual Criticism." *Bibliotheca Sacra* 128.509 (1971) 27–35.

Hodges, Zane Clark, and Arthur L. Farstad. *The Greek New Testament According to the Majority Text*. 2nd ed. Nashville: Thomas Nelson, 1985.

Holmes, Michael W. "From 'Original Text' to 'Initial Text': The Traditional Goal of New Testament Textual Criticism in Contemporary Discussion." In *The Text of the New Testament in Contemporary Research: Essays on the Status Quaestionis*, edited by Bart D. Ehrman and Michael W. Holmes, 637–88. New Testament Tools, Studies, and Documents 42. Leiden: Brill, 2013.

———, ed. *The Greek New Testament: Society of Biblical Literature Edition*. Atlanta: SBL, 2010.

———. "New Testament Textual Criticism." In *Introducing New Testament Interpretation*, edited by Scot McKnight, 53–74. Grand Rapids: Baker, 1989.

———. "Reasoned Eclecticism in New Testament Textual Criticism." In *The Text of the New Testament in Contemporary Research: Essays on the Status Quaestionis*, edited by Bart D. Ehrman and Michael W. Holmes, 336–60. SD 46. Grand Rapids: Eerdmans, 1995.

———. "Reasoned Eclecticism in New Testament Textual Criticism." In *The Text of the New Testament in Contemporary Research: Essays on the Status Quaestionis*, edited by Bart D. Ehrman and Michael W. Holmes, 771–802. NTTSD 42. Leiden: Brill, 2013.

———. "Review of *The Orthodox Corruption of Scripture: The Effect of Early Christological Controversies on the Text of the New Testament*." *Religious Studies Review* 20.3 (1994) 237.

———. "Review of *Perspectives on New Testament Textual Criticism: Collected Essays, 1962–2004*." *Religious Studies Review* 32.3 (2006) 191–92.

Horgan, Maurya P., and Paul J. Kobelski, eds. *To Touch the Text: Biblical and Related Studies in Honor of Joseph A. Fitzmyer*. New York: Crossroad, 1989.

Horton, Charles, ed. *The Earliest Gospels: The Origins and Transmission of the Earliest Christian Gospels—The Contribution of the Chester Beatty Gospel Codex P45*. Journal for the Study of the New Testament Supplement Series 258. London: T. & T. Clark, 2004.

Houghton, Hugh A. G., and David C. Parker, eds. *Textual Variation: Theological and Social Tendencies? Papers from the Fifth Birmingham Colloquium on the Textual Criticism of the New Testament*. Theological Studies, 3:6. Piscataway, NJ: Gorgias, 2008.

Hüffmeier, Annette. "The CBGM Applied to Variants from Acts." *TC: A Journal of Biblical Textual Criticism* 20 (2015). http://rosetta.reltech.org/TC/v15/Hurtado2010.pdf.

Hurtado, Larry W. "Going for the Bigger Picture: Eldon Epp as Textual Critic." *TC: A Journal of Biblical Textual Criticism* 15 (2010). http://jbtc.org/v15/Hurtado2010.pdf.

———. "In Gratitude to Eldon Jay Epp." https://larryhurtado.wordpress.com/2014/04/28/in-gratitude-to-eldon-jay-epp/.

———. "The New Testament in the Second Century: Text, Collections and Canon." In *Transmission and Reception: New Testament Text-Critical and Exegetical Studies*, edited by Jeff W. Childers and David C. Parker, 3–27. Theological Studies 3:4. Piscataway, NJ: Gorgias, 2006.

Jenkins, Philip. *Hidden Gospels: How the Search for Jesus Lost its Way*. Oxford: Oxford University Press, 2001.

Johnson, Luke Timothy. *The Real Jesus: The Misguided Quest for the Historical Jesus and the Truth of the Traditional Gospels*. New York: HarperCollins, 1996.

Jones, Timothy P. *Misquoting Truth: A Guide to the Fallacies of Bart Ehrman's Misquoting Jesus*. Downers Grove, IL: IVP, 2007.

Jongkind, Dirk, ed. *The Greek New Testament: Produced at Tyndale House Cambridge*. Cambridge: Cambridge University Press, 2017.

———. *An Introduction to the Greek New Testament, Produced at Tyndale House, Cambridge*. Wheaton, IL: Crossway, 2019.

———. "The Text and Lexicography of the New Testament in the Eighteenth and Nineteenth Centuries." In *The Enlightenment through the Nineteenth Century*. Vol.

3 of *A History of Biblical Interpretation*, edited by Alan J. Hauser and Duane F. Watson, 274–99. 3 vols. Grand Rapids: Eerdmans, 2017.

Kannaday, Wayne Campbell. *Apologetic Discourse and the Scribal Tradition: Evidence of the Influence of Apologetic Interests on the Text of the Canonical Gospels*. Text-Critical Studies 5. Atlanta: SBL, 2004.

Keith, Chris. "The Initial Location of the Pericope Adulterae in Fourfold Tradition." *Novum Testamentum* 51.3 (2009) 209–31.

Kelly, J. N. D. *Early Christian Doctrines*. 5th rev. ed. San Francisco: Harper & Row, 1978.

Kennedy, D. James, and Jerry Newcombe. *The Da Vinci Myth Versus the Gospel Truth*. Wheaton, IL: Crossway, 2006.

Kenyon, Frederic George. *Our Bible and the Ancient Manuscripts*. New York: Harper, 1940.

Kilpatrick, George Dunbar. "Atticism and the Text of the Greek New Testament." In *Neutestamentliche Aufsätze: Festschrift für Josef Schmid zum 70 Geburtstag*, edited by Josef Binzler et al., 125–37. Regensburg, Germany: Pustet, 1963.

———. "Eclecticism and Atticism." *Ephemerides Theologicae Lovanienses* 53.1 (1977) 107–12.

———. "The Transmission of the New Testament and its Reliability." *The Bible Translator* 9.3 (1958) 127–36.

Klein, William W., et al. *Introduction to Biblical Interpretation*. Dallas: Word, 1993.

Kloha, Jeffrey. "A Textual Commentary on Paul's First Epistle to the Corinthians." PhD Thesis, University of Leeds, 2006. http://etheses.whiterose.ac.uk/296/.

Knight, Jarrett W. "Reading between the Lines: 1 Peter 4:16, MS 424, and Some Methodological Blind Spots in the CBGM." *Journal of Biblical Literature* 138.4 (2019) 899-921.

Knust, Jennifer Wright. "In Pursuit of a Singular Text: New Testament Textual Criticism and the Desire for the True Original." *Religion Compass* 2.2 (2008) 180–94.

———. *Unprotected Texts: The Bible's Surprising Contradictions about Sex and Desire*. New York: HarperOne, 2011.

Koester, Helmut. "Apocryphal and Canonical Gospels." *Harvard Theological Review* 73.1–2 (1980) 105–30.

———. "New Testament Introduction: A Critique of a Discipline." In *Christianity, Judaism, and Other Greco-Roman Cults: Studies for Morton Smith at Sixty*, edited by Jacob Neusner, 1–20. Studies in Judaism in Late Antiquity 12. Leiden: Brill, 1975.

———. "The Text of the Synoptic Gospels in the Second Century." In *Gospel Traditions in the Second Century: Origins, Recensions, Text, and Transmission*, edited by William Lawrence Petersen, 19–37. Christianity and Judaism in Antiquity 3. Notre Dame: University of Notre Dame Press, 1989.

———. "ΓΝΩΜΑΙ ΔΙΑΦΟΡΟΙ: The Origin and Nature of Diversification in the History of Early Christianity." *Harvard Theological Review* 58.3 (1965) 279–318.

Komoszewski, J. Ed, et al., eds. *Reinventing Jesus: How Contemporary Skeptics Miss the Real Jesus and Mislead Popular Culture*. Grand Rapids: Kregel, 2006.

Köstenberger, Andreas J., and Michael J. Kruger. *The Heresy of Orthodoxy: How Contemporary Culture's Fascination with Diversity Has Reshaped Our Understanding of Early Christianity*. Wheaton, IL: Crossway, 2010.

Köstenberger, Andreas J., and Robert W. Yarbrough, eds. *Understanding the Times: New Testament Studies in the 21st Century, Essays in Honor of D. A. Carson on the Occasion of His 65th Birthday*. Wheaton, IL: Crossway, 2011.

Köstenberger, Andreas J., et al. *Truth in a Culture of Doubt: Engaging Skeptical Challenges to the Bible*. Nashville: B & H Academic, 2014.

Kruger, Michael J. "Do We Have a Trustworthy Text? Inerrancy and Canonicity, Preservation, and Textual Criticism." In *The Inerrant Word: Biblical, Historical, Theological, and Pastoral Perspectives*, edited by John MacArthur, 304–18. Wheaton, IL: Crossway, 2016.

Ladewig, Stratton L. "An Examination of the Orthodoxy of the Variants in Light of Bart Ehrman's *The Orthodox Corruption of Scripture*." ThM thesis, Dallas Theological Seminary, 2000.

Larsen, Matthew David. "Accidental Publication, Unfinished Texts and the Traditional Goals of New Testament Textual Criticism." *Journal for the Study of the New Testament* 39.4 (2017) 362–87.

Laurence, Richard. *Remarks upon the Systematical Classification of Manuscripts Adopted by Griesbach in His Edition of the Greek Testament*. Oxford: Oxford University Press, 1814.

Litwa, M. David, trans. *Refutation of All Heresies*. Writings from the Greco-Roman World 40. Atlanta: SBL, 2016.

Livingstone, Elizabeth A., ed. *Studia Patristica* 17:1. New York: Pergamon, 1982.

Longenecker, Richard N. *The Christology of Early Jewish Christianity*. Studies in Biblical Theology 2:17. Naperville, IL: Allenson, 1970.

MacArthur, John, ed. *The Inerrant Word: Biblical, Historical, Theological, and Pastoral Perspectives*. Wheaton, IL: Crossway, 2016.

Malik, Peter. "Myths about Copying: The Mistakes and Corrections Scribes Made." In *Myths and Mistakes in New Testament Textual Criticism*, edited by Elijah Hixson and Peter J. Gurry, 152–70. Downers Grove, IL: IVP Academic, 2019.

Marcello, Robert D. "Myths about Orthodox Corruption: Were Scribes Influenced by Theology and How Can We Tell?" In *Myths and Mistakes in New Testament Textual Criticism*, edited by Elijah Hixson and Peter J. Gurry, 211–27. Downers Grove, IL: IVP Academic, 2019.

McDonald, Lee Martin, and James A. Sanders, eds. *The Canon Debate: On the Origins and Formation of the Bible*. Peabody, MA: Hendrickson, 2002.

McGowan, Andrew Thomson Blake. *The Divine Authenticity of Scripture: Retrieving an Evangelical Heritage*. Downers Grove, IL: IVP Academic, 2007.

McKendrick, Scot, and Orlaith O'Sullivan, eds. *The Bible as Book: The Transmission of the Greek Text*. London: British Library, 2003.

McKnight, Scot, ed. *Introducing New Testament Interpretation*. Grand Rapids: Baker, 1989.

Meier, J. P. *The Roots of the Problem and the Person, Vol. 1. A Marginal Jew: Rethinking the Historical Jesus*. 5 vols. Anchor Bible Reference Library. New York: Doubleday, 1991.

Metzger, Bruce M. *The Canon of the New Testament: Its Origin, Development, and Significance*. Oxford: Clarendon, 1987.

———. "Explicit References in the Works of Origen to Variant Readings in New Testament Manuscripts." In *Biblical and Patristic Studies in Memory of Robert Pierce Casey*, edited by J. Neville Birdsall and Robert W. Thomson, 78–95. Freiburg: Herder, 1963.

———. "Patristic Evidence and the Textual Criticism of the New Testament." *New Testament Studies* 18.4 (1972) 379–400.

———. "Review of *The Living Text of the Gospels.*" *Princeton Seminary Bulletin* 20.2 (1999) 231–32.

———. "Review of *The Orthodox Corruption of Scripture: The Effect of Early Christological Controversies on the Text of the New Testament.*" *Princeton Seminary Bulletin* 15.2 (1994) 210–12.

———. *The Text of the New Testament: Its Transmission, Corruption, and Restoration.* 3rd enl. ed. Oxford: Oxford University Press, 1992.

———. *A Textual Commentary on the Greek New Testament.* 2nd ed. Stuttgart: Deutsche Bibelgesellschaft, 1994.

Metzger, Bruce M., and Bart D. Ehrman. *The Text of the New Testament: Its Transmission, Corruption, and Restoration.* 4th ed. Oxford: Oxford University Press, 2005.

Min, Kyoung Shik. *Die früheste Überlieferung des Matthäusevangeliums (bis zum 3./.4. Jh.).* Arbeiten zur neutestamentlichen Textforschung 34. Berlin: de Gruyter, 2005.

Mink, Gerd. "The Coherence-Based Genealogical Method." http://egora.uni-muenster.de/intf/service/downloads_en.shtml.

———. "The Coherence-Based Genealogical Method: What is it about?" http://egora.uni-muenster.de/intf/projekte/gsm_aus_en.shtml.

———. "Contamination, Coherence, and Coincidence in Textual Transmission: The Coherence-Based Genealogical Method (CBGM) as a Complement and Corrective to Existing Approaches." In *The Textual History of the Greek New Testament: Changing Views in Contemporary Research*, edited by Klaus Wachtel and Michael W. Holmes, 141–216. Text-Critical Studies 8. Atlanta: SBL, 2011.

———. "Problems of a Highly Contaminated Tradition, the New Testament: Stemmata of Variants as a Source of a Genealogy of Witnesses." In *Studies in Stemmatology II*, edited by Pieter Th. van Reenen et al., 13–85. Amsterdam: Benjamins, 2004.

———. "Zur Stemmatisierung neutestamentlicher Handschriften." *Bericht der Hermann Kunst-Stiftung zur Förderung der Neutestamentlicher Textforschung für die Jahre 1979–1981.* Münster: Institut für neutestamentliche Textforschung, 1982.

Mitchell, Margaret Mary, et al., eds. *Origins to Constantine.* 9 vols. Cambridge History of Christianity. Cambridge: Cambridge University Press, 2006.

Mitchell, Timothy N. "Myths about Autographs: What They Were and How Long They May Have Survived." In *Myths and Mistakes in New Testament Textual Criticism*, edited by Elijah Hixson and Peter J. Gurry, 26–47. Downers Grove, IL: IVP Academic, 2019.

———. "What are the NT Autographs?: An Examination of the Doctrine of Inspiration and Inerrancy in Light of Greco-Roman Publication." *Journal of the Evangelical Theological Society* 59.2 (2016) 287–307.

Moffatt, James. "Review of Professor Bauer's *Rechtgläubigkeit und Ketzerei im ältesten Christentum.*" *Expository Times* 45 (1933) 475.

Moir, Ian A. "Can We Risk Another 'Textus Receptus'?" *Journal of Biblical Literature* 100.4 (1981) 614–18.

Morgan, Fiona. "Complete Interview with Bart Ehrman." *Indy Week*, 9 March 2009, https://www.indyweek.com/indyweek/complete-interview-with-bart-ehrman/Content?oid=1214629.

Mugridge, Alan. *Copying Early Christian Texts: A Study of Scribal Practice.* Wissenschaftliche Untersuchungen zum Neuen Testament 362. Tübingen: Mohr/Siebeck, 2016.

Mullen, Roderic L. *The New Testament Text of Cyril of Jerusalem*. New Testament in the Greek Fathers 7. Atlanta: Scholars, 1997.

Neill, Stephen, and N. T. Wright. *The Interpretation of the New Testament, 1861–1986*. Oxford: Oxford University Press, 1988.

Nestle, Eberhard. *Einführung in das Griechische Neue Testament*. Göttingen: Vandenhoeck und Ruprecht, 1909.

Neusner, Jacob, ed. *Christianity, Judaism, and Other Greco-Roman Cults: Studies for Morton Smith at Sixty*. Studies in Judaism in Late Antiquity 12. Leiden: Brill, 1975.

Newman, Judith H., and John S. Kloppenborg, eds. *Editing the Bible: Assessing the Task Past and Present*. Society of Biblical Literature Sources for Biblical Study. Atlanta: SBL, 2012.

Nicole, Roger R., and J. Ramsey Michaels, eds. *Inerrancy and Common Sense*. Grand Rapids: Baker, 1980.

Nineham, Dennis. "In Memory of a Forgotten Scholar: John Mill, 1645–1707." *Theology* 111.861 (2008) 185–89.

Nolan, Frederick. *An Inquiry into the Integrity of the Greek Vulgate, or Received Text of the New Testament: In Which the Greek Manuscripts are Newly Classed, the Integrity of the Authorised Text Vindicated, and the Various Readings Traced to Their Origin*. London: F. C. and J. Rivington, 1815.

O'Day, Gail R. and Susan Hylen. *John*. Westminster Bible Companion. Louisville: Westminster John Knox, 2006.

Okholm, Dennis L., et al., eds. *Evangelicals & Scripture: Tradition, Authority and Hermeneutics*. Wheaton Theology Conference Series. Downers Grove, IL: IVP Academic, 2004.

Osborne, Grant R. "Redaction Criticism." In *New Testament Criticism and Interpretation*, edited by David Alan Black and David S. Dockery, 199–224. Grand Rapids: Zondervan, 1991.

Osburn, Carroll D. "Methodology in Identifying Patristic Citations in NT Textual Criticism." *Novum Testamentum* 47.4 (2005) 313–43.

———. *The Text of the Apostolos in Epiphanius of Salamis*. New Testament in the Greek Fathers 6. Atlanta: SBL, 2004.

Outler, Albert Cook. "Methods and Aims in the Study of the Development of Catholic Christianity." *Second Century* 1.1 (1981) 7–17.

Packer, James I. "Text Criticism and Inerrancy." *Christianity Today* 46.11 (2002) 102.

———. "Thirty Years' War: The Doctrine of Holy Scripture." In *Practical Theology and the Ministry of the Church, 1952–1984: Essays in Honor of Edmund P. Clowney*, edited by Harvie M. Conn, 25–44. Phillipsburg, NJ: Presbyterian and Reformed, 1990.

Parker, David C. *Codex Sinaiticus: The Story of the World's Oldest Bible*. London: British Library, 2010.

———. "Et Incarnatus Est." *Scottish Journal of Theology* 54.3 (2001) 330–43.

———. *An Introduction to the New Testament Manuscripts and Their Texts*. Cambridge: Cambridge University, 2008.

———. *The Living Text of the Gospels*. Cambridge: Cambridge University, 1997.

———. *Manuscripts, Texts, Theology: Collected Papers 1977–2007*. Arbeiten zur neutestamentlichen Textforschung 40. Berlin: de Gruyter, 2009.

———. "Review of *The Orthodox Corruption of Scripture: The Effect of Early Christological Controversies on the Text of the New Testament*." *Scottish Journal of Theology* 50.4 (1997) 506–7.

———. "Scripture is Tradition." *Theology* 94.757 (1991) 11–17.

———. "Textual Criticism and Theology." *Expository Times* 118.12 (2007) 583–89.

———. *Textual Scholarship and the Making of the New Testament*. Lyell Lectures, 2011. Oxford: Oxford University, 2012.

———. "Through a Screen Darkly: Digital Texts and the New Testament." *Journal for the Study of the New Testament* 25.4 (2003) 395–411.

Parvis, Merrill M. "The Nature and Tasks of New Testament Textual Criticism: An Appraisal." *Journal of Religion* 32.1 (1952) 165–74.

Patzia, Arthur G. *The Making of the New Testament: Origin, Collection, Text & Canon*. 2nd ed. Downers Grove, IL: IVP Academic, 2011.

Pearson, Birger A., ed. *The Future of Early Christianity: Essays in Honor of Helmut Koester*. Minneapolis: Fortress, 1991.

Petersen, William Lawrence, ed. *Gospel Traditions in the Second Century: Origins, Recensions, Text, and Transmission*. Christianity and Judaism in Antiquity 3. Notre Dame: University of Notre Dame, 1989.

———. "Review of *The Orthodox Corruption of Scripture: The Effect of Early Christological Controversies on the Text of the New Testament*." *Journal of Religion* 74.4 (1994) 562–64.

———. "Review of *The Quest for the Original Text of the New Testament*." *Journal of Biblical Literature* 113.3 (1994) 529–31.

———. "What Text Can New Testament Textual Criticism Ultimately Reach?" In *Patristic and Text-Critical Studies: The Collected Essays of William L. Petersen*. edited by Joseph Verheyden and Jan Krans, 219–35. New Testament Tools, Studies, and Documents 40. Leiden: Brill, 2012.

Petersen, William Lawrence, et al., eds. *Sayings of Jesus: Canonical and Non-Canonical: Essays in Honour of Tjitze Baarda*. Supplements to Novum Testamentum 89. Leiden: Brill, 1997.

Peterson, Jacob W. "Math Myths: How Many Manuscripts We Have and Why More Isn't Always Better." In *Myths and Mistakes in New Testament Textual Criticism*, edited by Elijah Hixson and Peter J. Gurry, 48–69. Downers Grove, IL: IVP Academic, 2019.

Petzer, Jacobus H. "The History of the New Testament—Its Reconstruction, Significance and Use in New Testament Textual Criticism." In *New Testament Textual Criticism, Exegesis, and Early Church History: A Discussion of Methods*, edited by Barbara Aland and Joël Delobel, 11–36. Kampen, The Netherlands: Pharos, 1994.

Pickering, Wilbur N. "The Greek New Testament According to Family 35." https://www.amazon.com/Greek-New-Testament-According-Family/dp/0989827372.

———. *The Identity of the New Testament Text*. 4th edition. Nashville: Thomas Nelson, 1977.

———. "The Identity of the New Testament Text IV." http://www.walkinhiscommandments.com/pickering3b.htm.

———. "In Defense of the Objective Authority of the Sacred Text." http://www.walkinhiscommandments.com/Pickering/Authority/In%20Defense%20of%20the%20Objective%20Authority%20of%20the%20Sacred%20Text.pdf.

Porter, Stanley E., ed. *Handbook to Exegesis of the New Testament*. New Testament Tools and Studies 25. Leiden: Brill, 1997.
Porter, Stanley E., and Mark Boda, eds. *Translating the New Testament: Text, Translation, Theology*. McMaster New Testament Studies. Grand Rapids: Eerdmans, 2009.
Prothro, James B. "Myths about Classical Literature: Responsibly Comparing the New Testament to Ancient Works." In *Myths and Mistakes in New Testament Textual Criticism*, edited by Elijah Hixson and Peter J. Gurry, 70–89. Downers Grove, IL: IVP Academic, 2019.
Quarles, Charles L. "ΜΕΤΑ ΤΗΝ ΕΓΕΡΣΙΝ ΑΥΤΟΥ: A Scribal Interpolation in Matthew 27:53?" *TC: A Journal of Biblical Textual Criticism* 20 (2015) 1–15.
Racine, Jean-Francois. *The Text of Matthew in the Writings of Basil of Caesarea*. New Testament in the Greek Fathers 5. Atlanta: SBL, 2004.
Reenen, Pieter Th. van, et al., eds. *Studies in Stemmatology II*. Amsterdam: Benjamins, 2004.
Riches, John, ed. *The New Cambridge History of the Bible, vol. 4: From 1750 to the Present*. 4 vols. Cambridge: Cambridge University, 2015.
Riddle, Donald Wayne. "Textual Criticism as a Historical Discipline." *Anglican Theological Review* 18.4 (1936) 220–33.
Roberts, Alexander, et al., eds. *The Ante-Nicene Fathers: Translations of the Writings of the Fathers down to AD 325*. 10 vols. Buffalo, NY: Christian Literature, 1885–1886.
Roberts, Colin H. *Manuscript, Society and Belief in Early Christian Egypt*. The Schweich Lectures, 1977. Oxford: Oxford University, 1979.
Robertson, A. T. *An Introduction to the Textual Criticism of the New Testament*. Nashville: Broadman, 1925.
Robinson, Maurice A. "Absent from the Handbooks? The Role of the Holy Spirit in New Testament Textual Criticism." Paper presented at the Annual Meeting of the Evangelical Theological Society. Denver, CO, November 2018.
———. "The Case for Byzantine Priority." In *Rethinking New Testament Textual Criticism*, edited by David Alan Black, 125–39. Grand Rapids: Baker Academic, 2002.
———. "The Case for Byzantine Priority." *TC: A Journal of Biblical Textual Criticism* 6 (2001). http://www.reltech.org/TC/v06/Robinson2001.html.
———. "Discussion on CBGM." http://evangelicaltextualcriticism.blogspot.com/2014/11/your-greek-new-testament-and-revisions.html.
———. "The Integrity of the Early New Testament Text: A Collation-Based Comparison Utilizing the Papyri of the Second and Third Centuries." Paper presented at the Annual Meeting of the Evangelical Theological Society. Valley Forge, PA, November 2005.
———. "Review of *The Quest for the Original Text of the New Testament*." *Faith and Mission* 10.2 (1993) 93–99.
Robinson, Maurice A., and William G. Pierpont, eds. *The New Testament in the Original Greek According to the Byzantine/Majority Textform*. Atlanta: Original Word, 1991.
———. *The New Testament in the Original Greek: Byzantine Textform*. Southborough, MA: Chilton, 2005.
Robinson, Thomas A. *The Bauer Thesis Examined: The Geography of Heresy in the Early Christian Church*. Lewiston, NY: Mellen, 1988.
Rodgers, Peter R. "Review of *Perspectives on New Testament Textual Criticism: Collected Essays 1962–2004*." *Novum Testamentum* 48.3 (2006) 292–93.

Ropes, James Hardy. *The Synoptic Gospels*. Cambridge, MA: Harvard University Press, 1934.

Royse, James Ronald. *Scribal Habits in Early Greek New Testament Papyri*. New Testament Tools, Studies and Documents 36. Leiden: Brill, 2008.

Schrader, Elizabeth. "Is Martha an Interpolation into John's Gospel?" http://evangelicaltextualcriticism.blogspot.com/2019/08/is-martha-interpolation-into-johns.html.

———. "Is Martha an Interpolation into John's Gospel? Part II." http://evangelicaltextualcriticism.blogspot.com/2019/09/is-martha-interpolation-into-johns_7.html.

———. "Is Martha an Interpolation into John's Gospel? Part III." http://evangelicaltextualcriticism.blogspot.com/2019/09/is-martha-interpolation-into-johns_7.html.

———. "Was Martha of Bethany Added to the Fourth Gospel in the Second Century?" *Harvard Theological Review* 110.3 (2017) 360–92.

Scrivener, Frederick H. A. *A Plain Introduction to the Criticism of the New Testament for the Use of Biblical Students*. 4th ed. Edited by Edward Miller. 2 vols. London: George Bell, 1894.

Sevrin, Jean-Marie, ed. *The New Testament in Early Christianity: La Réception des Écrits Néotestamentaires dans le Christianisme Primitif*. Bibliotheca Ephemeridum Theologicarum Lovaniensium 86. Leuven: Leuven University, 1989.

Shah, Abidan Paul. "The Alexandrian Presumption of Authenticity Regarding the Matthew 27:49 addition." In *Digging for the Truth: Collected Essays Regarding the Byzantine Text of the Greek New Testament: A Festschrift in Honor of Maurice A. Robinson*, edited by Mark Billington and Peter Streitenberger, 92–99. Norden, Germany: FocusYourMission KG, 2014.

———. "Bats in the Belfry: How the CBGM Destroys Any Valid Methodology of NT Textual Criticism." Paper presented at the Annual Meeting of the Southeastern Region of the Evangelical Theological Society, Lynchburg, VA, April 2016.

———. "From Mill to Muenster: How Many Variants in the Manuscript Tradition of the New Testament?" Paper presented at the Annual Meeting of the Evangelical Theological Society, Baltimore, MD, November 2013.

Sheler, Jeffrey L., et al. "In Search of Jesus: Some Scholars Seek Answers in History and Redefine the Meaning of His Life and Deeds." *U.S. News and World Report*, 8 April 1996, 47–53.

Silva, Moisés. "The New Testament Use of the Old Testament: Text, Form, and Authority." In *Scripture and Truth*, edited by D. A. Carson and John D. Woodbridge, 143–65. Grand Rapids: Zondervan, 1983.

———. "Review of *The Living Text of the Gospels*." *Westminster Theological Journal* 62.2 (2000) 295–302.

Soulen, Richard N., and R. Kendall Soulen. *Handbook of Biblical Criticism*. 4th ed. Louisville: Westminster John Knox, 2011.

Sparks, Kenton L. *God's Word in Human Words: An Evangelical Appropriation of Critical Biblical Scholarship*. Grand Rapids: Baker Academic, 2008.

Stein, Robert H. *Studying the Synoptic Gospels: Origin and Interpretation*. Grand Rapids: Baker Academic, 2001.

Stewart, Robert B., ed. *The Reliability of the New Testament: Bart D. Ehrman and Daniel B. Wallace in Dialogue*. Minneapolis: Fortress, 2011.

Strutwolf, Holger. "Original Text and Textual History." In *The Textual History of the Greek New Testament: Changing Views in Contemporary Research*, edited by Klaus Wachtel and Michael W. Holmes, 23–42. Text-Critical Studies 8. Atlanta: SBL, 2011.

Stuart, Douglas. "Inerrancy and Textual Criticism." In *Inerrancy and Common Sense*, edited by Roger R. Nicole and J. Ramsey Michaels, 97–117. Grand Rapids: Baker, 1980.

Suggs, M. Jack. "The Use of Patristic Evidence in the Search for a Primitive New Testament Text." *New Testament Studies* 4.2 (1958) 139–47.

Swete, Henry Barclay. *An Introduction to the Old Testament in Greek; With an Appendix Containing the Letter of Aristeas*. Edited by H. St. J. Thackeray. Cambridge: Cambridge University, 1900.

Thiselton, Anthony C. *New Horizons in Hermeneutics*. Grand Rapids: Zondervan, 1992.

———. "Review of *Junia: The First Woman Apostle*." *Ecclesiology* 5.2 (2009) 266–67.

Thomas, Robert L. "Did the Jesus Seminar Draw from Faulty Assumptions?" *Los Angeles Times*, 13 April 1991 F18–19. https://www.latimes.com/archives/la-xpm-1991-04-13-ca-74-story.html.

———. "Redaction Criticism." In *The Jesus Crisis: The Inroads of Historical Criticism into Evangelical Scholarship*, edited by Robert L. Thomas and F. David Farnell, 233–67. Grand Rapids: Kregel, 1998.

Thomas, Robert L., and F. David Farnell, eds. *The Jesus Crisis: The Inroads of Historical Criticism into Evangelical Scholarship*. Grand Rapids: Kregel, 1998.

Tilly, Michael, and Tobias Nicklas, eds. *The Book of Acts As Church History: Text, Textual Traditions and Ancient Interpretations/Apostelgeschichte als Kirchengeschichte: Text, Texttraditionen und antike Auslegungen*. Beihefte zur Zeitschrift für die Neutestamentliche Wissenschaft und die Kunde der Älteren Kirche. New York: de Gruyter, 2003.

Tischendorf, Constantine. *The New Testament: The Authorised English Version; With Introduction, and Various Readings from the Three Most Celebrated Manuscripts of the Original Greek Text*. Tauchnitz Edition 1000. Leipzig: Tauchnitz, 1869.

Tregelles, Samuel Prideaux. *An Account of the Printed Text of the Greek New Testament: With Remarks on its Revision upon Critical Principles: Together with a Collation of the Critical Texts of Griesbach, Scholz, Lachmann, and Tischendorf, With that in Common Use*. London: Bagster, 1854.

Turner, Cuthbert H. "Marcan Usage: Notes, Critical and Exegetical, on the Second Gospel." *Journal of Theological Studies* 26 (1925) 337–46.

Turner, E. G. *Greek Manuscripts of the Ancient World*. Oxford: Clarendon, 1971.

———. *Greek Papyri: An Introduction*. Princeton: Princeton University Press, 1968.

———. "Roman Oxyrhynchus." *Journal of Egyptian Archaeology* 38 (1952) 78–93.

Turner, Henry Ernest William. *The Pattern of Christian Truth: A Study in the Relations between Orthodoxy and Heresy in the Early Church*. Bampton Lectures 1954. London: Mowbray, 1954.

Vaganay, Léon, and Christian-Bernard Amphoux. *An Introduction to New Testament Textual Criticism*. 2nd ed. revised and updated by Christian-Bernard Amphoux. Translated by Jenny Heimerdinger. English ed. amplified and updated by Christian-Bernard Amphoux and Jenny Heimerdinger. Cambridge: Cambridge University, 1991.

Verheyden, Joseph, and Jan Krans, eds. *Patristic and Text-Critical Studies: The Collected Essays of William L. Petersen.* New Testament Tools, Studies, and Documents 40. Leiden: Brill, 2012.

Vincent, Marvin Richardson. *A History of Textual Criticism of the New Testament.* New York: Macmillan, 1900.

Wachtel, Klaus. "The Byzantine Text of the Gospels: Recension or Process?" Paper presented at the NTTC session of the Annual Meeting of SBL, New Orleans, November 2009. http://evangelicaltextualcriticism.blogspot.com/2009/12/wachtel-on-byzantine-text-of-gospels.html.

———. "The Coherence-Based Genealogical Method: A New Way to Reconstruct the Text of the Greek New Testament." In *Editing the Bible: Assessing the Task Past and Present*, edited by Judith H. Newman and John S. Kloppenborg, 123–38. Society of Biblical Literature Sources for Biblical Studies. Atlanta: SBL, 2012.

———. "The Coherence Method and History." *TC: A Journal of Biblical Textual Criticism* 20 (2015) 1–6. http://jbtc.org/v20/TC-2015-CBGM-history.pdf.

———. "Towards a Redefinition of External Criteria: The Role of Coherence in Assessing the Origin of Variants." In *Textual Variation: Theological and Social Tendencies? Papers from the Fifth Birmingham Colloquium on the Textual Criticism of the New Testament*, edited by Hugh A. G. Houghton and David C. Parker, 109–27. Texts and Studies 3:6. Piscataway, NJ: Gorgias, 2008.

Wachtel, Klaus, and Michael W. Holmes, eds. *The Textual History of the Greek New Testament: Changing Views in Contemporary Research.* Text-Critical Studies 8. Atlanta: SBL, 2011.

Wallace, Daniel B. "Challenges in New Testament Textual Criticism for the Twenty-First Century." *Journal of the Evangelical Theological Society* 52.1 (2009) 79–100.

———. "The Gospel According to Bart: A Review Article of *Misquoting Jesus* by Bart Ehrman." *Journal of the Evangelical Theological Society* 49.2 (2006) 327–49.

———. "Inspiration, Preservation, and New Testament Textual Criticism." *Grace Theological Journal* 12 (1991) 21–50.

———. "The Number of Textual Variants: An Evangelical Miscalculation." http://danielbwallace.com/2013/09/09/the-number-of-textual-variants-an-evangelical-miscalculation/.

———. *Revisiting the Corruption of the New Testament: Manuscript, Patristic, and Apocryphal Evidence.* Text and Canon of the New Testament 1. Grand Rapids: Kregel, 2011.

Wasserman, Tommy. "The Coherence-Based Genealogical Method as a Tool for Explaining Textual Changes in the Greek New Testament." *Novum Testamentum* 57.2 (2015) 206–18.

———. "Criteria for Evaluating Readings in New Testament Textual Criticism." In *The Text of the New Testament in Contemporary Research: Essays on the Status Quaestionis*, edited by Bart D. Ehrman and Michael W. Holmes, 579–612. New Testament Tools, Studies, and Documents 42. Leiden: Brill, 2013.

———. "The Implications of Textual Criticism for Understanding the 'Original Text.'" In *Mark and Matthew I. Comparative Readings: Understanding the Earliest Gospels in Their First-Century Settings*, edited by Eve-Marie Becker and Anders Runesson, 77–96. Wissenschaftliche Untersuchungen zum Neuen Testament 271. Tübingen: Mohr/Siebeck, 2011.

———. "Misquoting Manuscripts? The Orthodox Corruption of Scripture Revisited." In *The Making of Christianity: Conflicts, Contacts, and Constructions: Essays in Honor of Bengt Holmberg*, edited by Magnus Zetterholm and Samuel Byrskog, 325–50. ConBNT 47. Winona Lake, IN: Eisenbrauns, 2012.

———. "Theologisch-christologische Varianten in der frühen Überlieferung des Neuen Testaments? A 'Magisterarbeit' by Ivo Tamm from Münster under Barbara Aland. http://evangelicaltextualcriticism.blogspot.com/2006/03/theologisch-christologische-varianten.html.

Wasserman, Tommy, and Peter J. Gurry. *A New Approach to Textual Criticism: An Introduction to the Coherence-Based Genealogical Method*. Resources for Biblical Study 80. Atlanta: SBL, 2017.

Weren, Wim, and Dietrich-Alex Koch, eds. *Recent Developments in Textual Criticism: New Testament, Other Early Christian and Jewish Literature*. Studies in Theology and Religion 8. Assen, The Netherlands: Royal Van Gorcum, 2003.

Westcott, Brooke Foss, and Fenton John Anthony Hort. *The New Testament in the Original Greek*. London: Macmillan, 1881.

———. *The New Testament in the Original Greek: Introduction and Appendix*. London: Macmillan, 1882.

Wilkins, Michael J., and James Porter Moreland, eds. *Jesus under Fire*. Grand Rapids: Zondervan, 1995.

Williams, Peter J. "Ehrman's Equivocation and the Inerrancy of the Original Text." In *The Enduring Authority of the Christian Scriptures*, edited by D. A. Carson, 389–406. Grand Rapids: Eerdmans, 2016.

———. "Review of *Perspectives on New Testament Textual Criticism: Collected Essays 1962-2004*." *Journal for the Study of the New Testament* 28.5 (2006) 146–47.

Wisse, Frederik W. "The Nature and Purpose of Redactional Changes in Early Christian Texts: The Canonical Gospels." In *Gospel Traditions in the Second Century: Origins, Recensions, Text, and Transmission*, edited by William Lawrence Petersen, 39–53. Christianity and Judaism in Antiquity 3. Notre Dame: University of Notre Dame, 1989.

———. "Textual Limits to Redactional Theory in the Pauline Corpus." In *Gospel Origins and Christian Beginnings: In Honor of James M. Robinson*, edited by James E. Goehring et al., 167–78. Forum Fascicles 2. Sonoma, CA: Polebridge, 1990.

Witherington, Ben. "Bart Ehrman's on *Did Jesus Exist?* Part One," *Patheos (blog)*, 5 June 2012. http://www.patheos.com/blogs/bibleandculture/2012/06/05/bart-ehrmans-on-did-jesus-exist-part-one/.

Woodbridge, John D. "Evangelical Self-Identity and the Doctrine of Biblical Inerrancy." In *Understanding the Times: New Testament Studies in the 21st Century, Essays in Honor of D.A. Carson on the Occasion of His 65th Birthday*, edited by Andreas J. Köstenberger and Robert W. Yarbrough, 104–40. Wheaton, IL: Crossway, 2011.

Zetterholm, Magnus, and Samuel Byrskog, eds. *The Making of Christianity: Conflicts, Contacts, and Constructions: Essays in Honor of Bengt Holmberg*. Coniectanea Biblica: New Testament Series 47. Winona Lake, IN: Eisenbrauns, 2012.

Zuntz, Günther. *The Text of the Epistles: A Disquisition upon the Corpus Paulinum*. Schweich Lectures 1946. Oxford: Oxford University, 1953.

www.ingramcontent.com/pod-product-compliance
Lightning Source LLC
Chambersburg PA
CBHW062038220426
43662CB00010B/1547